The Modern Civil Aircraft Guide

The Modern Civil Aircraft Guide

Editor: David Donald

BLITZ EDITIONS

Some of this material has previously appeared
in the Orbis reference set 'Airplane'.

Published by Blitz Editions
an imprint of Bookmart Ltd
Registered Number 2372865
Trading as Bookmart Ltd
Desford Road
Enderby
Leicester LE9 5AD

ISBN 1 85605 500 0

Editorial and design by Brown Packaging Books Ltd
Bradley's Close
74–77 White Lion Street
London N1 9PF

Editor: David Donald

Printed in The Slovak Republic

Contents

Bristol Freighter Mk 21/Bristol Super Freighter Mk 32

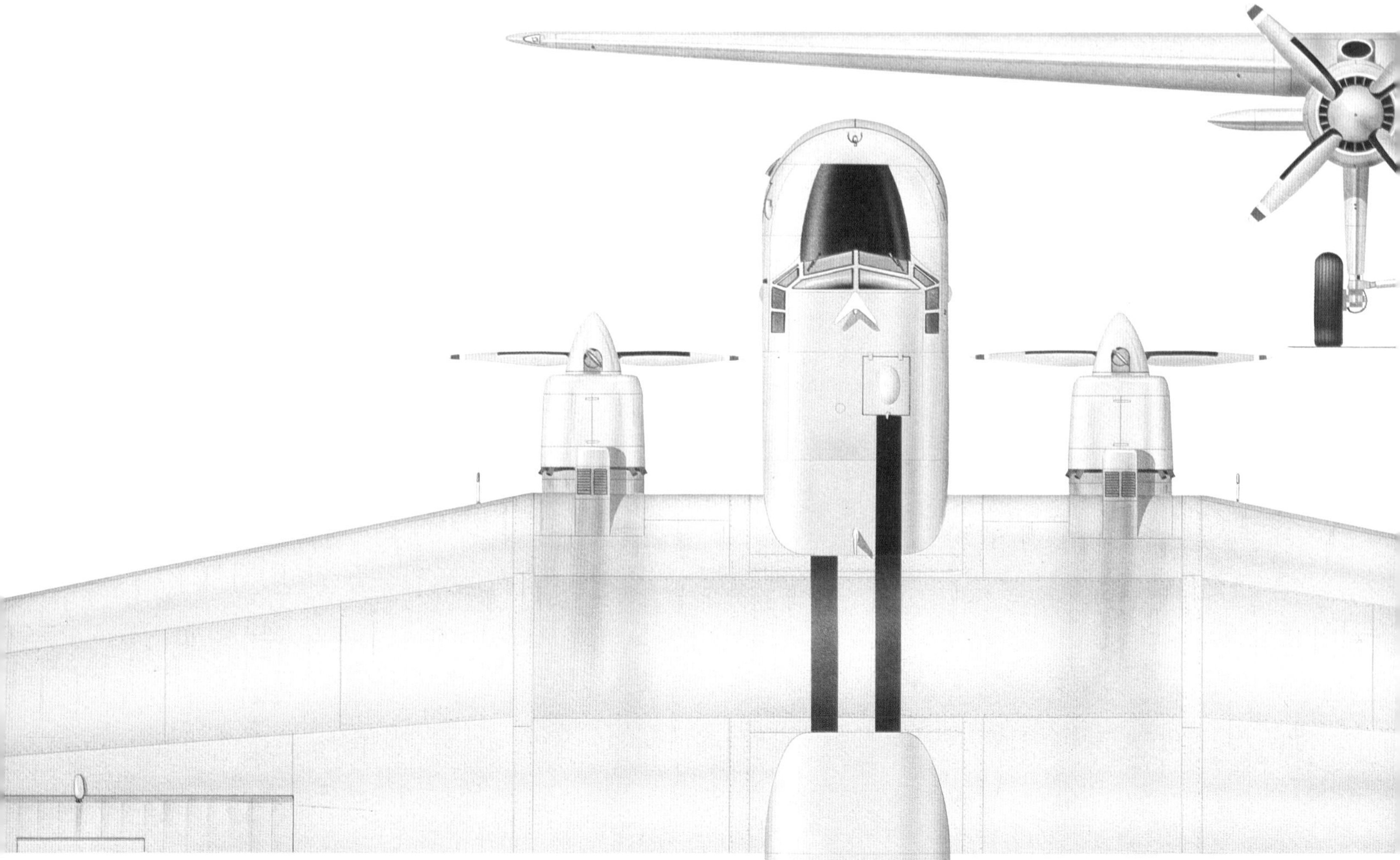

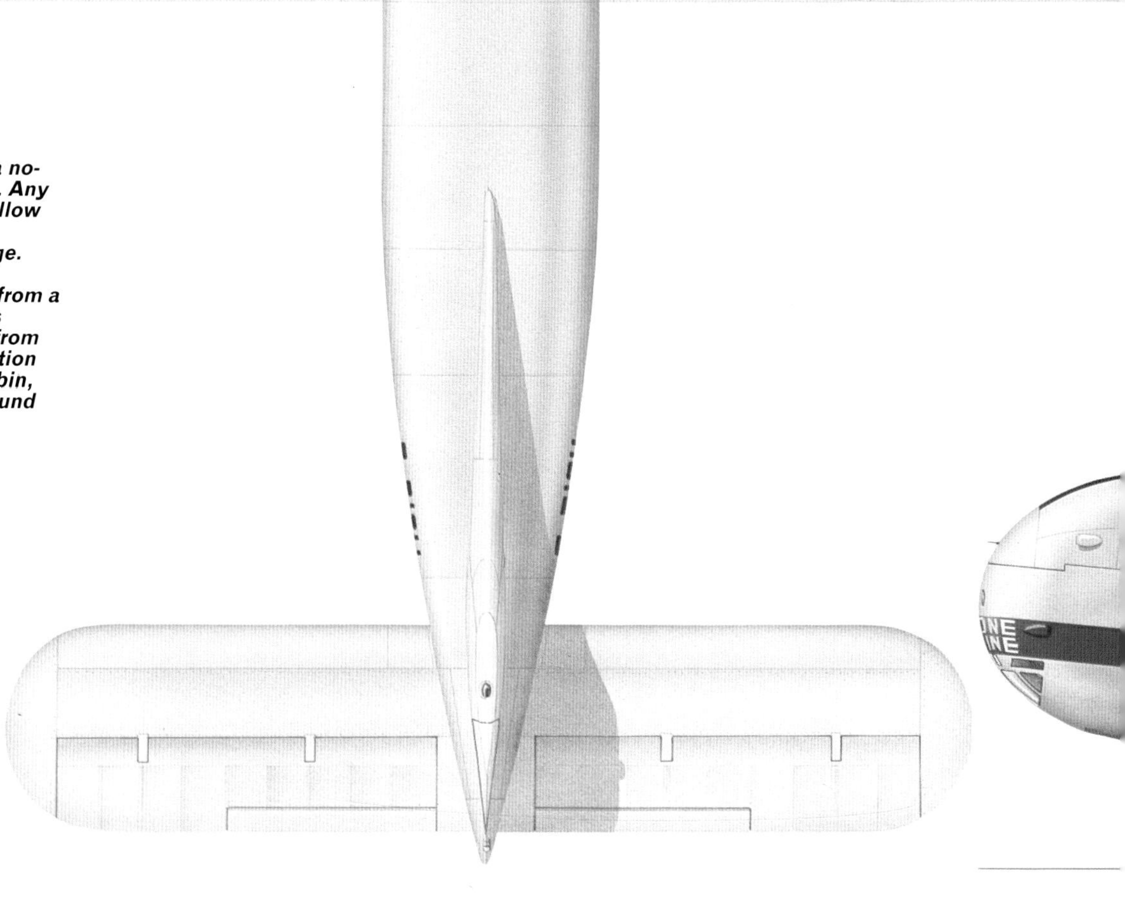

The Bristol 170 was designed to reflect a no-nonsense approach to the requirements. Any needless complexities were left out to allow ease of maintenance under primitive conditions, hence the fixed undercarriage. The expansive wing won no prizes for performance, but could lift a good load from a small strip, while the undercarriage was sturdy enough to withstand operations from most surfaces. The high-wing configuration allowed a flat floor to the main cargo cabin, and also kept the nose as low to the ground as possible for ease of access.

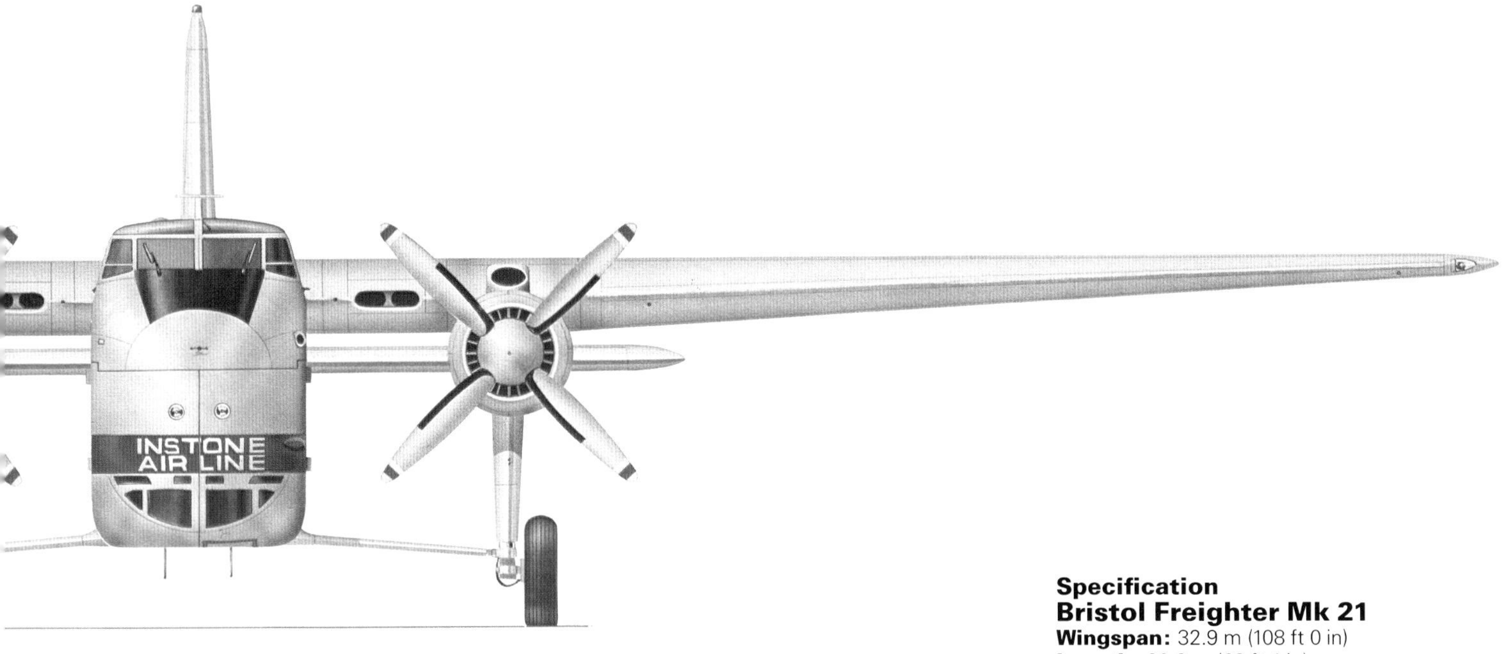

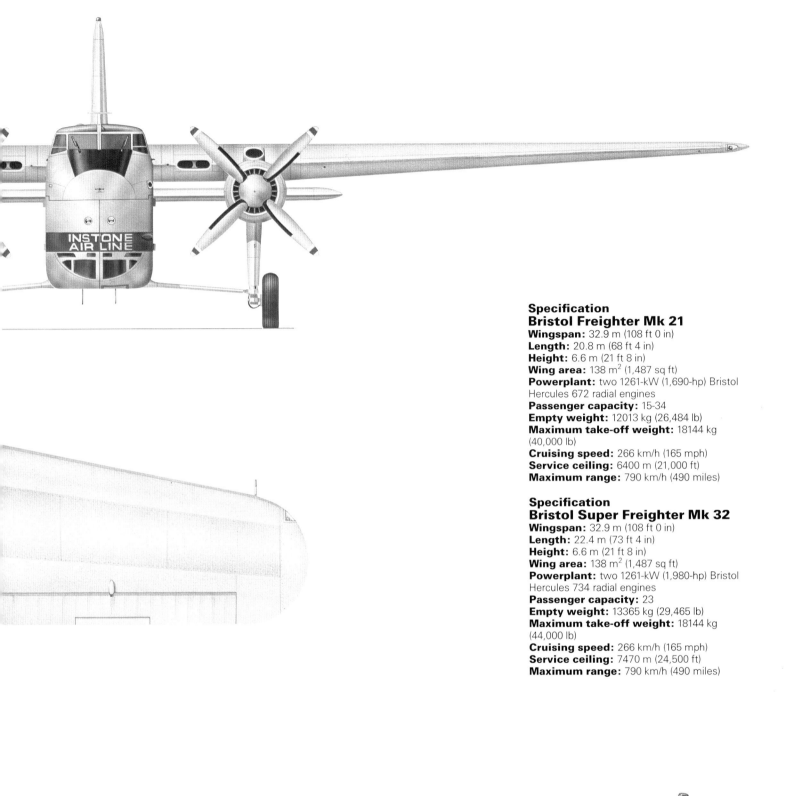

Specification
Bristol Freighter Mk 21
Wingspan: 32.9 m (108 ft 0 in)
Length: 20.8 m (68 ft 4 in)
Height: 6.6 m (21 ft 8 in)
Wing area: 138 m^2 (1,487 sq ft)
Powerplant: two 1261-kW (1,690-hp) Bristol Hercules 672 radial engines
Passenger capacity: 15-34
Empty weight: 12013 kg (26,484 lb)
Maximum take-off weight: 18144 kg (40,000 lb)
Cruising speed: 266 km/h (165 mph)
Service ceiling: 6400 m (21,000 ft)
Maximum range: 790 km/h (490 miles)

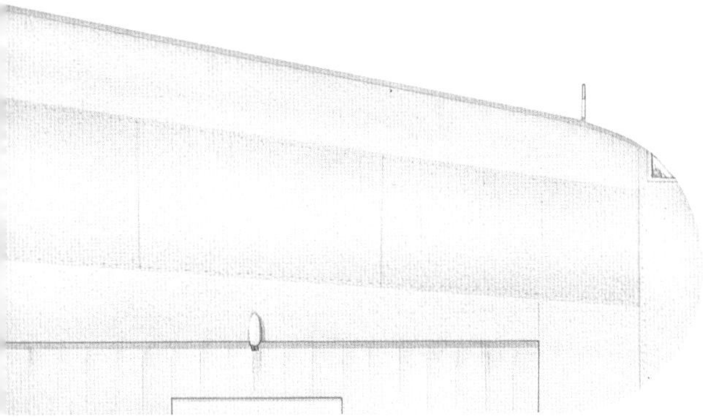

Specification
Bristol Super Freighter Mk 32
Wingspan: 32.9 m (108 ft 0 in)
Length: 22.4 m (73 ft 4 in)
Height: 6.6 m (21 ft 8 in)
Wing area: 138 m^2 (1,487 sq ft)
Powerplant: two 1261-kW (1,980-hp) Bristol Hercules 734 radial engines
Passenger capacity: 23
Empty weight: 13365 kg (29,465 lb)
Maximum take-off weight: 18144 kg (44,000 lb)
Cruising speed: 266 km/h (165 mph)
Service ceiling: 7470 m (24,500 ft)
Maximum range: 790 km/h (490 miles)

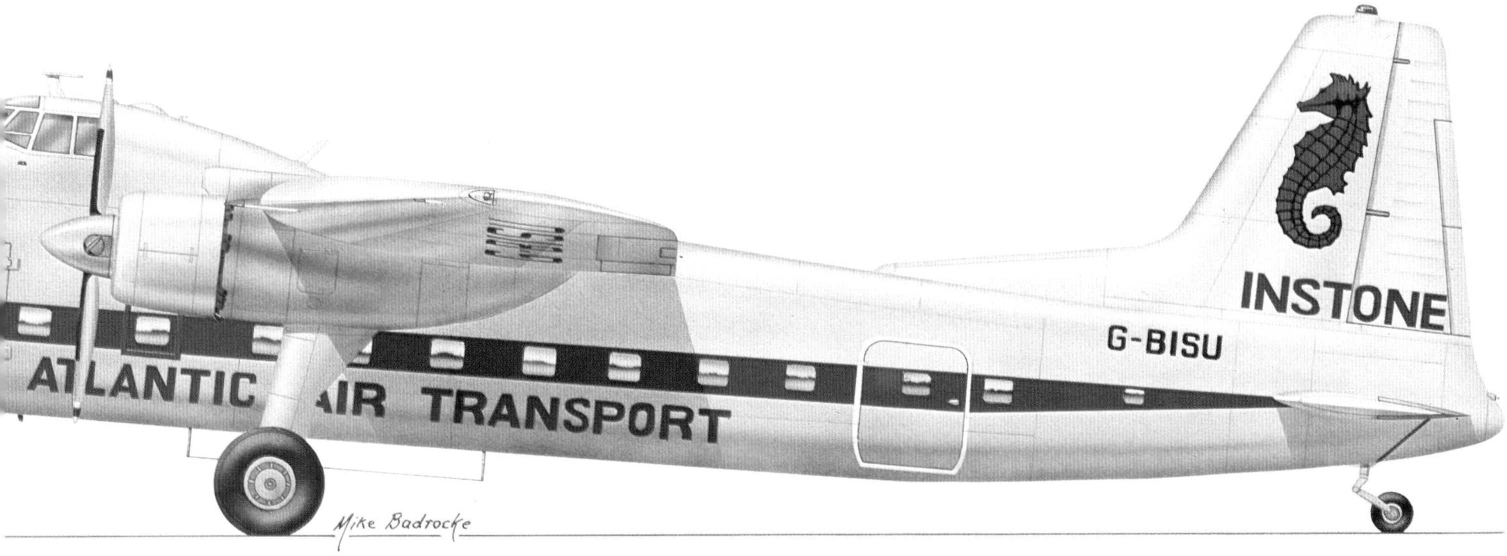

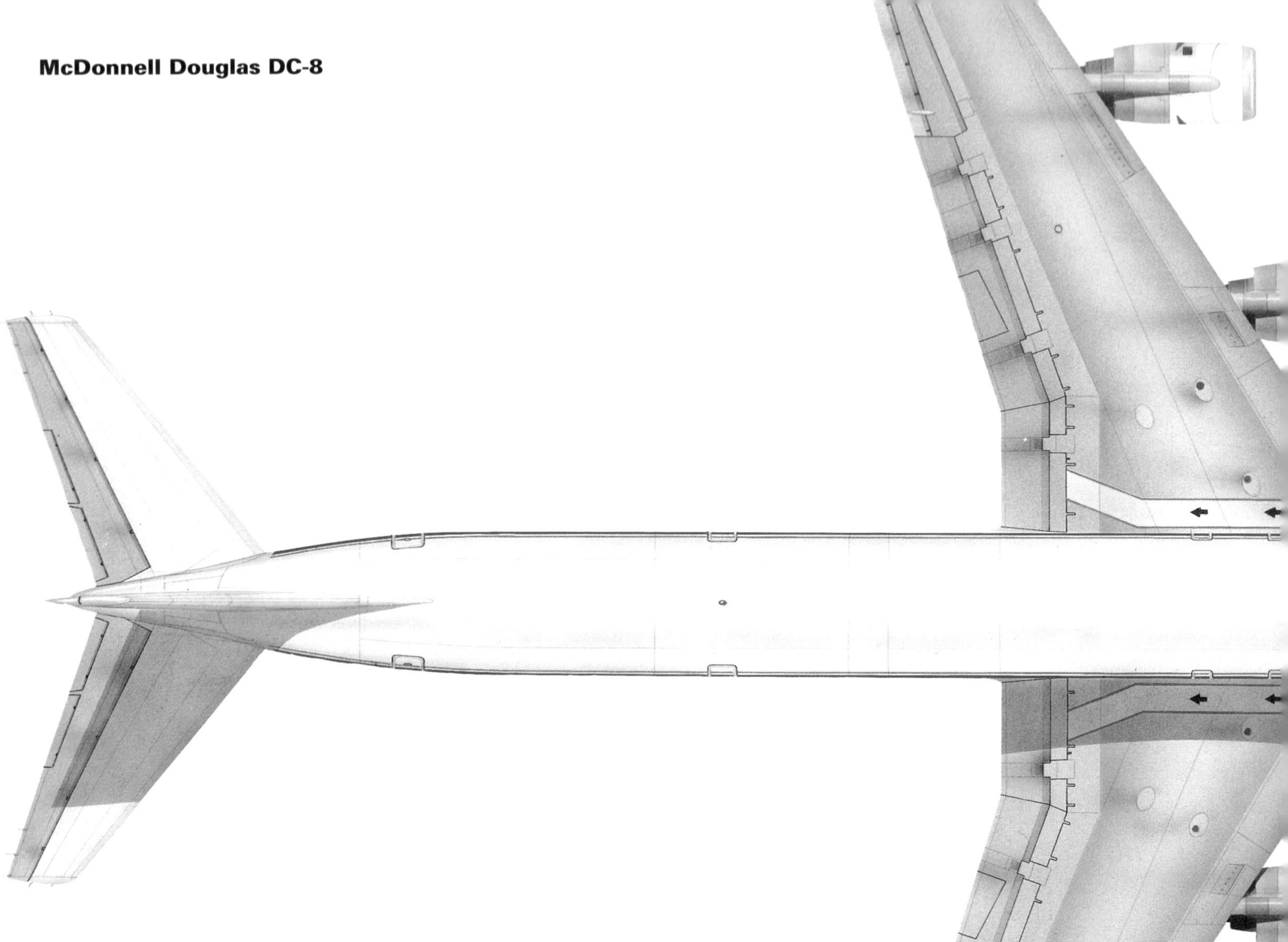

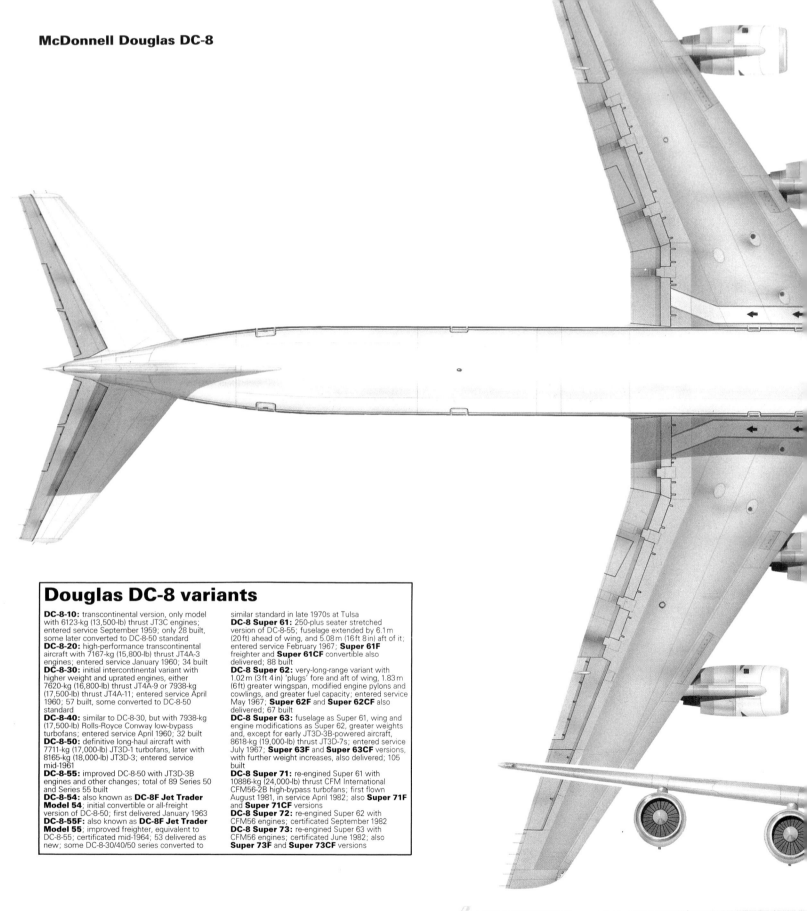

Douglas DC-8 variants

DC-8-10: transcontinental version, only model with 6123-kg (13,500-lb) thrust JT3C engines; entered service September 1959; only 28 built, some later converted to DC-8-50 standard
DC-8-20: high-performance transcontinental aircraft with 7167-kg (15,800-lb) thrust JT4A-3 engines; entered service January 1960; 34 built
DC-8-30: initial intercontinental variant with higher weight and uprated engines, either 7620-kg (16,800-lb) thrust JT4A-9 or 7938-kg (17,500-lb) thrust JT4A-11; entered service April 1960; 57 built, some converted to DC-8-50 standard
DC-8-40: similar to DC-8-30, but with 7938-kg (17,500-lb) Rolls-Royce Conway low-bypass turbofans; entered service April 1960; 32 built
DC-8-50: definitive long-haul aircraft with 7711-kg (17,000-lb) JT3D-1 turbofans, later with 8165-kg (18,000-lb) JT3D-3; entered service mid-1961
DC-8-55: improved DC-8-50 with JT3D-3B engines and other changes; total of 89 Series 50 and Series 55 built
DC-8-54: also known as **DC-8F Jet Trader Model 54**; initial convertible or all-freight version of DC-8-50; first delivered January 1963
DC-8-55F: also known as **DC-8F Jet Trader Model 55**; improved freighter, equivalent to DC-8-55; certificated mid-1964; 53 delivered as new; some DC-8-30/40/50 series converted to similar standard in late 1970s at Tulsa
DC-8 Super 61: 250-plus seater stretched version of DC-8-55; fuselage extended by 6.1 m (20 ft) ahead of wing, and 5.08 m (16 ft 8 in) aft of it; entered service February 1967; **Super 61F** freighter and **Super 61CF** convertible also delivered; 88 built
DC-8 Super 62: very-long-range variant with 1.02 m (3 ft 4 in) 'plugs' fore and aft of wing, 1.83 m (6 ft) greater wingspan, modified engine pylons and cowlings, and greater fuel capacity; entered service May 1967; **Super 62F** and **Super 62CF** also delivered; 67 built
DC-8 Super 63: fuselage as Super 61, wing and engine modifications as Super 62, greater weights and, except for early JT3D-3B-powered aircraft, 8618-kg (19,000-lb) thrust JT3D-7s; entered service July 1967; **Super 63F** and **Super 63CF** versions, with further weight increases, also delivered; 105 built
DC-8 Super 71: re-engined Super 61 with 10886-kg (24,000-lb) thrust CFM International CFM56-2B high-bypass turbofans; first flown August 1981, in service April 1982; also **Super 71F** and **Super 71CF** versions
DC-8 Super 72: re-engined Super 62 with CFM56 engines; certificated September 1982
DC-8 Super 73: re-engined Super 63 with CFM56 engines; certificated June 1982; also **Super 73F** and **Super 73CF** versions

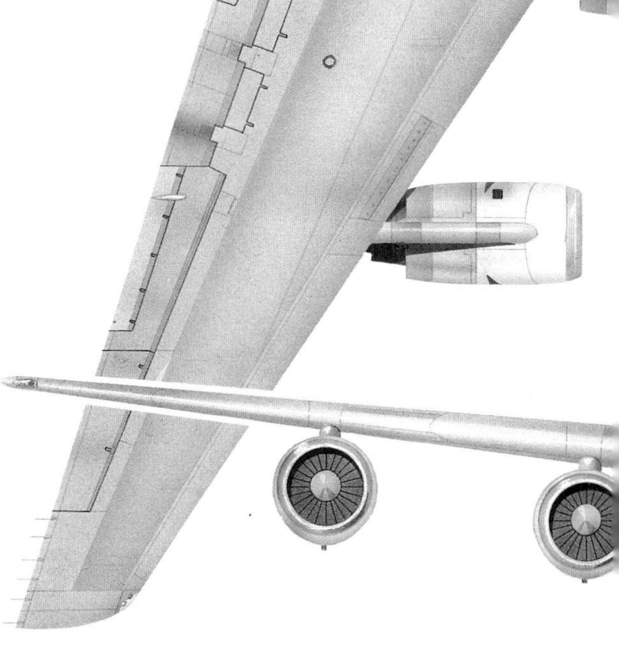

Specification
McDonnell Douglas DC-8 Super 71
Type: long-range passenger transport
Powerplant: four CFM International CFM56-2-1C turbofan engines each developing 10887-kg (24,000-lb) thrust
Performance: maximum level speed 965 km/h (600 mph); cruising speed 854 km/h (531 mph) at 10670 m (35,000 ft); initial cruising altitude 10550 m (34,600 ft); take-off field length 2698 m (8,850 ft); range with maximum passenger payload 7485 km (4,650 miles)
Weights: empty 73800 kg (162,700 lb); maximum payload 30240 kg (66,665 lb); fuel weight 71093 kg (156,733 lb); maximum take-off weight 147415 kg (325,000 lb); maximum landing weight 108860 kg (240,000 lb)
Dimensions: span 43.36 m (142 ft 3 in); length 57.22 m (187 ft 5 in); height 12.93 m (42 ft 5 in); wing area 271.92 m^2 (2,927 sq ft)

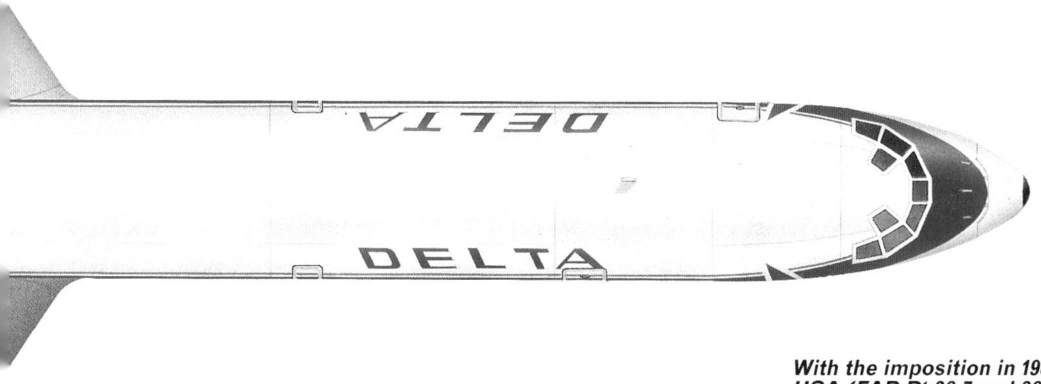

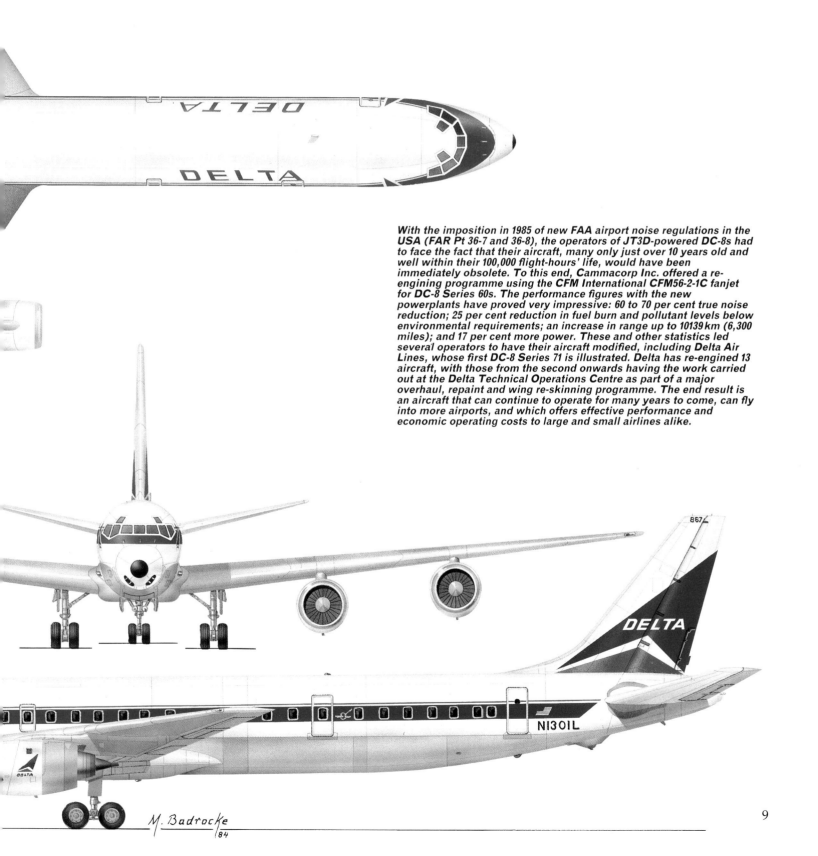

With the imposition in 1985 of new FAA airport noise regulations in the USA (FAR Pt 36-7 and 36-8), the operators of JT3D-powered DC-8s had to face the fact that their aircraft, many only just over 10 years old and well within their 100,000 flight-hours' life, would have been immediately obsolete. To this end, Cammacorp Inc. offered a re-engining programme using the CFM International CFM56-2-1C fanjet for DC-8 Series 60s. The performance figures with the new powerplants have proved very impressive: 60 to 70 per cent true noise reduction; 25 per cent reduction in fuel burn and pollutant levels below environmental requirements; an increase in range up to 10139 km (6,300 miles); and 17 per cent more power. These and other statistics led several operators to have their aircraft modified, including Delta Air Lines, whose first DC-8 Series 71 is illustrated. Delta has re-engined 13 aircraft, with those from the second onwards having the work carried out at the Delta Technical Operations Centre as part of a major overhaul, repaint and wing re-skinning programme. The end result is an aircraft that can continue to operate for many years to come, can fly into more airports, and which offers effective performance and economic operating costs to large and small airlines alike.

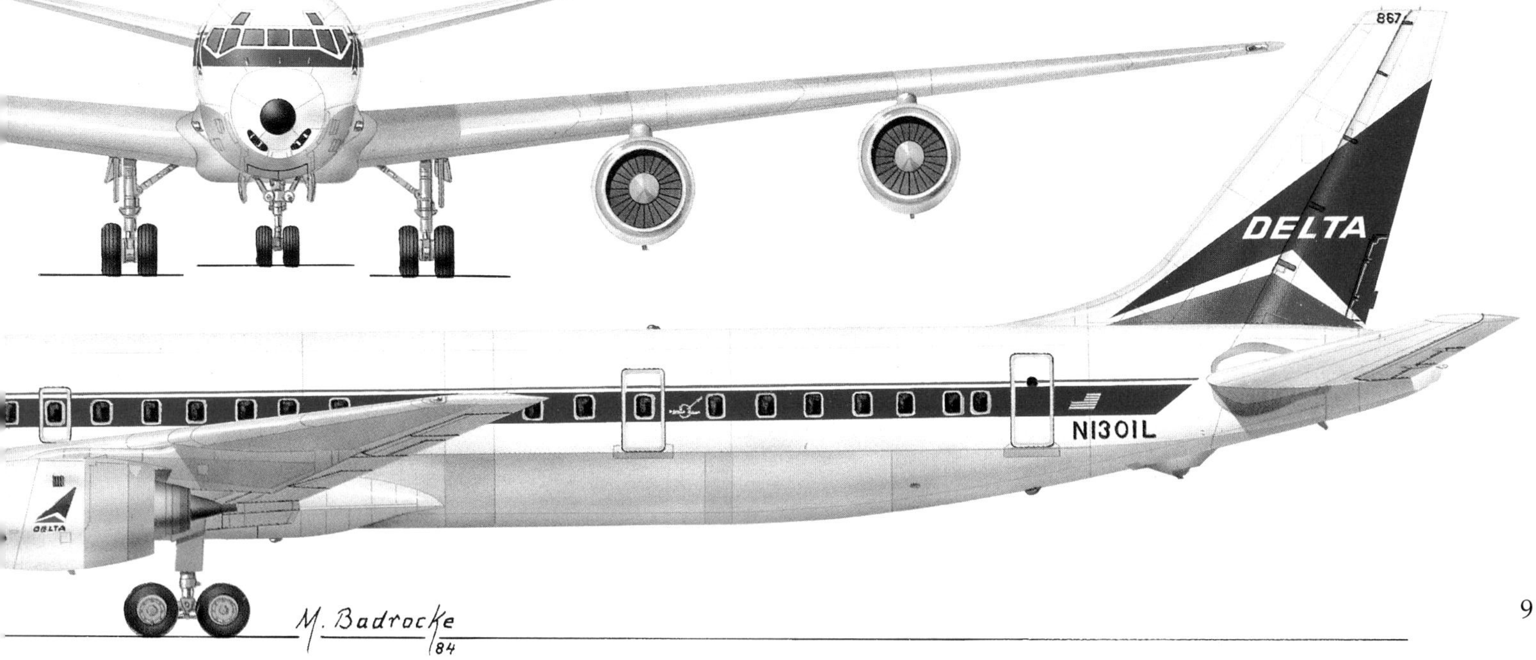

Sud-Aviation Caravelle III

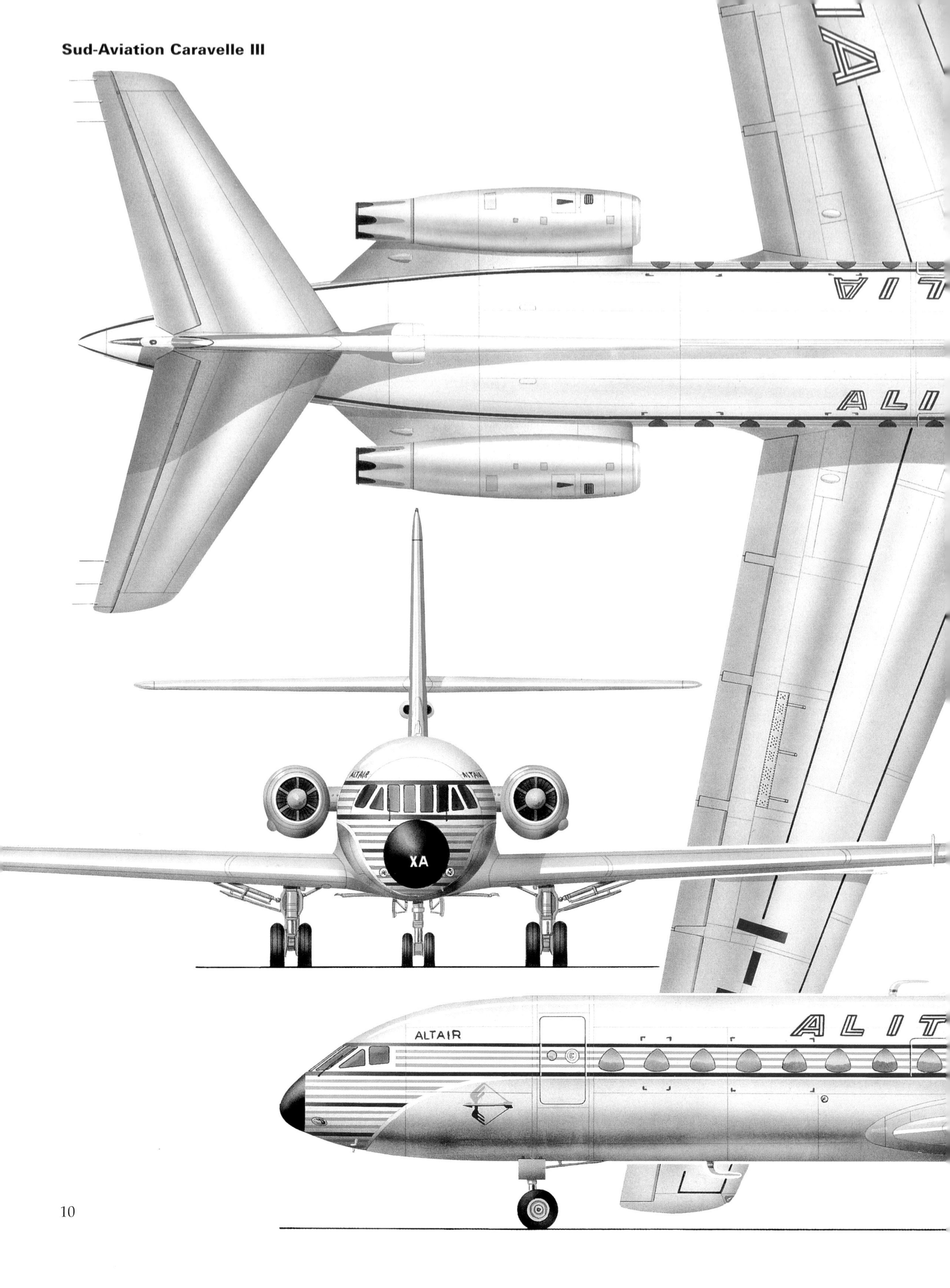

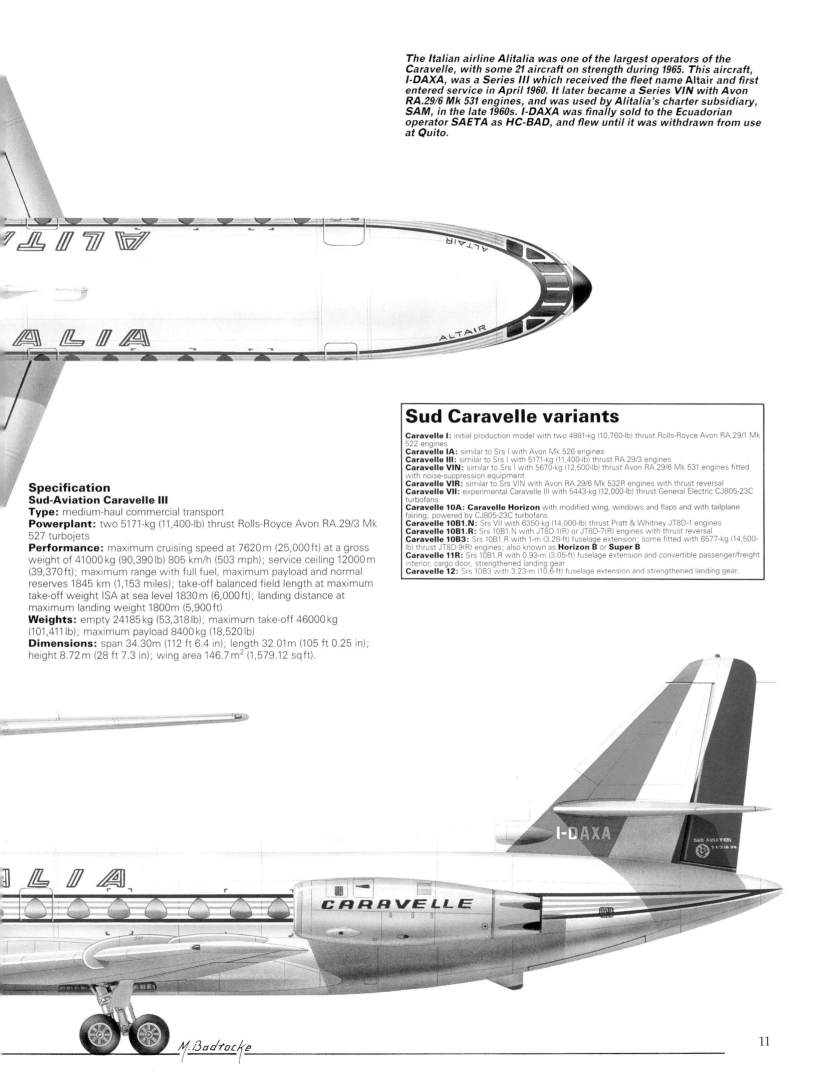

The Italian airline Alitalia was one of the largest operators of the Caravelle, with some 21 aircraft on strength during 1965. This aircraft, I-DAXA, was a Series III which received the fleet name Altair and first entered service in April 1960. It later became a Series VIN with Avon RA.29/6 Mk 531 engines, and was used by Alitalia's charter subsidiary, SAM, in the late 1960s. I-DAXA was finally sold to the Ecuadorian operator SAETA as HC-BAD, and flew until it was withdrawn from use at Quito.

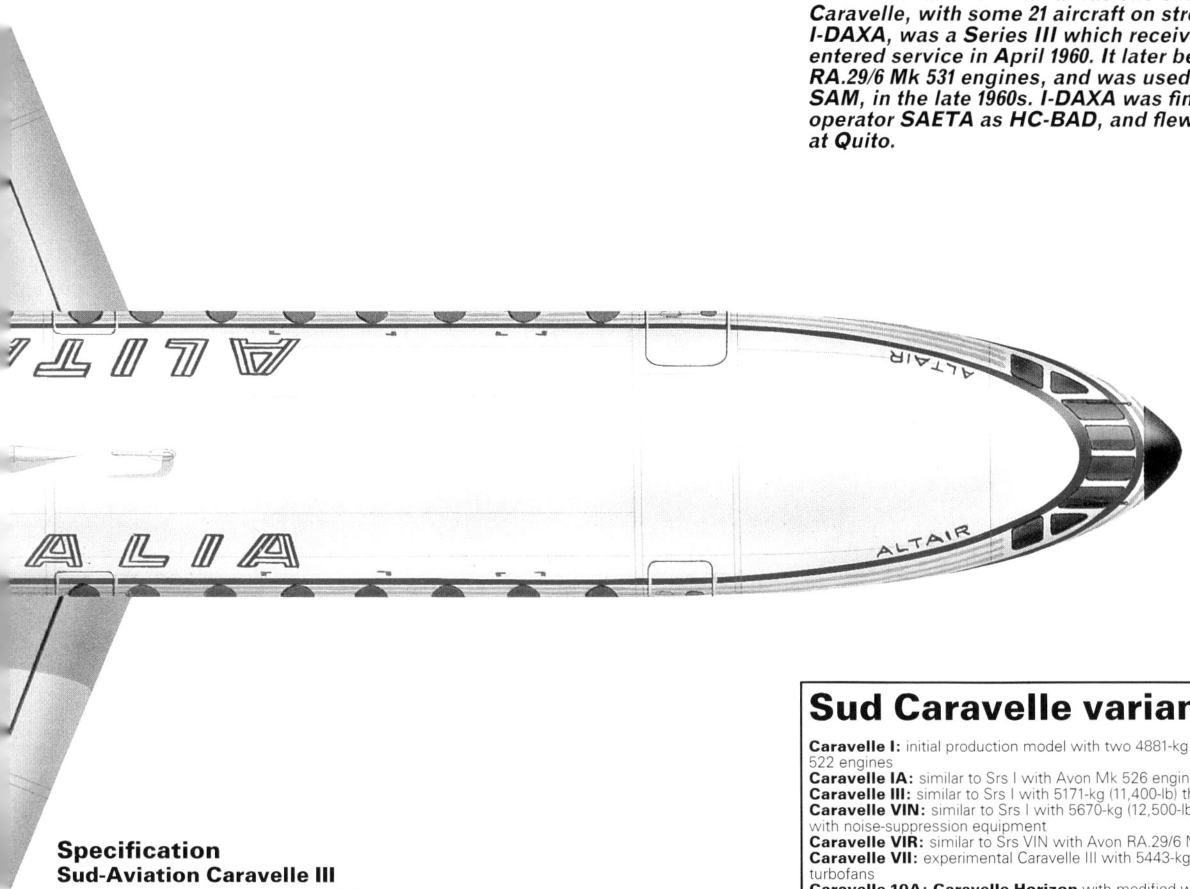

Sud Caravelle variants

Caravelle I: initial production model with two 4881-kg (10,760-lb) thrust Rolls-Royce Avon RA.29/1 Mk 522 engines
Caravelle IA: similar to Srs I with Avon Mk 526 engines
Caravelle III: similar to Srs I with 5171-kg (11,400-lb) thrust RA.29/3 engines
Caravelle VIN: similar to Srs I with 5670-kg (12,500-lb) thrust Avon RA.29/6 Mk 531 engines fitted with noise-suppression equipment
Caravelle VIR: similar to Srs VIN with Avon RA.29/6 Mk 532R engines with thrust reversal
Caravelle VII: experimental Caravelle III with 5443-kg (12,000-lb) thrust General Electric CJ805-23C turbofans
Caravelle 10A: Caravelle Horizon with modified wing, windows and flaps and with tailplane fairing; powered by CJ805-23C turbofans
Caravelle 10B1.N: Srs VII with 6350-kg (14,000-lb) thrust Pratt & Whitney JT8D-1 engines
Caravelle 10B1.R: Srs 10B1.N with JT8D-1(R) or JT8D-7(R) engines with thrust reversal
Caravelle 10B3: Srs 10B1.R with 1-m (3.28-ft) fuselage extension; some fitted with 6577-kg (14,500-lb) thrust JT8D-9(R) engines; also known as **Horizon B** or **Super B**
Caravelle 11R: Srs 10B1.R with 0.93-m (3.05-ft) fuselage extension and convertible passenger/freight interior, cargo door, strengthened landing gear
Caravelle 12: Srs 10B3 with 3.23-m (10.6-ft) fuselage extension and strengthened landing gear.

Specification
Sud-Aviation Caravelle III
Type: medium-haul commercial transport
Powerplant: two 5171-kg (11,400-lb) thrust Rolls-Royce Avon RA.29/3 Mk 527 turbojets
Performance: maximum cruising speed at 7620 m (25,000 ft) at a gross weight of 41000 kg (90,390 lb) 805 km/h (503 mph); service ceiling 12000 m (39,370 ft); maximum range with full fuel, maximum payload and normal reserves 1845 km (1,153 miles); take-off balanced field length at maximum take-off weight ISA at sea level 1830 m (6,000 ft); landing distance at maximum landing weight 1800m (5,900 ft)
Weights: empty 24185 kg (53,318 lb); maximum take-off 46000 kg (101,411 lb); maximum payload 8400 kg (18,520 lb)
Dimensions: span 34.30m (112 ft 6.4 in); length 32.01m (105 ft 0.25 in); height 8.72 m (28 ft 7.3 in); wing area 146.7 m^2 (1,579.12 sq ft).

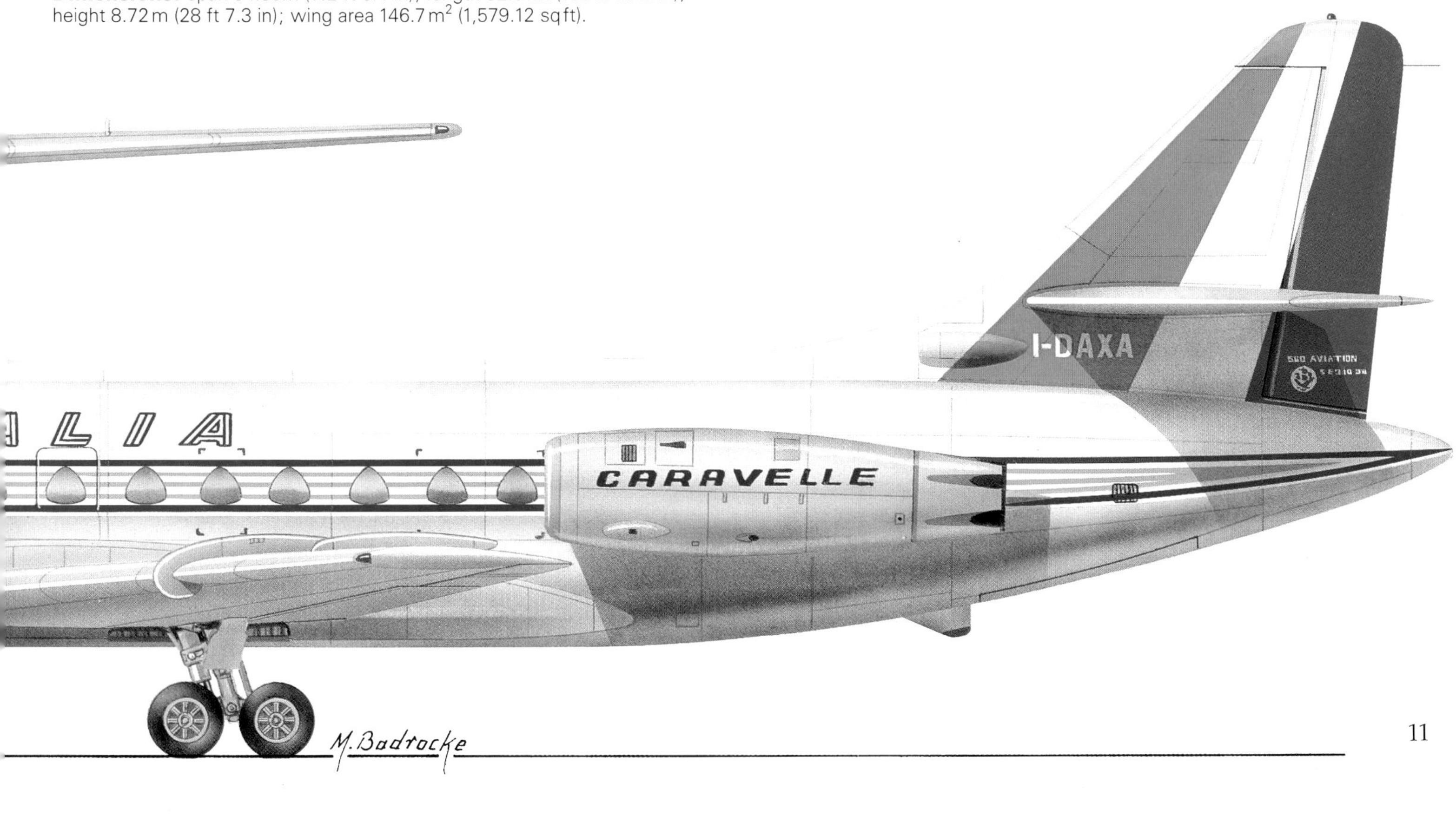

Shin Meiwa US-1A

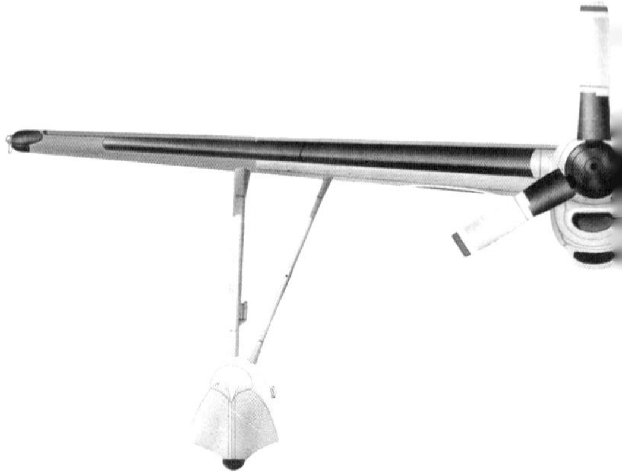

*The Shin Meiwa **US-1A** has been standing **SAR** duty with the 71st Kokutai at Iwakuni since 1 July 1976. A total of 14 has been ordered and once the final aircraft is in service the squadron will have a complement of 10 'boats. The **US-1**s are tasked with search and rescue duties along Japan's extensive Pacific coastline, offering the unique ability to land on the water and retrieve up to 20 seated and 12 stretcher patients. This aircraft was the third production **US-1** delivered.*

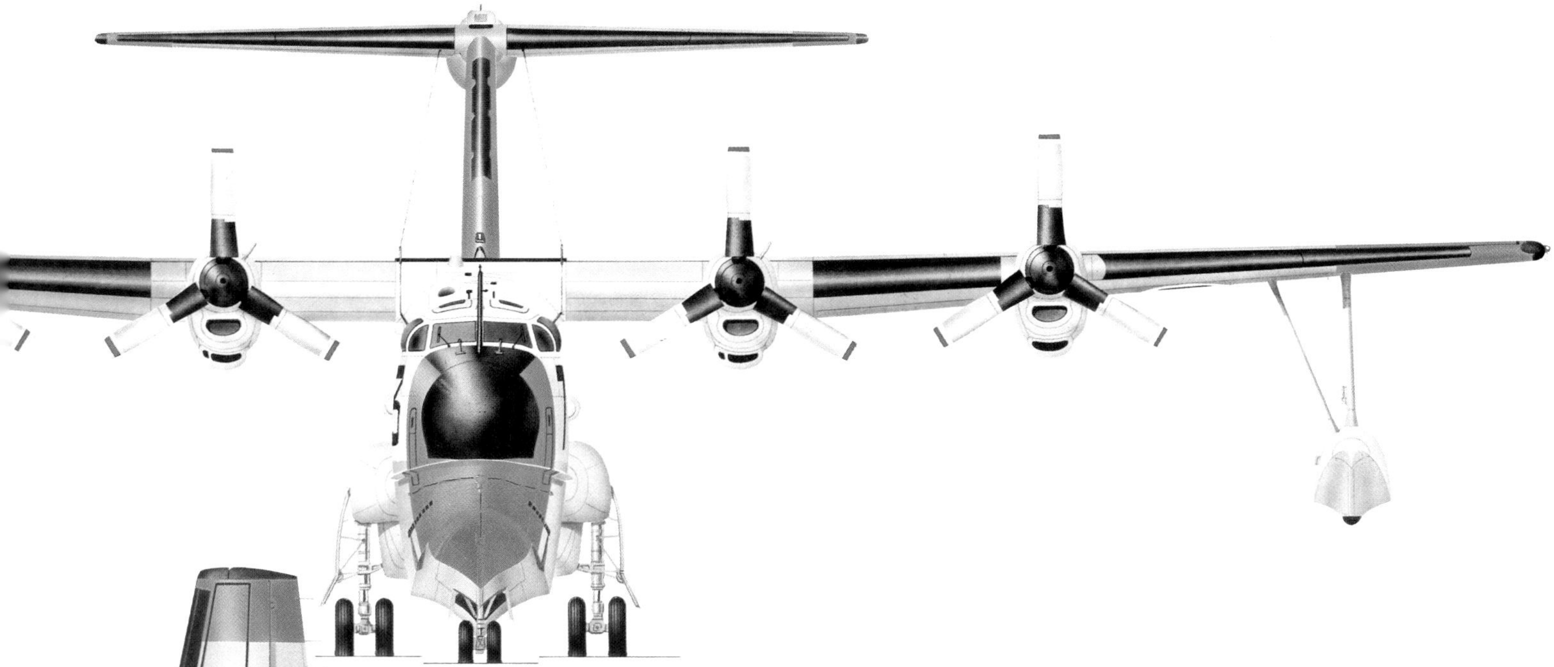

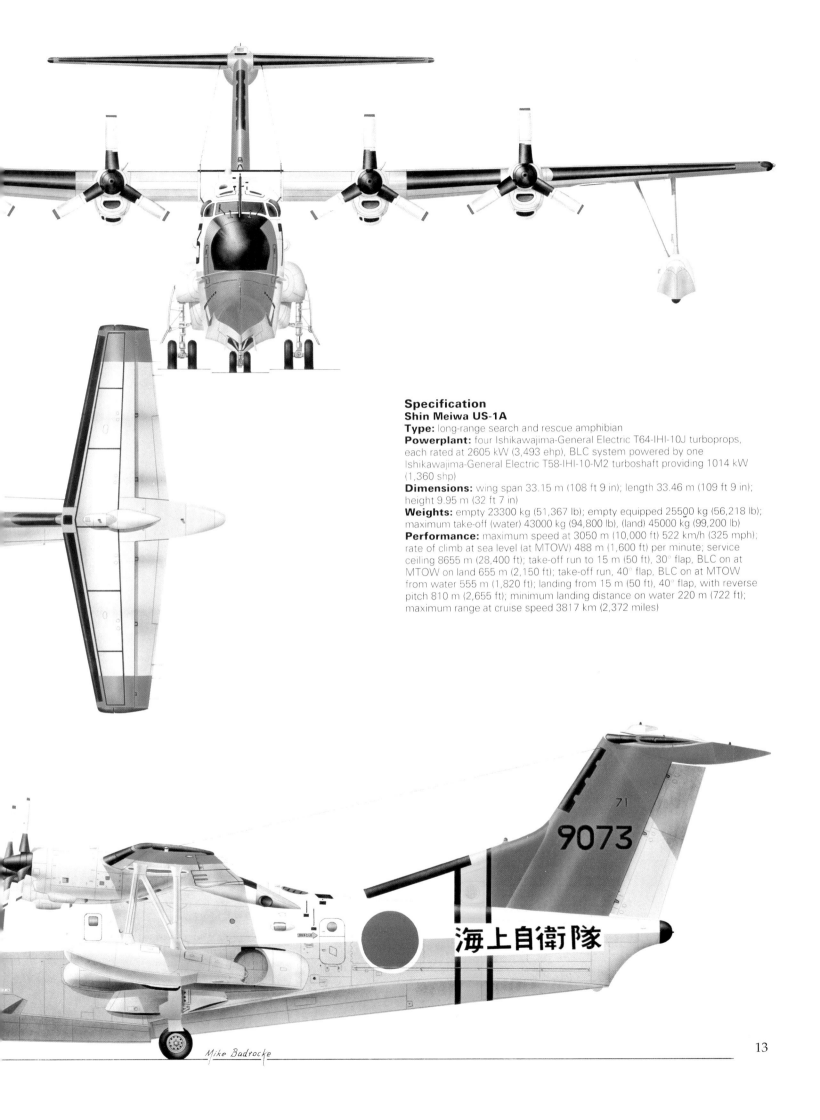

Specification
Shin Meiwa US-1A
Type: long-range search and rescue amphibian
Powerplant: four Ishikawajima-General Electric T64-IHI-10J turboprops, each rated at 2605 kW (3,493 ehp), BLC system powered by one Ishikawajima-General Electric T58-IHI-10-M2 turboshaft providing 1014 kW (1,360 shp)
Dimensions: wing span 33.15 m (108 ft 9 in); length 33.46 m (109 ft 9 in); height 9.95 m (32 ft 7 in)
Weights: empty 23300 kg (51,367 lb); empty equipped 25500 kg (56,218 lb); maximum take-off (water) 43000 kg (94,800 lb), (land) 45000 kg (99,200 lb)
Performance: maximum speed at 3050 m (10,000 ft) 522 km/h (325 mph); rate of climb at sea level (at MTOW) 488 m (1,600 ft) per minute; service ceiling 8655 m (28,400 ft); take-off run to 15 m (50 ft), 30° flap, BLC on at MTOW on land 655 m (2,150 ft); take-off run, 40° flap, BLC on at MTOW from water 555 m (1,820 ft); landing from 15 m (50 ft), 40° flap, with reverse pitch 810 m (2,655 ft); minimum landing distance on water 220 m (722 ft); maximum range at cruise speed 3817 km (2,372 miles)

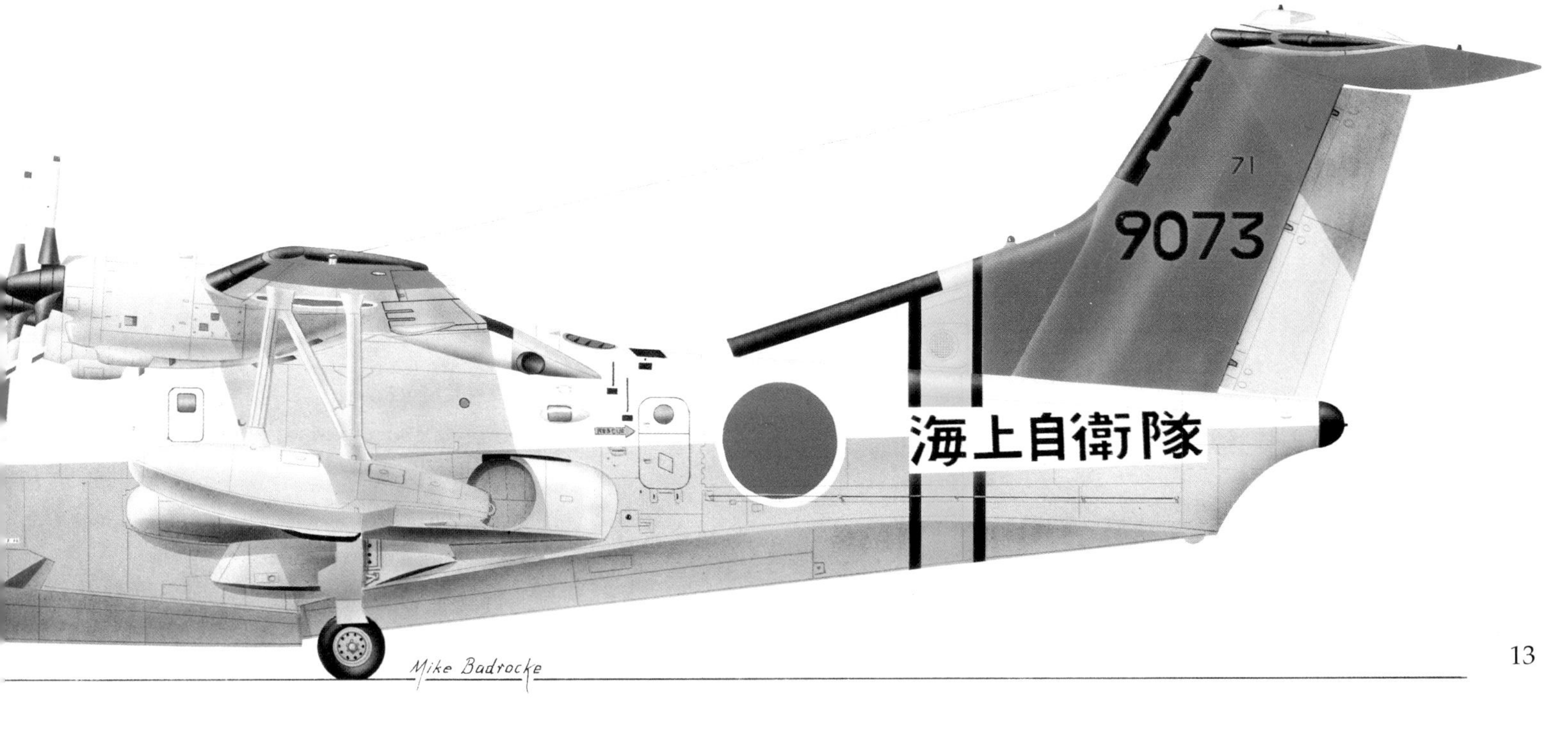

Boeing 727-200

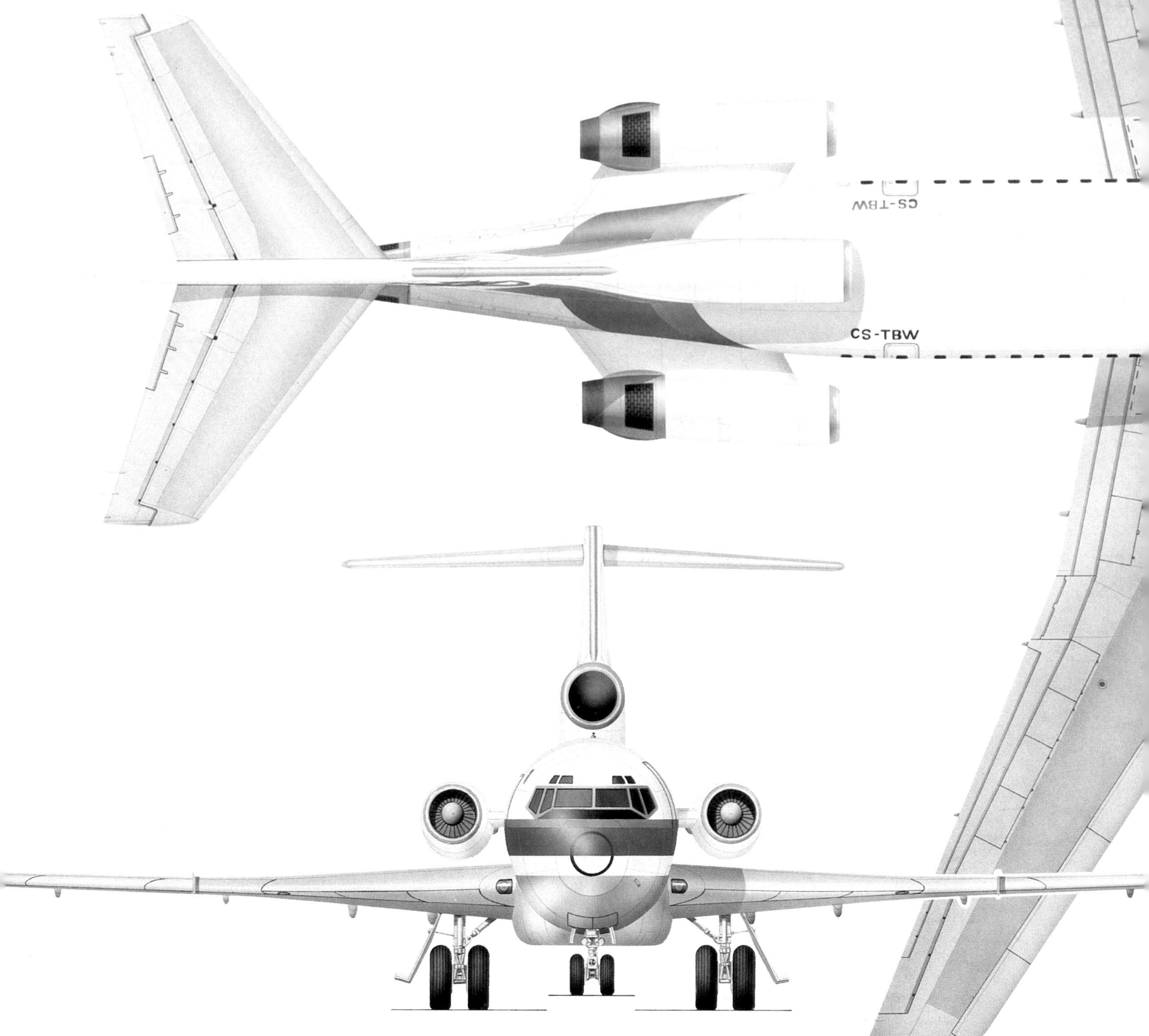

***CS-TBW** is the 13th Boeing 727 supplied to **TAP**, **T**ransportes **A**ereos **P**ortugueses, the national airline of Portugal. **TAP**'s early 727s were short-bodied 082s, or convertible 727-172**C** aircraft, but the latest are of the current standard model, the precise series being 727-282. Altogether these advanced 727s are fast, capable and extremely trouble-free aircraft, their most serious faults being relatively old engines which result in noise and fuel consumption that compares unfavourably with today's aircraft, such as the Boeing 757 or **A**irbus **I**ndustrie **A**310. The dark grills on all three engines are the outlets for the thrust-reversers. On the trailing edge of the 32°-swept wing are inboard high-speed ailerons (between the inboard and outboard sections of triple-slotted flap) and outboard ailerons used at low speeds only, all operating in conjunction with the spoilers seen on the upper surface. Just visible in the side view under the no. 1 engine nozzle is the hydraulically operated aft stairway; many airlines sealed this stairway shut after a hijacker with over a million **US** dollars parachuted through it!*

Boeing Model 727 variants

Model 727-100: first production model, there being no prototypes; fuselage length 40.59 m (133 ft 2 in); standard transport for up to 131 passengers, with three Pratt & Whitney JT8D-1 or D-7 turbofans, with later models having JT8D-9s; maximum take-off weight of 72576 kg (160,000 lb), with later variants certified to 76668 kg (169,000 lb)
Model 727-100C: convertible passenger cargo model with freight door, strengthened floor and floor beams, but otherwise identical to Model 727-100; optional payloads of 94 mixed-class passengers, or of 52 passengers and baggage plus 10297 kg (22,700 lb) of cargo on four pallets, or of 17237 kg (38,000 lb) of cargo on eight pallets
Model 727-100QC: installation of roller-bearing floors for palletised galley and seating and/or palletized freight; conversion from cargo to all-passenger achievable within 30 minutes; freighter with conversion increased ramp weight to 77112 kg (170,000 lb), maximum take-off weight of 76658 kg (169,000 lb), and maximum landing weight of 64411 kg (142,000 lb)
Model 727-100 Business Jet: optional fittings for luxury or business travel; extra fuel tanks in lower cargo compartments to provide a range with 40504 litres (10,700 US gal) of about 6680 km (4,150 miles) with a 1814-kg (4,000-lb) payload; option for dual Carousel IV or Litton LTN501 inertial navigation systems and long-range weather radar
Model 727-200: stretched version with fuselage length of 41.50 m (136 ft 2 in), and basic accommodation for 163 passengers and a maximum capacity of 189; structurally strengthened; revised centre engine air inlet; three JT8D-9 turbofans, each rated at 6577-kg (14,500-lb) thrust to 84°F, as standard with options of JT8D-11s or JT8D-15s
Advanced Model 727-200: increased ramp weight to 86638 kg (191,000 lb) and fitted with sound-suppression; improved avionics with options for INS, Flight Management, dual FD-108 flight directors or Collins FD-110, or Sperry Z-15 flight directors, and Sperry SP-150 Model 5 auto-pilot
Advanced Model 727-200F: pure freighter model with JT8D-17A turbofans; the fuselage has no windows, and up to 11 pallets can be loaded through a port-side hatch in the forward fuselage; the first customer was Federal Express, which ordered 15 in September 1981 for delivery from July 1983

Specification

Boeing 727-200
Type: medium-range passenger or mixed-traffic airliner
Powerplant: three Pratt & Whitney JT8D-9A (6577 kg/14,500 lb thrust), JT8D-15 (7031 kg/15,500 lb) or JT8D-17 (7893 kg/17,400 lb) turbofans
Performance: maximum cruising speed 964 km/h (599 mph); range at long-range cruise speed of 872 km/h (542 mph) with maximum fuel 4392 km (2,729 miles)
Weights: empty equipped 46675 kg (102,000 lb); maximum take-off 95027 kg (209,500 lb)
Dimensions: span 32.92 m (108 ft 0 in); length 46.69 m (153 ft 2 in); height 10.36 m (34 ft 0 in); wing area 157.9 m^2 (1,700 sq ft)
Accommodation: flight crew of three, variable cabin crew for up to 189 passengers, typical mixed-class seating being 14 first plus 131 tourist

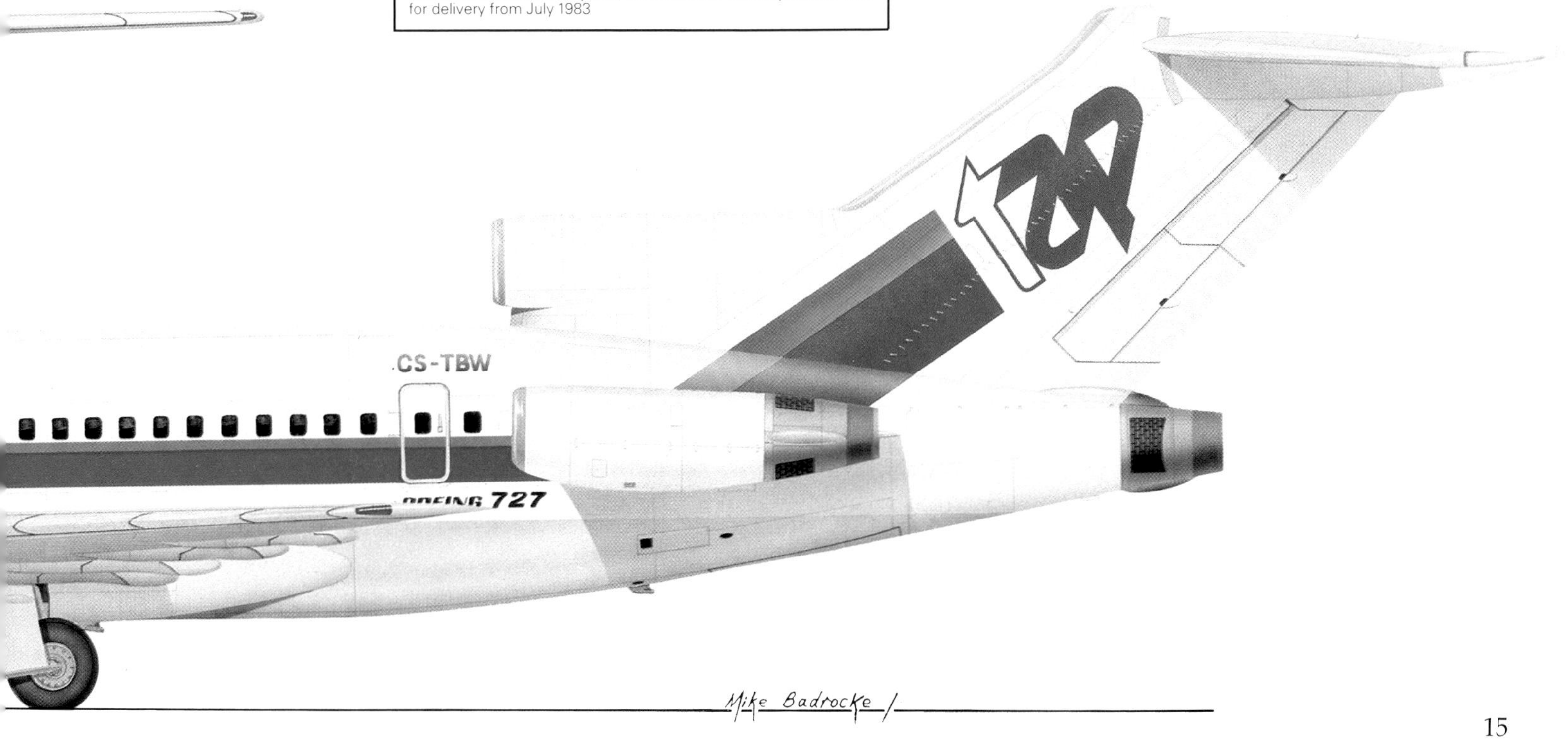

The performance of the MU-2 has made it an attractive proposition for customers, proving considerably faster than the Beech King Air on less power. Other attributes include the high-set wing, making the fuselage low set. In turn this saves weight in terms of undercarriage and integral steps, while increasing comfort. Naturally the Japanese Ground Self Defence Forces were an early customer, finding the type well-suited to liaison and patrol duties. This is the radar-equipped MU-2E which serves in the rescue patrol role.

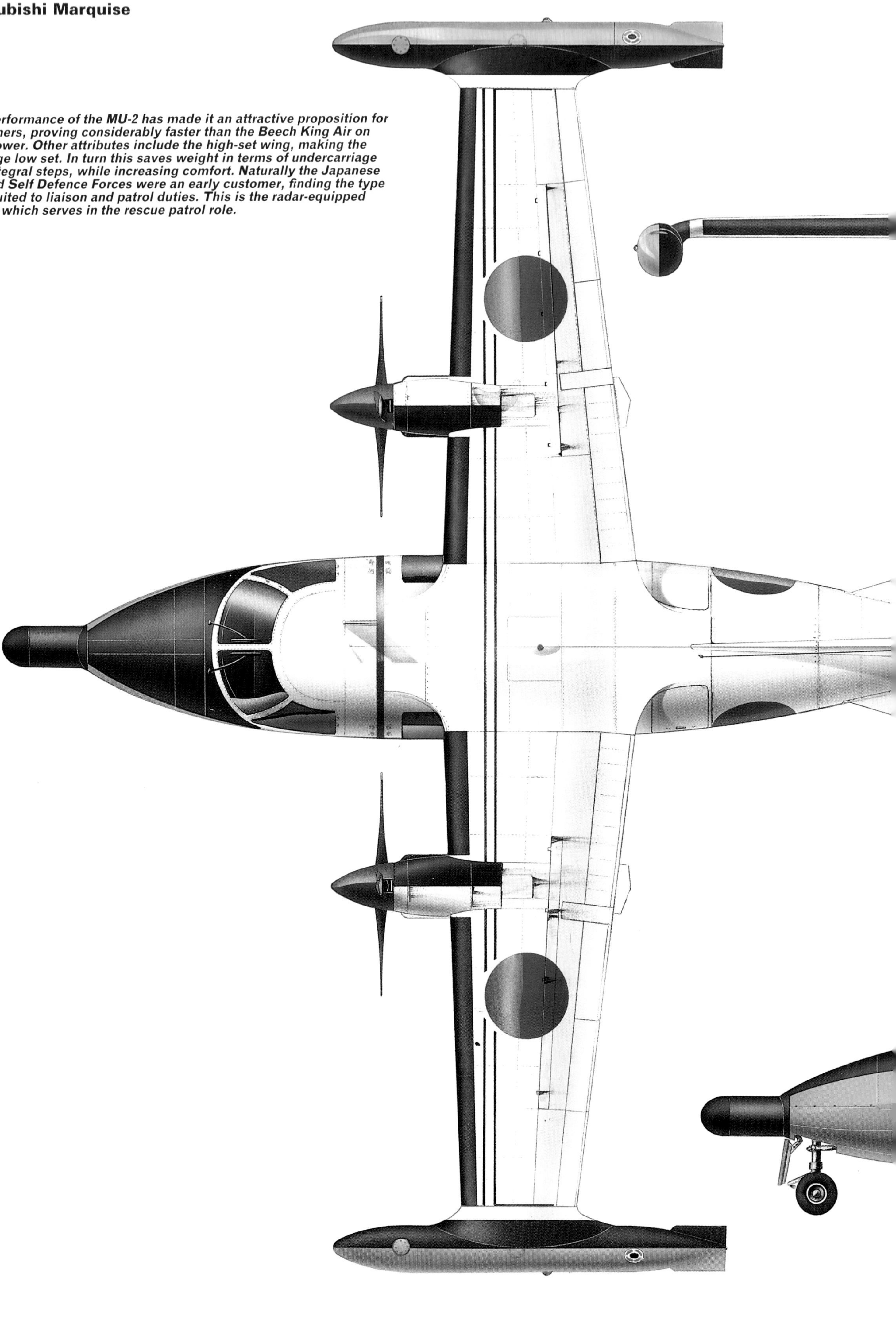

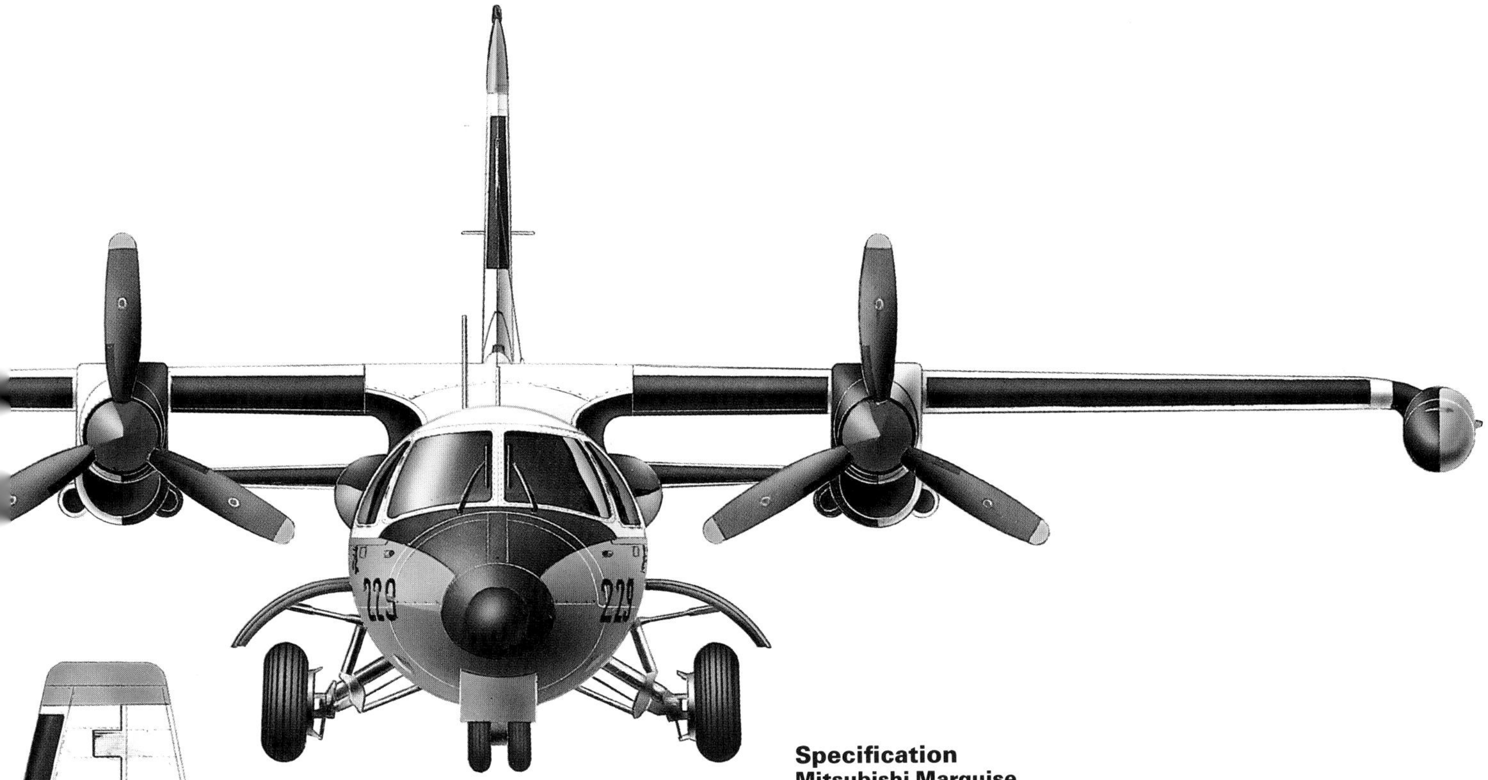

Specification
Mitsubishi Marquise
Wingspan: 11.94 m
Length: 12.02 m
Height: 4.17 m
Wing area: 16.55 m^2
Powerplant: 2 × 715 shp Garrett TPE331-10-501M turboprop engines
Passenger capacity: 7-9
Empty weight: 3470 kg
Maximum take-off weight: 5250 kg
Maximum cruising speed: 571 km/h
Service ceiling: 9070 m
Maximum range: 2584 km

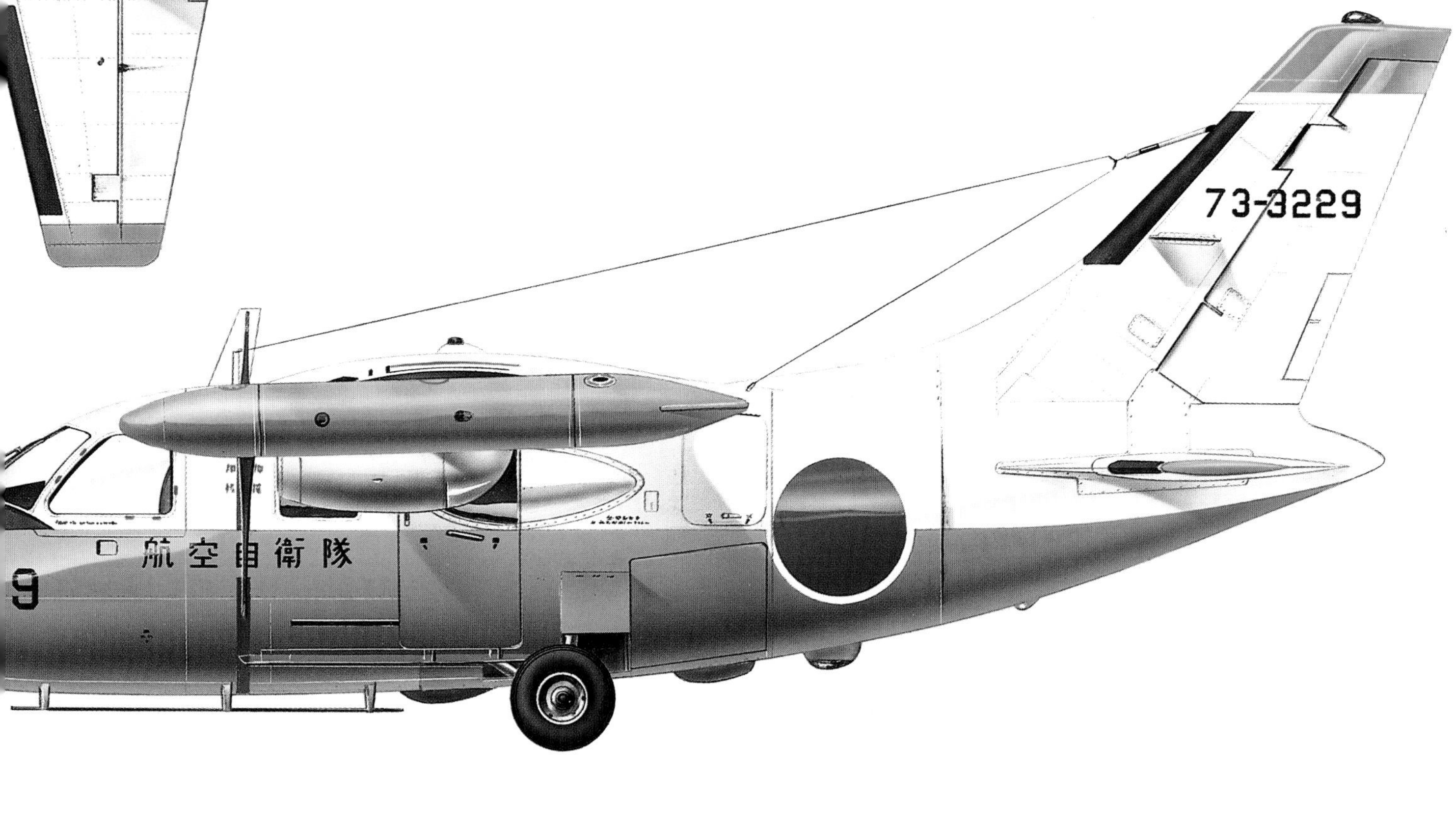

Hawker Siddeley Trident 1C/1E/2E/3B

Specification
Hawker Siddeley Trident 1C

Powerplant: three Rolls-Royce Spey 505-5F turbofan engines each rated at 43.8 kN (9,850 lb) thrust
Performance: economic cruising speed 931.7 km/h (579 mph); maximum cruising speed 981.6 km/h (610 mph); range with maximum payload 2172 km (1,350 miles)
Weights: empty 30877 kg (68,071 lb); maximum take-off 53207 kg (117,300 lb)
Dimensions: wing span 27.1 m (89 ft 10 in); length 35.0 m (114 ft 9 in); height 8.2 m (27 ft 0 in); wing area 126.1 m^2 (1,358 sq ft)

Hawker Siddeley Trident 1E

Powerplant: three Rolls-Royce Spey 511-5 turbofan engines each rated at 50.7 kN (11,400 lb) thrust
Performance: economic cruising speed 933.3 km/h (580 mph); maximum cruising speed 949.4 km/h (590 mph); maximum range 4345 km (2,700 miles)
Weights: empty 31615 kg (69,700 lb); maximum take-off 58968-61499 kg (130,000-135,580 lb)
Dimensions: wing span 28.9 m (95 ft 0 in); length 35.0 m (114 ft 9 in); height 8.2 m (27 ft 0 in); wing area 134.3 m^2 (1,446 sq ft)

Hawker Siddeley Trident 2E

Powerplant: three Rolls-Royce Spey 512-5W turbofan engines each rated at 53.0 kN (11,930 lb) thrust
Performance: economic cruising speed 959.1 km/h (596 mph); maximum cruising speed 973.6 km/h (605 mph); range with maximum payload 4345 km (2,700 miles)
Weights: empty 33203 kg (73,200 lb); maximum take-off 64638 kg (142,500 lb)
Dimensions: wing span 29.8 m (98 ft 0 in); length 35.0 m (114 ft 9 in); height 8.2 m (27 ft 0 in); wing area 135.2 m^2 (1,456 sq ft)

Hawker Siddeley Trident 3B

Powerplant: three Rolls-Royce Spey 512-5W turbofan engines each rated at 53.0 kN (11,930 lb) thrust plus one 23.2 kN (5,250 lb) thrust Rolls-Royce RB.162 auxiliary powerplant
Performance: economic cruising speed 869 km/h (540 mph); maximum cruising speed 885.1 km/h (550 mph); maximum range 3600 km (2,235 miles)
Weights: empty 37084 kg (81,778 lb); maximum take-off 68040 kg (150,000 lb)
Dimensions: wing span 29.8 m (98 ft 0 in); length 39.9 m (131 ft 2 in); height 8.6 m (28 ft 3 in); wing area 138.6 m^2 (1,493 sq ft)

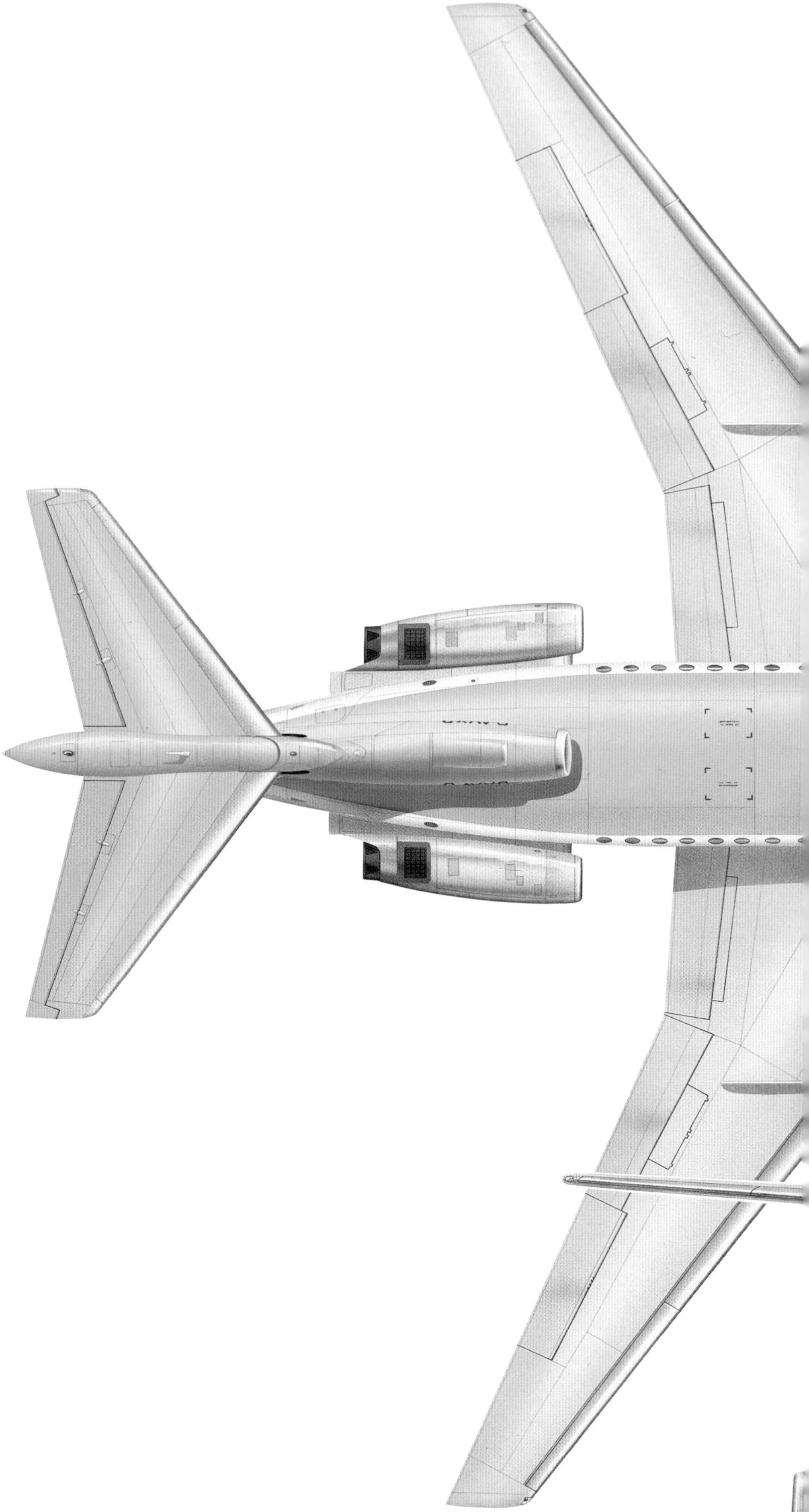

1952 saw the foundation of BKS (Barnaby-Keegan-Stephens) air services as a Dakota operator. The airline grew over the years until in November 1970 it changed its name to Northeast, to underline its ties with that region. It operated a total of four Trident 1E-140s from 1969 onwards, including one originally ordered by Channel Airways. Scheduled domestic routes and holiday charters abroad were flown mainly from Newcastle, Leeds and Tees-side airport. These aircraft were unique in having two overwing emergency exits to permit a high-density seating layout of up to 139 seats. The brightly-painted Tridents were known as 'yellowbirds'. By 1967 the airline had become part of the British Air Services network, which had been set up by BEA to take over the other British regional operators. In 1973 Northeast and its Tridents were absorbed by British Airways.

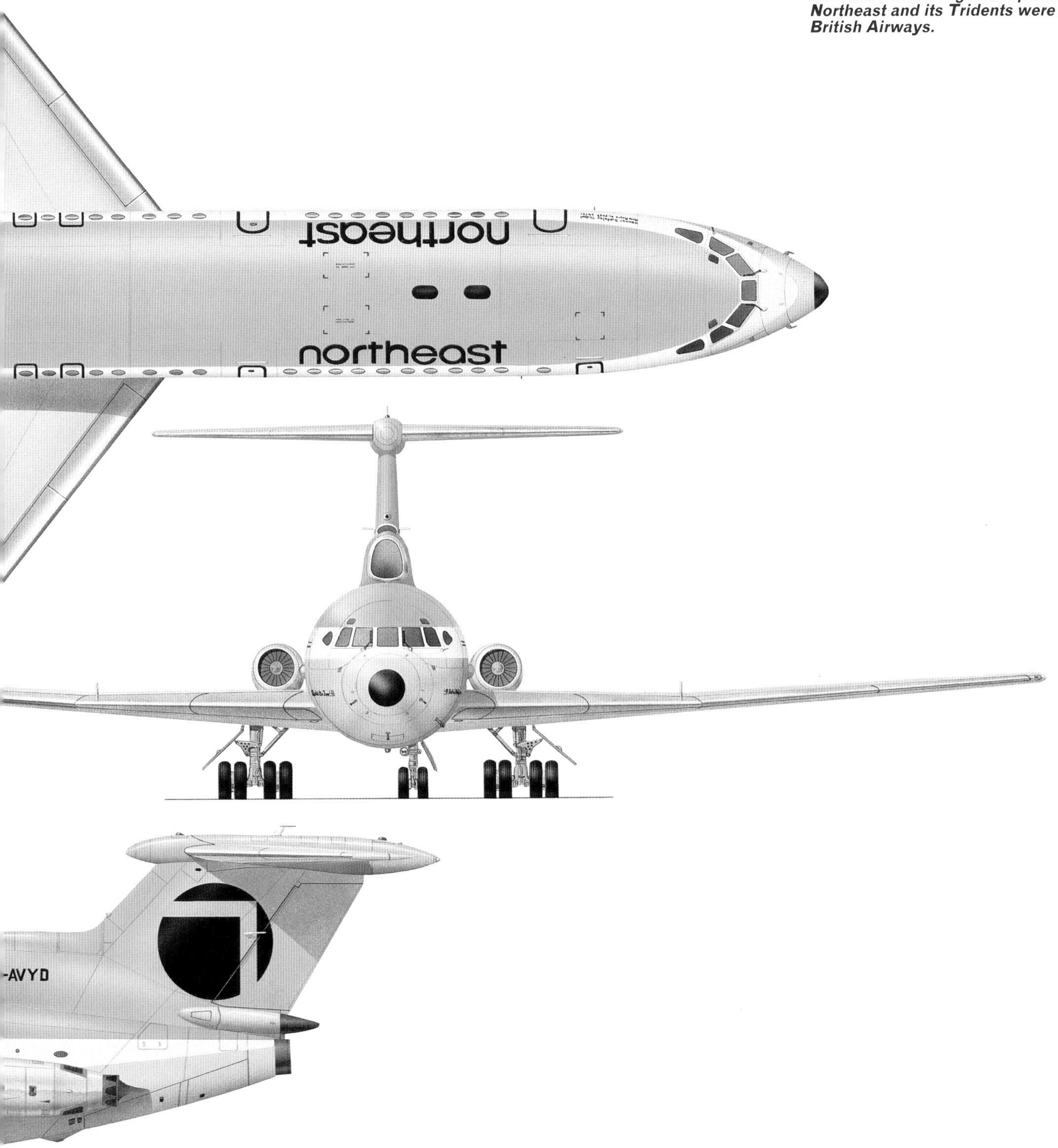

Ilyushin Il-62M

Specification
Ilyushin Il-62M
Wingspan: 43.20 m (141 ft 9 in)
Length: 53.12 m (174 ft 3½ in)
Height: 12.35 m (40 ft 6¼ in)
Wing area: 279.55 m^2 (3,009 sq ft)
Powerplant: four Soloviev D-30KU turbofans each rated at 107.9 kN (24,250 lb st)
Passenger capacity: 174
Maximum zero-fuel weight: 94600 kg (208,550 lb)
Maximum take-off weight: 165000 kg (231,500 lb)
Cruising speed: 486 kts (900 km/h, 559 mph)
Range: with maximum payload and fuel reserves, 4,210 nm (7800 km, 4846 miles)

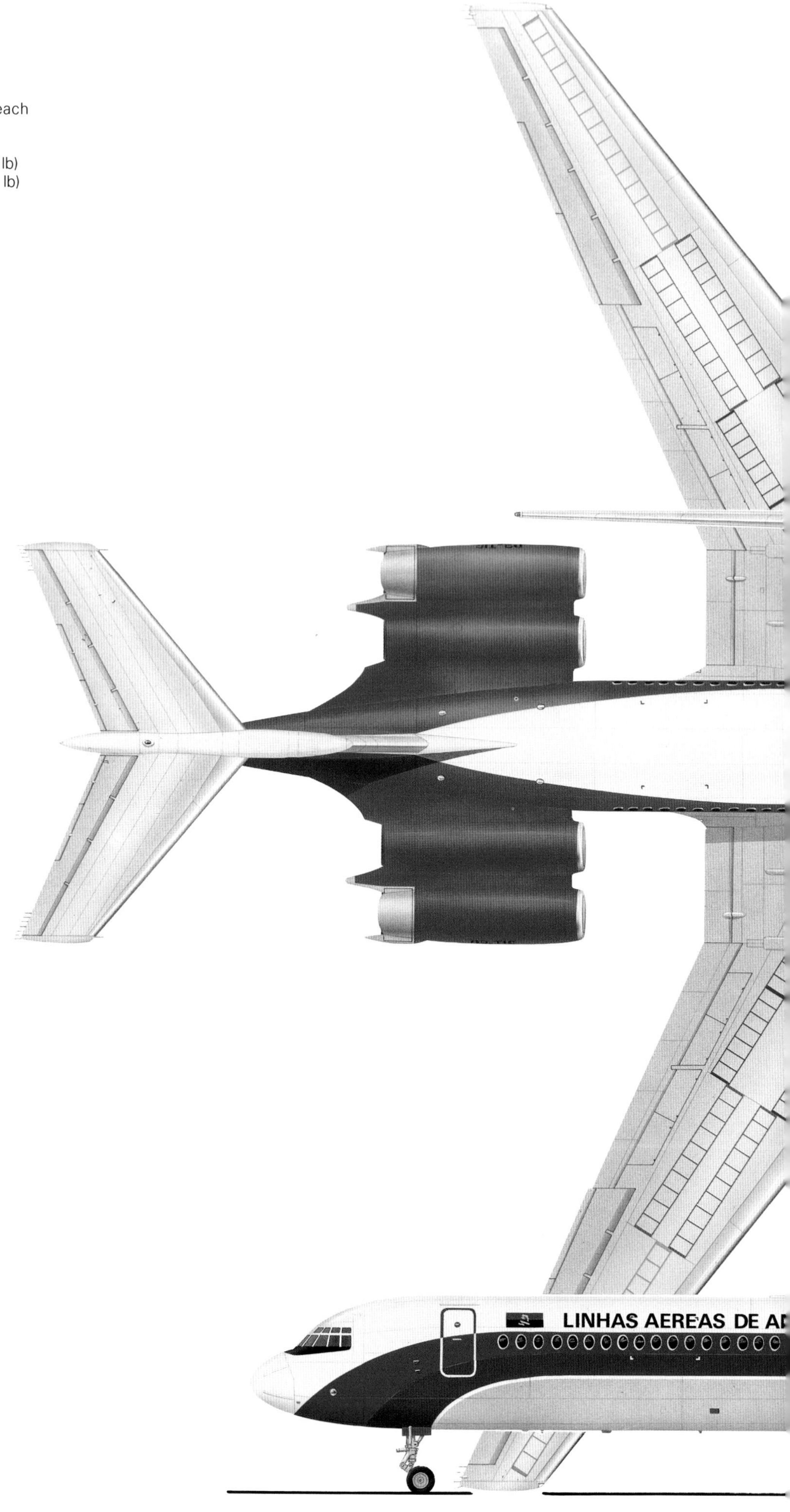

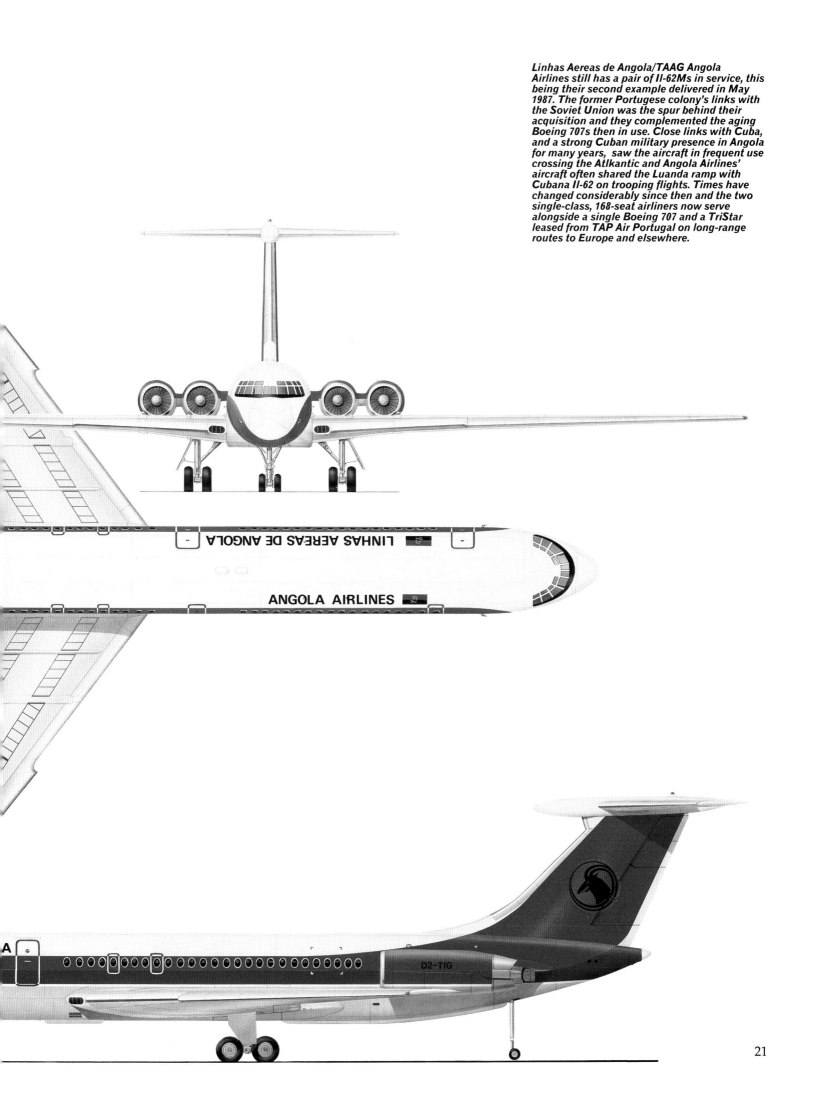

Linhas Aereas de Angola/TAAG Angola Airlines still has a pair of Il-62Ms in service, this being their second example delivered in May 1987. The former Portugese colony's links with the Soviet Union was the spur behind their acquisition and they complemented the aging Boeing 707s then in use. Close links with Cuba, and a strong Cuban military presence in Angola for many years, saw the aircraft in frequent use crossing the Atlkantic and Angola Airlines' aircraft often shared the Luanda ramp with Cubana Il-62 on trooping flights. Times have changed considerably since then and the two single-class, 168-seat airliners now serve alongside a single Boeing 707 and a TriStar leased from TAP Air Portugal on long-range routes to Europe and elsewhere.

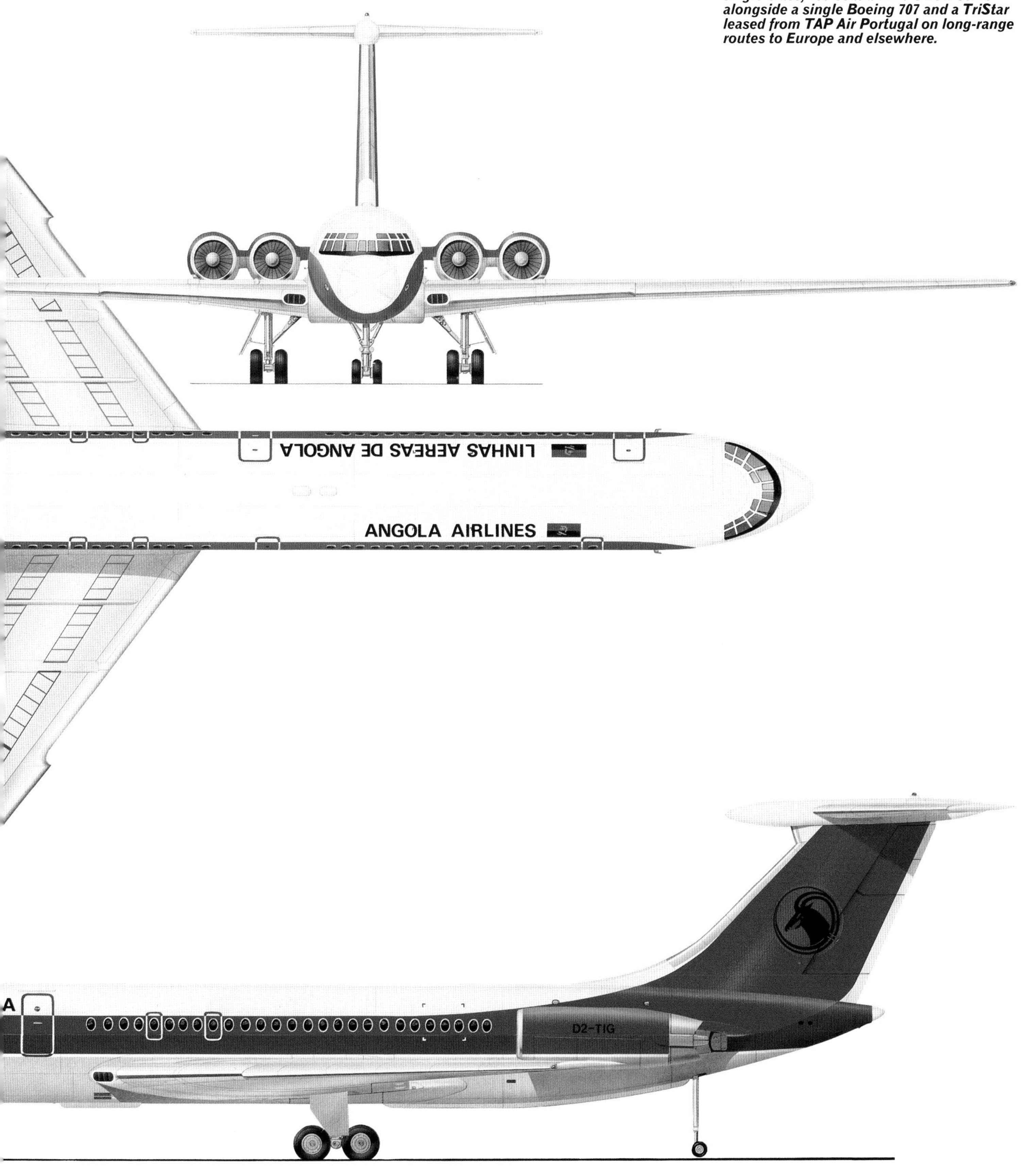

Boeing Model 720-048

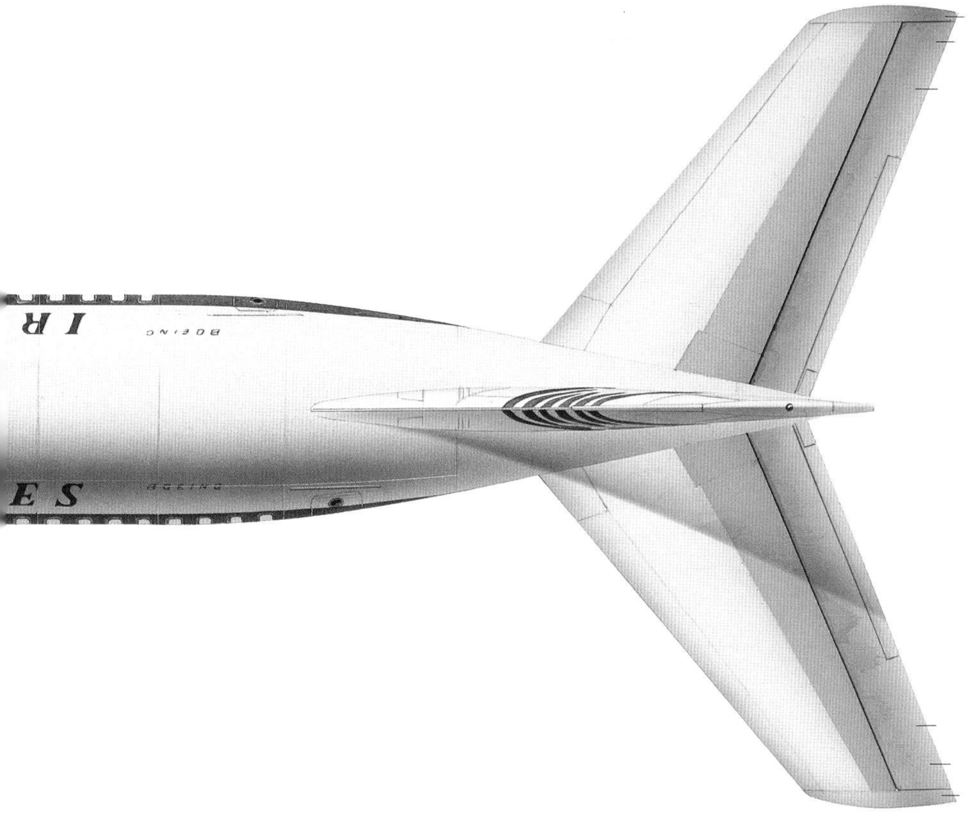

Specification

Boeing Model 720-048

Type: medium-range passenger transport
Powerplant: four Pratt & Whitney JT3C-7 turbojets, each rated at 55.62 kN (12,500 lb) thrust
Performance: maximum speed 1010 km/h (628 mph); maximum cruising speed at 7620 m (25,000 ft) 945 km/h (587 mph); economical cruising speed at 12192 m (40,000 ft) 897 km/h (557 mph); rate of climb at sea level 731 m (2,400 ft) per minute; service ceiling 12192 m (40,000 ft); take-off distance to 15 m (50 ft) 2865 m (9,400 ft); landing distance from 15 m (50 ft) 1890 m (6,200 ft); landing run 790 m (2,590 ft); stalling speed, flaps down 183 km/h (114 mph); range with maximum fuel, no reserves 8433 km (5,240 miles); range with maximum payload, no reserves 6815 km (4,235 miles)
Weights: operating empty 50259 kg (110,800 lb); maximum take-off 103874 kg (229,000 lb); maximum payload 12792 kg (28,200 lb); fuel load 51292 litres (13,550 US gal)
Dimensions: wing span 39.87 m (130 ft 10 in); length 41.68 m (136 ft 9 in); height 12.67 m (41 ft 7 in); tailplane span 12.09 m (39 ft 8 in); wing area 234.2 m^2 (2,521 sq ft)

Irish carrier Aer Lingus began its association with Boeing products with the Model 720. Three Series 048s were purchased (EI-ALA/B/C), and used for the transatlantic route. This may seem surprising, but the distance from Shannon in the west of Ireland to the United States was short enough for the Model 720 to conquer. This aircraft was the first delivered, joining the airline on 24 October 1960. It had the name St Patrick bestowed on it as flagship of the fleet. St Briget followed on 24 January 1961, and the third, St Brendan, on 6 April. The deliveries of Boeing 707-348Cs beginning in June 1964 allowed the 720 to retire from the US route, and it assumed shorter-range and inclusive-tour duties. The trio was sold to other operators between September 1972 and May 1973.

Tupolev Tu-134A

Specification

Tupolev Tu-134A
Type: short/medium-range passenger transport
Powerplant: two Soloviev D-30 Srs II turbofans, rated at 66.7 kN (14,990 lb) thrust each
Performance: maximum cruising speed 885 km (550 mph); service ceiling 11900 m (39,000 ft); take-off length 2400 m (7,875 ft); landing length 2200 m (7,218 ft); range with maximum payload 1890 km (1,174 miles); range with 5000-kg (11,025-lb) payload 3020 km (1,876 miles)
Weights: operating empty 29050 kg (64,045 lb); maximum take-off 47000 kg (103,600 lb)
Dimensions: span 29.00 m (95 ft 1¾ in); length 37.05 m (121 ft 6½ in); height 9.14 m (30 ft 0 in); wing area 127.3 m^2 (1,370.3 sq ft)

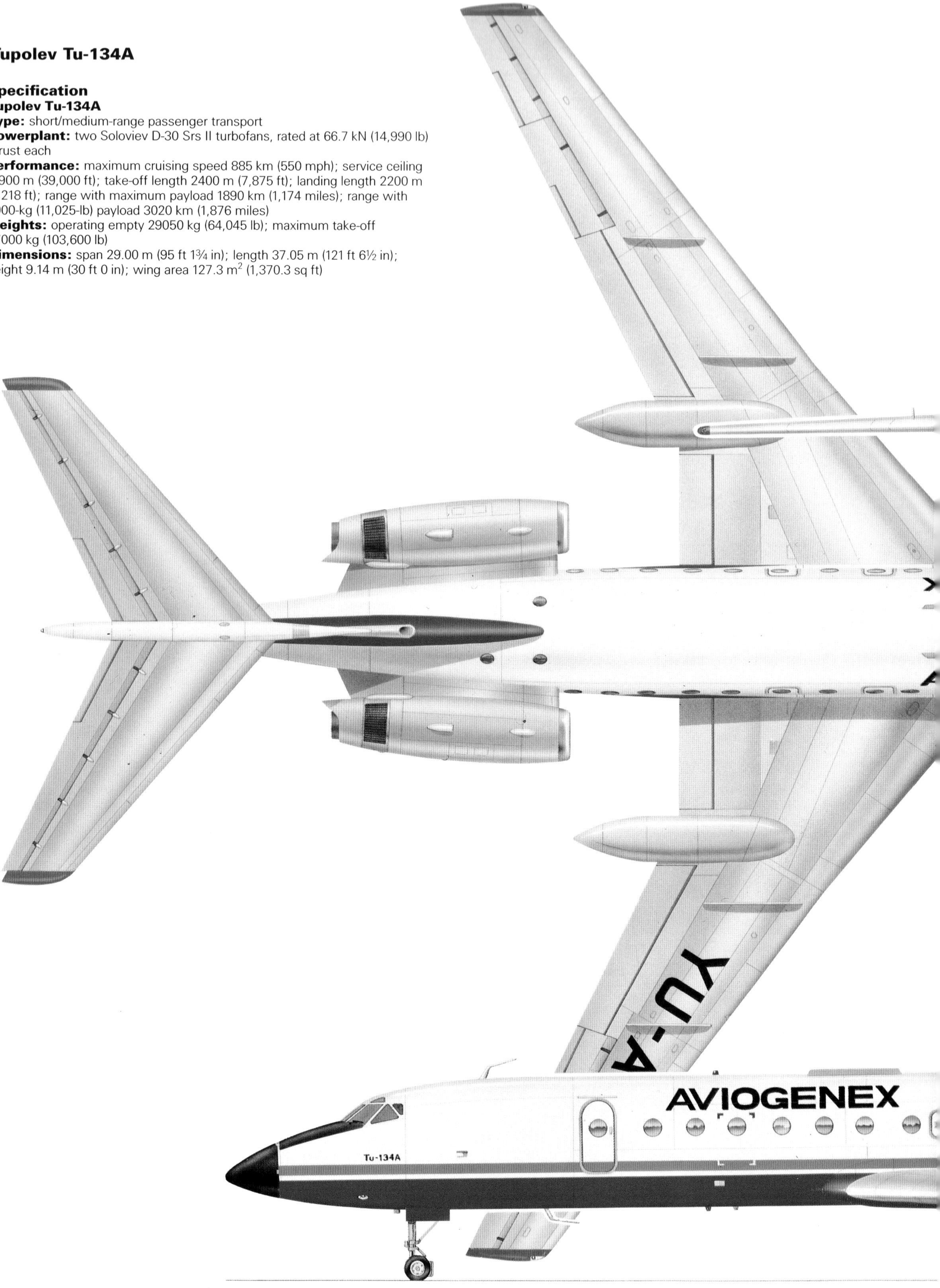

Formed in 1968 as Genex Airlines, Aviogenex is the air transport division of the Yugoslavian General Export organisation. It flies passenger charter flights in Europe and the Mediterranean, in association with Yugotours. The fleet was split between US and Soviet types, the latter represented by four Tu-134A-3 aircraft, converted from Tu-134As by the addition of fuel-efficient Soloviev D-30-III engines. Delivered in 1971-72, the Tu-134s were configured in a single-class arrangement for 86 passengers in high-density seating. Each aircraft was named after a Yugoslavian town: this aircraft is Titograd, the others being Beograd, Zagreb and Skopje. They were replaced between 1986-90 by Boeing 737-200s, and returned to the USSR.

Specification
BAe (Hawker Siddeley) 748 Series 2A
Type: short range passenger/freight transport
Powerplant: two Rolls-Royce Dart RDa.7 Mk 535-2 turboprops, 1700 kW (2,280 ehp) each
Performance: cruising speed 452 km/h (281 mph); maximum rate of climb 433 m (1,420 ft) per minute; service ceiling 7620 m (25,000 ft); take-off length 1225 m (4,020 ft); range with maximum payload 1361 m (846 miles); range with maximum fuel 3132 km (1,946 miles)
Weights: operating basic 12159 kg (26,806 lb); maximum take-off 21092 kg (46,500 lb)
Dimensions: span 30.02 m (98 ft 6 in); length 20.42 m (67 ft 0 in); height 7.57 m (24 ft 10 in); wing area 75.35 m^2 (810.75 sq ft)

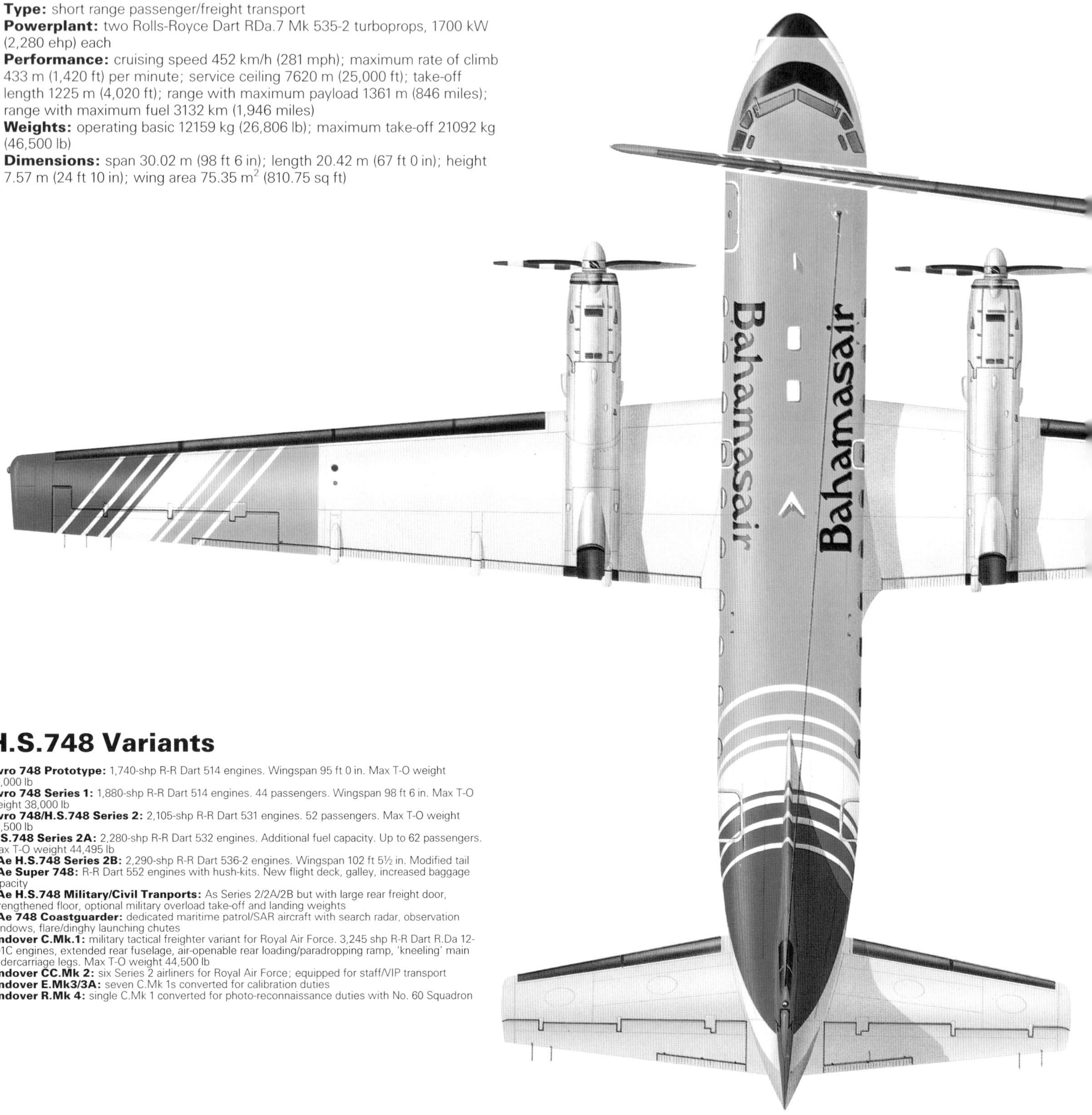

H.S.748 Variants

Avro 748 Prototype: 1,740-shp R-R Dart 514 engines. Wingspan 95 ft 0 in. Max T-O weight 33,000 lb
Avro 748 Series 1: 1,880-shp R-R Dart 514 engines. 44 passengers. Wingspan 98 ft 6 in. Max T-O weight 38,000 lb
Avro 748/H.S.748 Series 2: 2,105-shp R-R Dart 531 engines. 52 passengers. Max T-O weight 43,500 lb
H.S.748 Series 2A: 2,280-shp R-R Dart 532 engines. Additional fuel capacity. Up to 62 passengers. Max T-O weight 44,495 lb
BAe H.S.748 Series 2B: 2,290-shp R-R Dart 536-2 engines. Wingspan 102 ft 5½ in. Modified tail
BAe Super 748: R-R Dart 552 engines with hush-kits. New flight deck, galley, increased baggage capacity
BAe H.S.748 Military/Civil Tranports: As Series 2/2A/2B but with large rear freight door, strengthened floor, optional military overload take-off and landing weights
BAe 748 Coastguarder: dedicated maritime patrol/SAR aircraft with search radar, observation windows, flare/dinghy launching chutes
Andover C.Mk.1: military tactical freighter variant for Royal Air Force. 3,245 shp R-R Dart R.Da 12-201C engines, extended rear fuselage, air-openable rear loading/paradropping ramp, 'kneeling' main undercarriage legs. Max T-O weight 44,500 lb
Andover CC.Mk 2: six Series 2 airliners for Royal Air Force; equipped for staff/VIP transport
Andover E.Mk3/3A: seven C.Mk 1s converted for calibration duties
Andover R.Mk 4: single C.Mk 1 converted for photo-reconnaissance duties with No. 60 Squadron

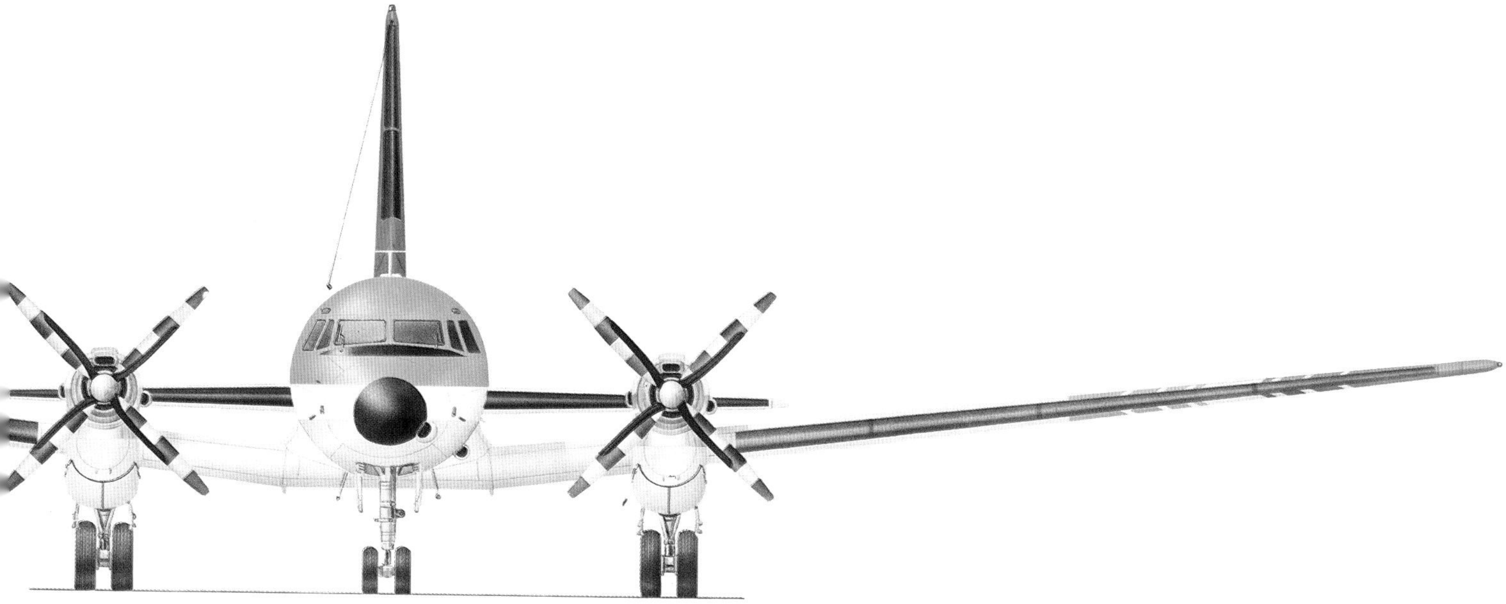

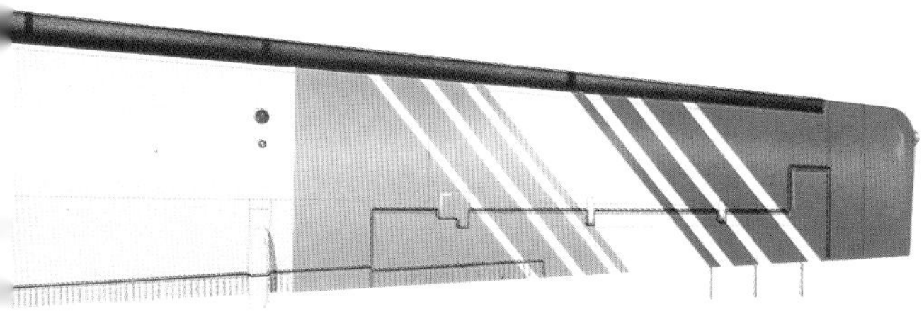

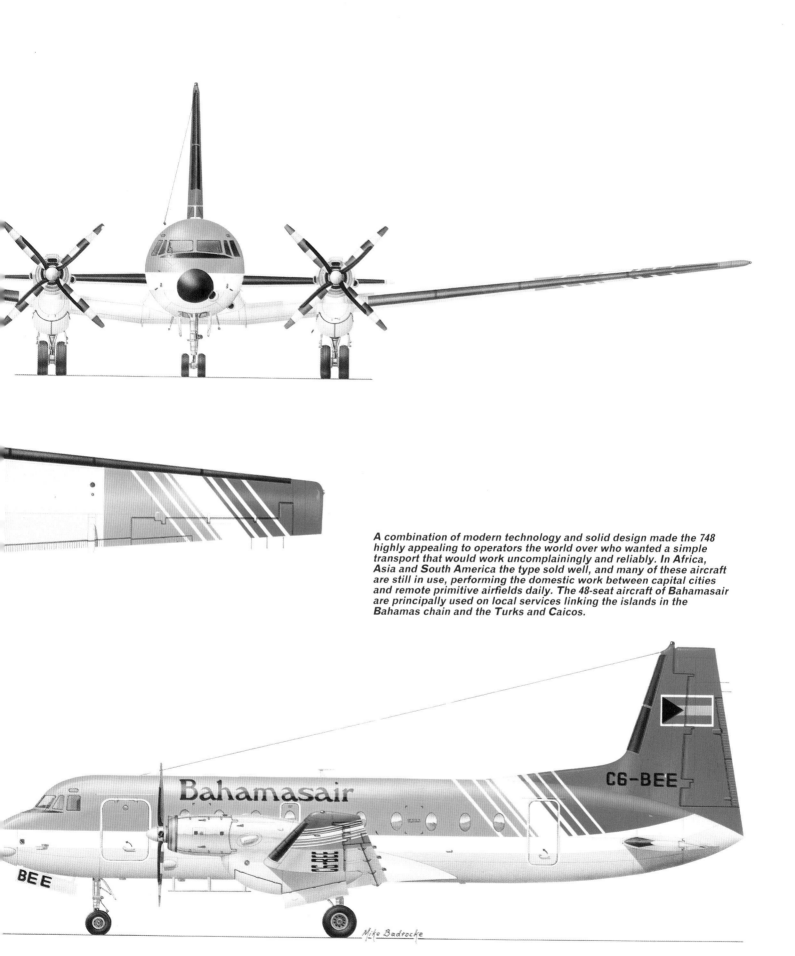

A combination of modern technology and solid design made the 748 highly appealing to operators the world over who wanted a simple transport that would work uncomplainingly and reliably. In Africa, Asia and South America the type sold well, and many of these aircraft are still in use, performing the domestic work between capital cities and remote primitive airfields daily. The 48-seat aircraft of Bahamasair are principally used on local services linking the islands in the Bahamas chain and the Turks and Caicos.

Boeing Advanced Model 737-200

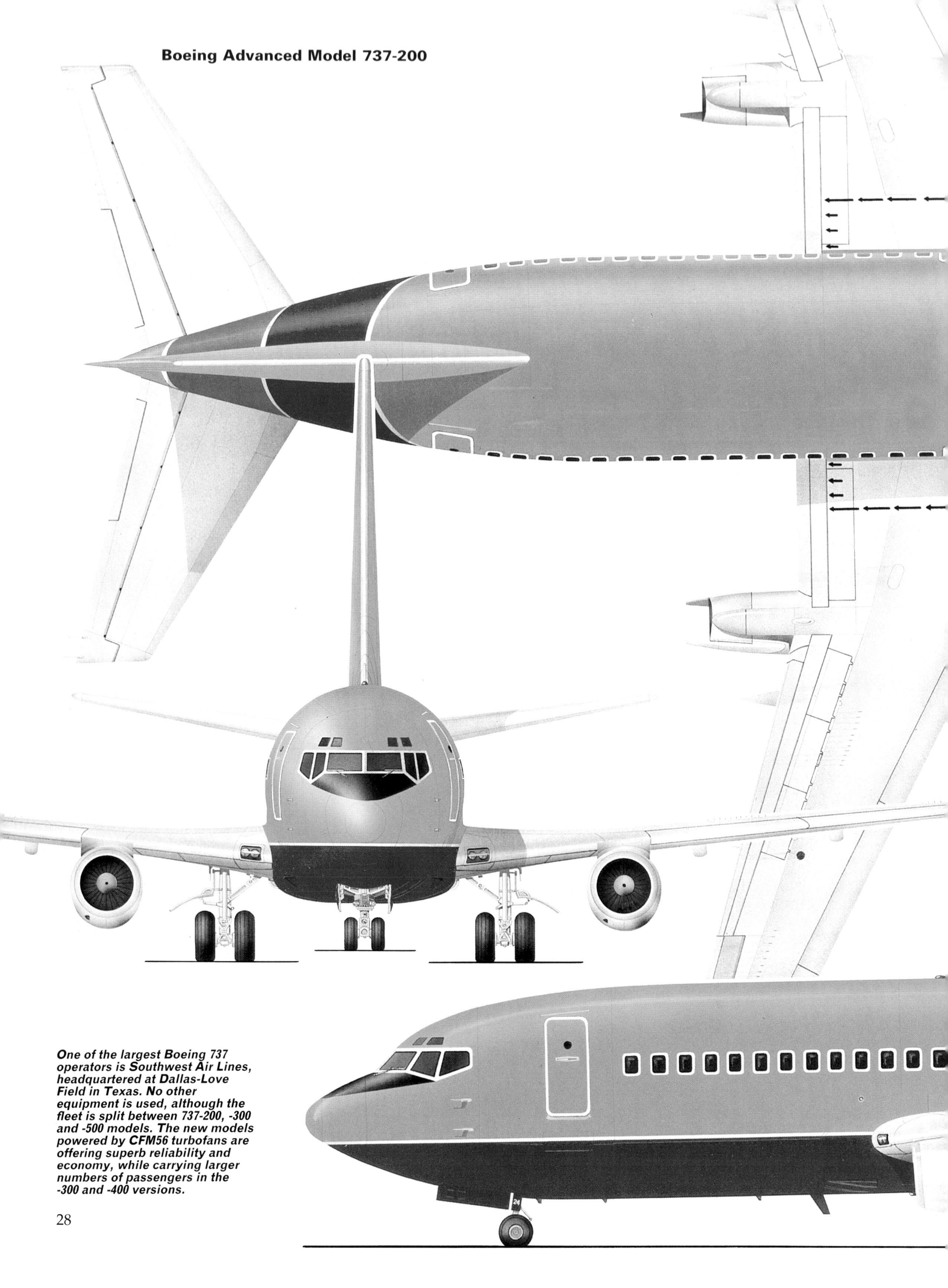

One of the largest Boeing 737 operators is Southwest Air Lines, headquartered at Dallas-Love Field in Texas. No other equipment is used, although the fleet is split between 737-200, -300 and -500 models. The new models powered by CFM56 turbofans are offering superb reliability and economy, while carrying larger numbers of passengers in the -300 and -400 versions.

Specification

Boeing Advanced Model 737-200

Type: 115/130-seat short/medium-range airliner

Powerplant: standard, two Pratt & Whitney JT8D-9A turbofans, each of 6577-kg (14,500-lb) thrust; optionally, two 7030-kg (15,500-lb) thrust JT8D-15/15A or 7258-kg (16,000-lb) thrust JT8D-17/17A turbofans

Performance: (standard weight option with JT8D-17s) maximum cruising speed 909 km/h (565 mph) at 7620 m (25,000 ft); long-range cruising speed 774 km/h (481 mph) at 10670 m (35,000 ft); range with 115 passengers 3423 km (2,127 miles); take-off field length 1975 m (6,475 ft); landing field length 1350 m (4,430 ft)

Weights: empty 27765 kg (61,210 lb); maximum take-off 53071 kg (117,000 lb); optional maximum take-off 58333 kg (128,600lb); maximum landing 46721 kg (103,000 lb)

Dimensions: span 28.35 m (93 ft 0 in); length overall 30.48 m (100 ft 0 in); height 11.28 m (37 ft 0 in); wing area 91.04 m^2 (980.0 sq ft)

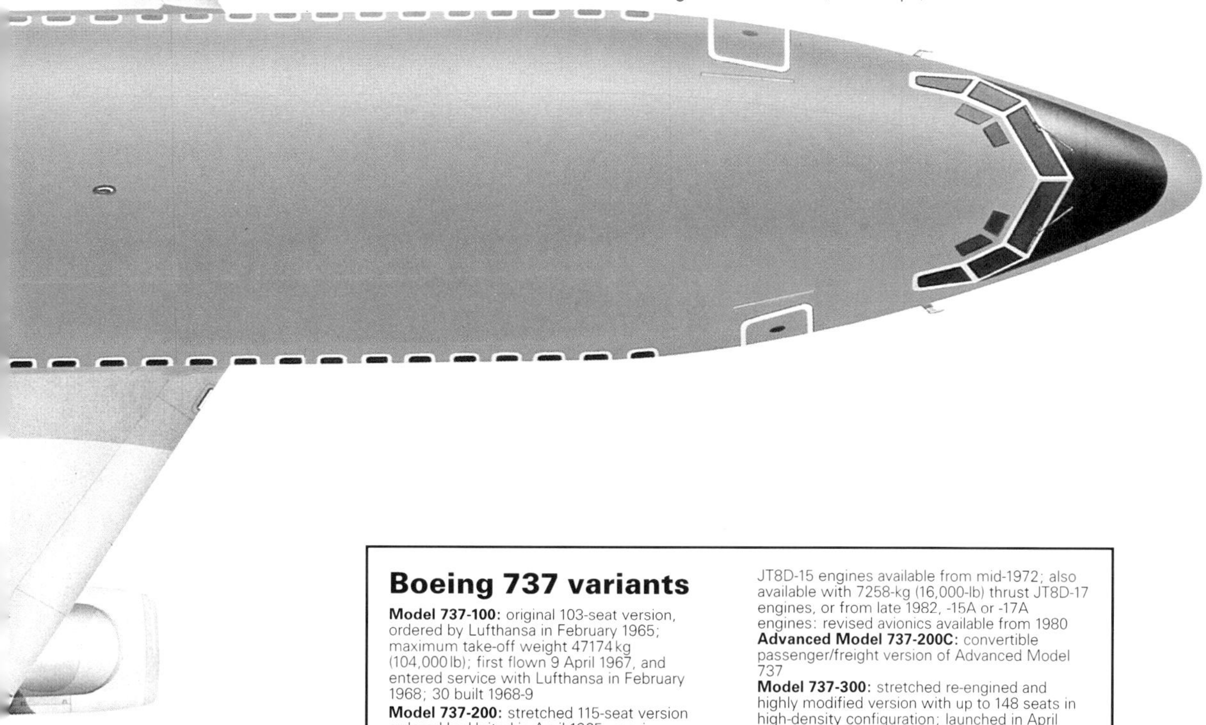

Boeing 737 variants

Model 737-100: original 103-seat version, ordered by Lufthansa in February 1965; maximum take-off weight 47174 kg (104,000 lb); first flown 9 April 1967, and entered service with Lufthansa in February 1968; 30 built 1968-9

Model 737-200: stretched 115-seat version ordered by United in April 1965; maximum take-off weight 51484 kg (113,500 lb); first flown June 1967, and entered service with United in April 1968; 250-plus Model 737-200s and Model 737-200Cs delivered between 1968 and mid-1971

Model 737-200C: convertible passenger/freight version, with freight door in forward fuselage and strengthened floor with cargo fixtures; also available in **Model 737-200QC** quick-change form

Advanced Model 737-200: improved version, standard from mid-1971; maximum take-off weight options from 53071 kg (117,000 lb) to 58333 kg (128,600 lb); JT8D-15 engines available from mid-1972; also available with 7258-kg (16,000-lb) thrust JT8D-17 engines, or from late 1982, -15A or -17A engines; revised avionics available from 1980

Advanced Model 737-200C: convertible passenger/freight version of Advanced Model 737

Model 737-300: stretched re-engined and highly modified version with up to 148 seats in high-density configuration; launched in April 1981

Model 737-400: further stretched version with 154 seats in standard mixed-class layout

Model 737-500: short fuselage model with derated engines for longer-range sectors

T-43A: US Air Force navigation trainer developed from Advanced Model 737; first flown in June 1973 and last of 19 delivered in July 1974; equipped with all navigation systems of aircraft such as the B-52, C-5A, E-3A, E-4A and C-135; accommodation for 16 students and three instructors

Model 737 Surveiller: maritime patrol version, equipped with Motorola side-looking airborne radar in rear fuselage – three for Indonesia

BN-2B Islander II/BN-2A Mk III Trislander

Specification
BN-2B Islander II
Wingspan: 14.94 m (49 ft)
Length: 10.86 m (35 ft 7 in)
Height: 4.18 m (13 ft 8 in)
Wing area: 30.19 m^2 (325 sq ft)
Powerplant: two 194-kW (260-hp) Avco Lycoming O-540-E4C5 or 224-kW (300-hp) IO-540-K1B5 piston engines
Passenger capacity: 10
Empty weight: 1866 kg (4,114 lb)
Maximum take-off weight: 2993 kg (6,600 lb)
Maximum speed: 274 km/h (170 mph)
Service ceiling: 6005 m (19,700 ft)
Maximum range: 1400 km (870 miles)

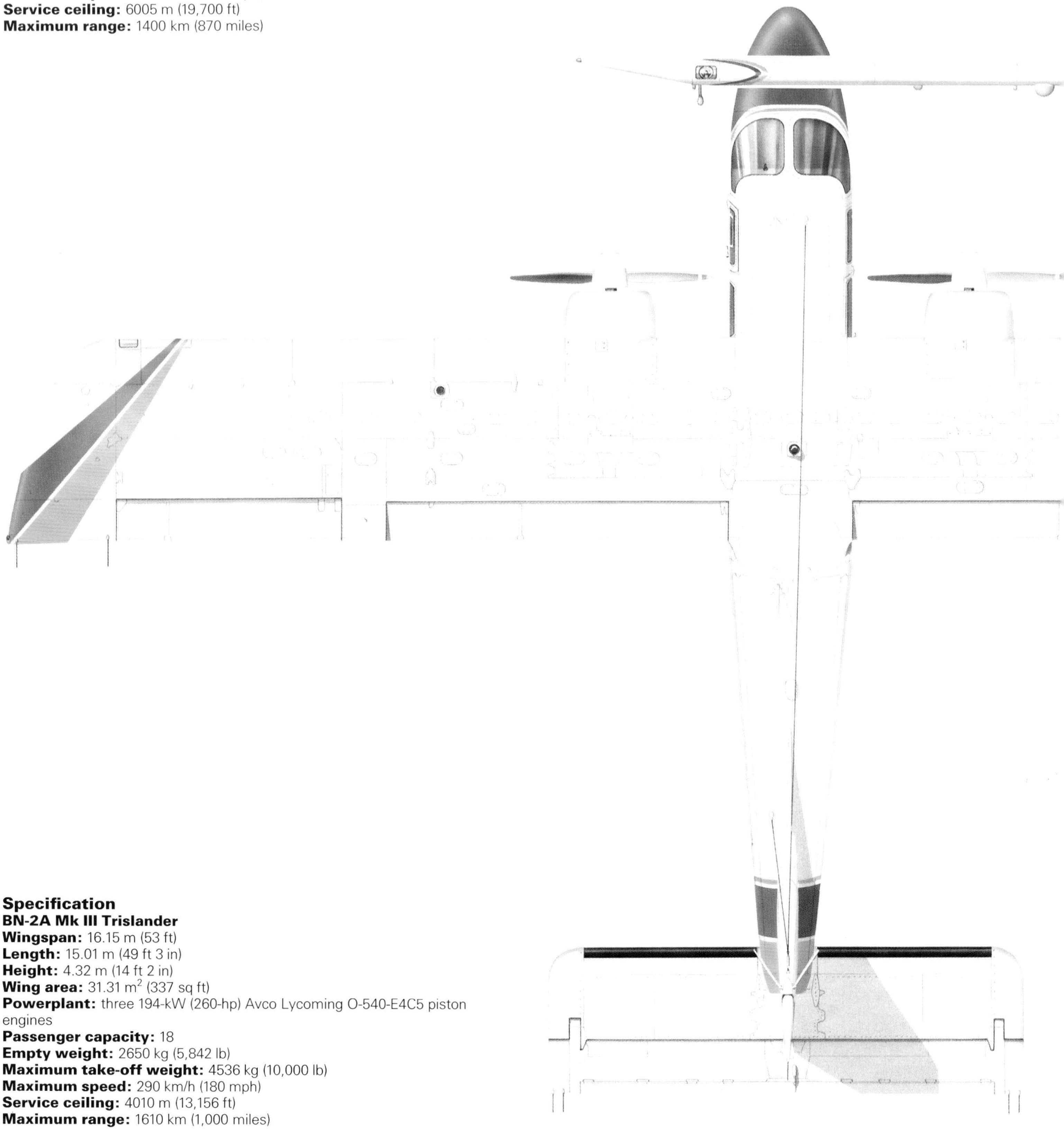

Specification
BN-2A Mk III Trislander
Wingspan: 16.15 m (53 ft)
Length: 15.01 m (49 ft 3 in)
Height: 4.32 m (14 ft 2 in)
Wing area: 31.31 m^2 (337 sq ft)
Powerplant: three 194-kW (260-hp) Avco Lycoming O-540-E4C5 piston engines
Passenger capacity: 18
Empty weight: 2650 kg (5,842 lb)
Maximum take-off weight: 4536 kg (10,000 lb)
Maximum speed: 290 km/h (180 mph)
Service ceiling: 4010 m (13,156 ft)
Maximum range: 1610 km (1,000 miles)

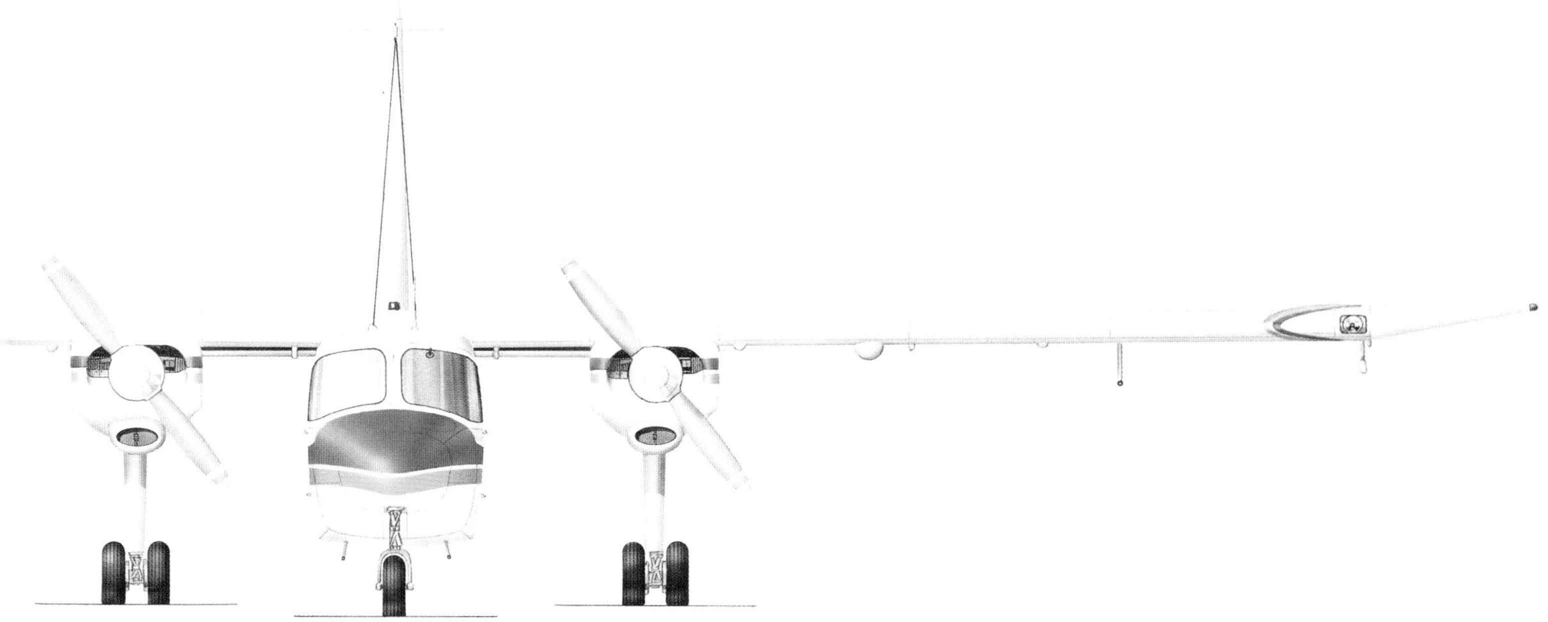

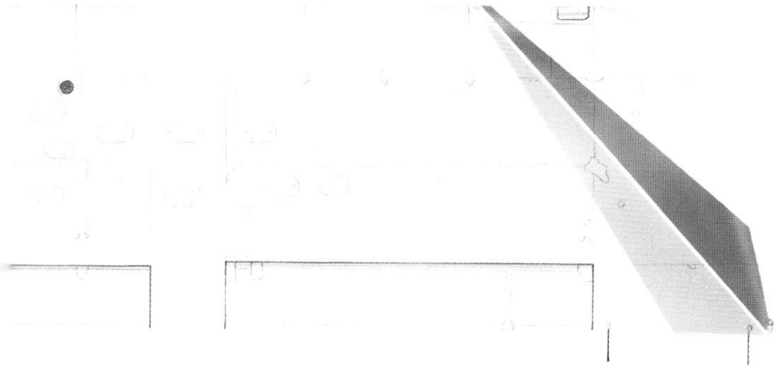

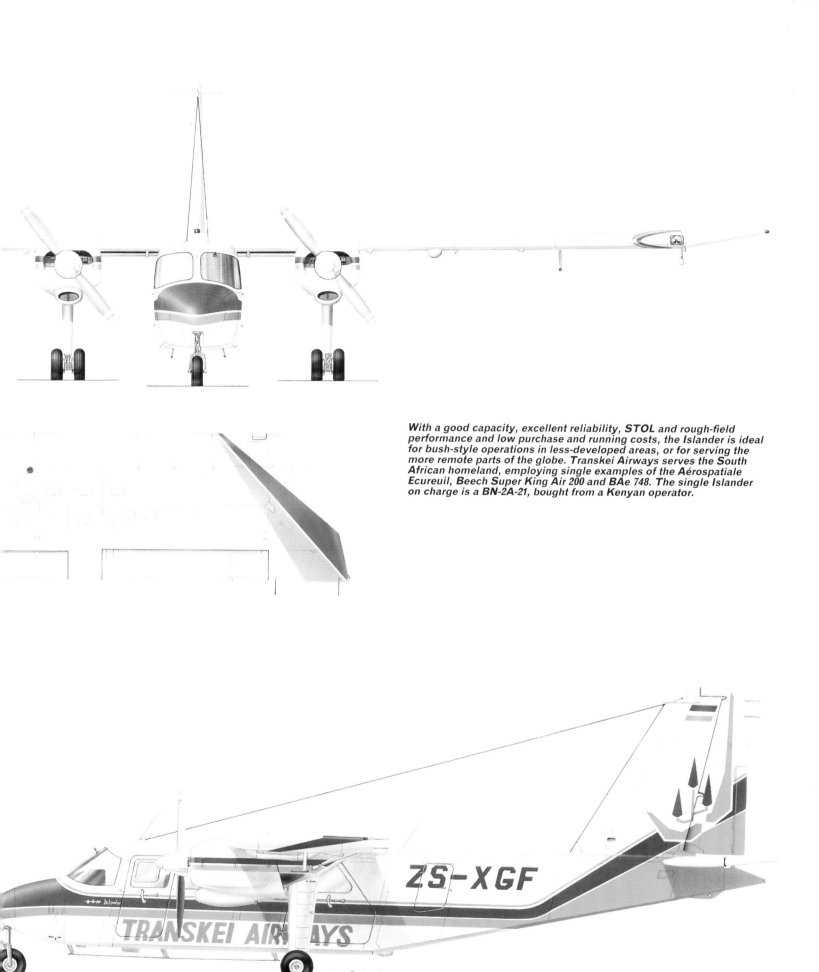

With a good capacity, excellent reliability, STOL and rough-field performance and low purchase and running costs, the Islander is ideal for bush-style operations in less-developed areas, or for serving the more remote parts of the globe. Transkei Airways serves the South African homeland, employing single examples of the Aérospatiale Ecureuil, Beech Super King Air 200 and BAe 748. The single Islander on charge is a BN-2A-21, bought from a Kenyan operator.

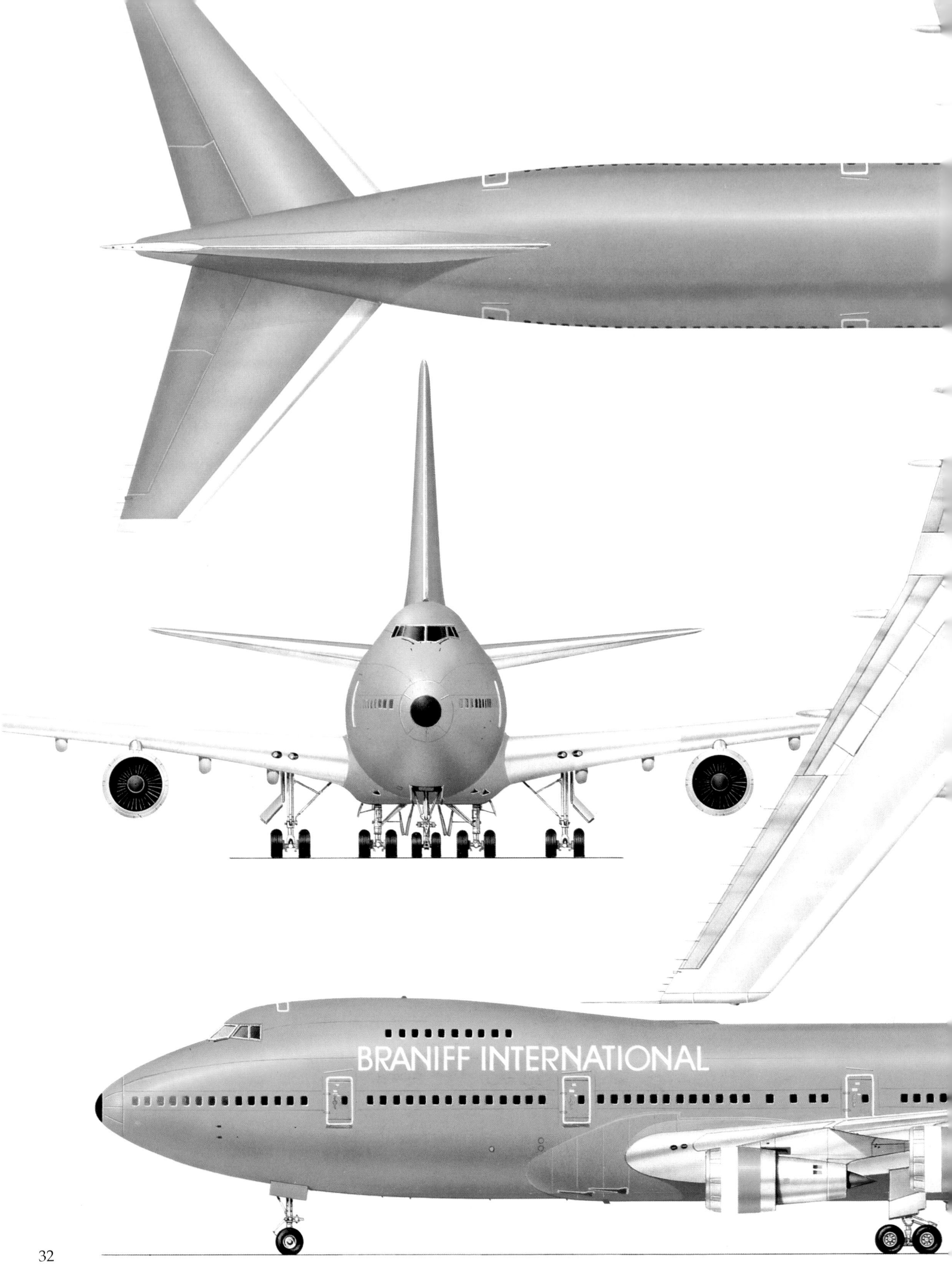
BRANIFF INTERNATIONAL

Among the most gaudy 747s were two of the Braniff machines which operated the ***B****ig* ***O****range service between* ***D****allas and* ***L****ondon-***G****atwick until the airline became bankrupt in 1982. A new Braniff emerged as a domestic operator and the 747s (including one 747****SP****) were sold. This aircraft was a* ***S****eries 100, the initial production model with* ***JT9D****-3 engines. Later versions would increase weight and range.*

Boeing 747-127
Specification

Type: long-range commercial transport
Powerplant: four 20412-kg (45,000-lb) Pratt & Whitney JT9D-3A turbofans; later models JT9D, CF6-50, -45 or -80, or RB.211 turbofans each of 25400-kg (56,000-lb) thrust
Performance: maximum speed at maximum weight 969 km/h (601 mph); maximum cruising speed 939 km/h (583 mph); maximum payload 74030 kg (163,200 lb) for range of 6460 km (4,014 miles), later versions up to 69990 kg (154,300 lb) for 10040 km (6,239 miles) or 115500 kg (254,640 lb) of cargo
Weights: empty 167300 kg (363,300 lb); maximum take-off 322100 kg (710,000 lb) (later versions 377840 kg/833,000 lb)
Dimensions: span 59.64 m (195 ft 8 in); length 70.66 m (231 ft 10 in); height 19.94 m (65 ft 5 in); wing area 510.95 m^2 (5,500 sq ft)

Reims Cessna FA.152 Aerobat

Specification

Reims Cessna FA.152 Aerobat
Type: aerobatic basic trainer
Powerplant: one 80-kW (180-hp) Avco Lycoming O-235-N2C piston engine driving a fixed-pitch metal propeller
Performance: maximum speed at sea level 200 km/h (125 mph); cruising speed at 75 per cent power 194 km/h (121 mph); typical range at 75 per cent power and 2591 m (8,500 ft) altitude with standard tanks 574 km (310 nautical miles) or 3 hours; service ceiling 4480 m (14,700 ft); take-off distance over 15.2-m (50-ft) obstacle 408 m (1,340 ft); stall speed, flaps down and power off 80 km/h (50 mph)
Weights: maximum ramp weight 760 kg (1,675 lb); maximum take-off 757 kg (1,670 lb); standard empty in basic configuration 513 kg (1,131 lb); standard fuel capacity with long-range tanks 148 litres (39 gal)
Dimensions: span 10.11 m (33 ft 2 in); length 7.34 m (24 ft 1 in); height 2.60 m (8 ft 6 in)
Crew and accommodation: one instructor and one pupil in side-by-side seating

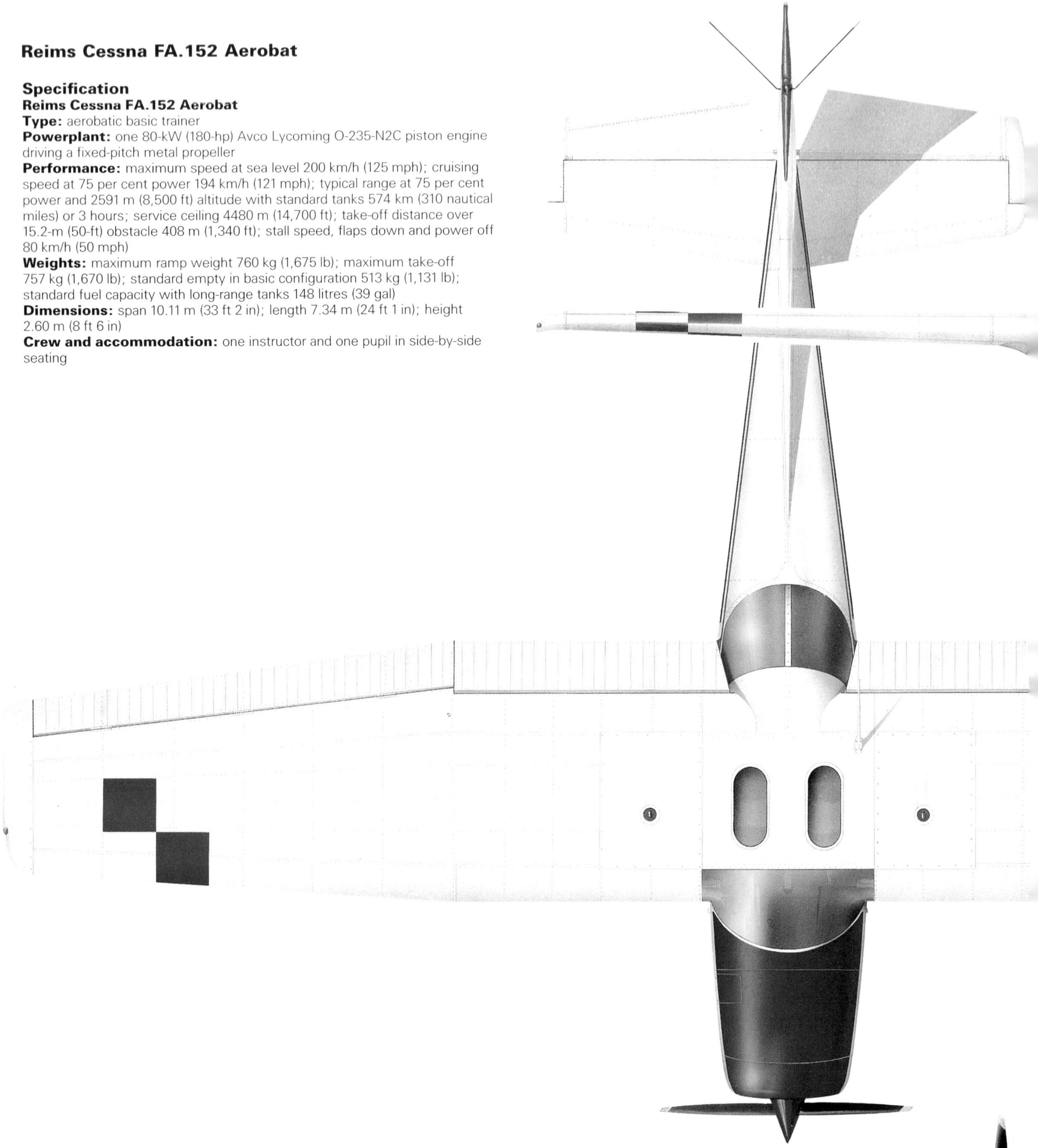

In 1970 Cessna introduced a new, specialised version of its most successful Model 150 Trainer. Designed for limited aerobatics, the A.150 Aerobat had a strengthened airframe, full flap and shoulder safety harnesses, a 'g' meter, quick release doors, cabin roof skylight windows and a special checkerboard colour scheme. In each subsequent year an Aerobat version of the basic aircraft was marketed and the type was available to European purchasers from the Reims factory in France. G-DFTS, illustrated, is an FA.152 Aerobat which was operated by the Denham Flight Training School after delivery from Reims in November 1977.

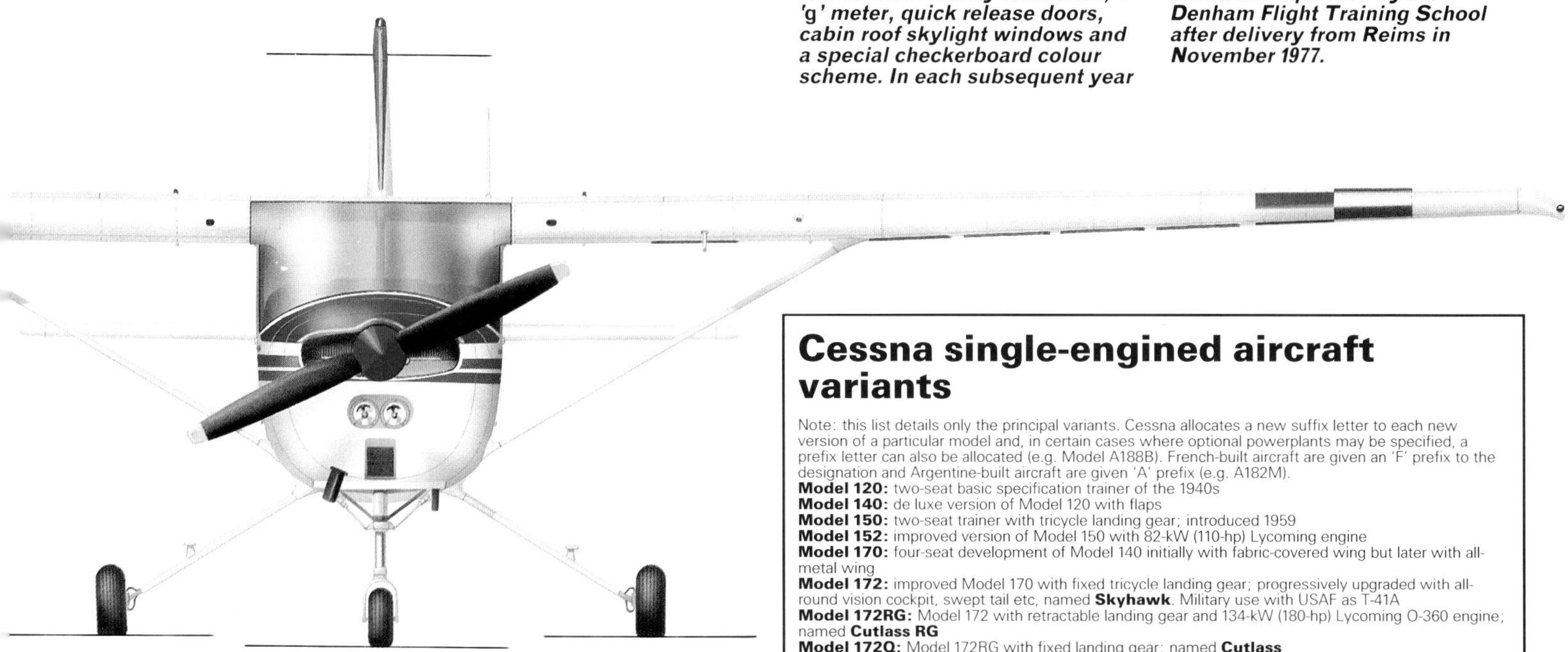

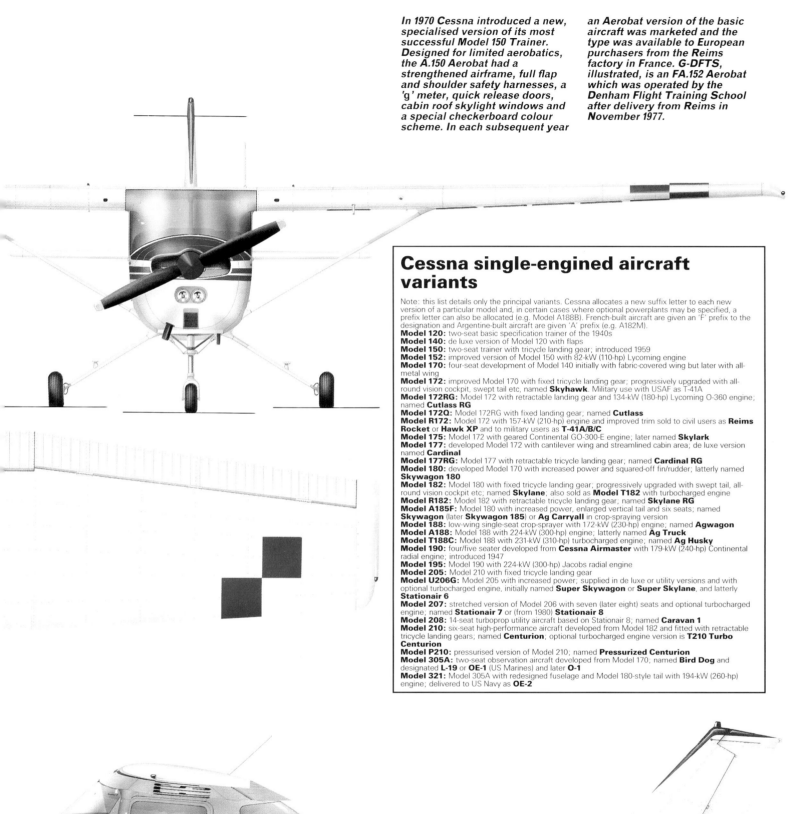

Cessna single-engined aircraft variants

Note: this list details only the principal variants. Cessna allocates a new suffix letter to each new version of a particular model and, in certain cases where optional powerplants may be specified, a prefix letter can also be allocated (e.g. Model A188B). French-built aircraft are given an 'F' prefix to the designation and Argentine-built aircraft are given 'A' prefix (e.g. A182M).

Model 120: two-seat basic specification trainer of the 1940s
Model 140: de luxe version of Model 120 with flaps
Model 150: two-seat trainer with tricycle landing gear; introduced 1959
Model 152: improved version of Model 150 with 82-kW (110-hp) Lycoming engine
Model 170: four-seat development of Model 140 initially with fabric-covered wing but later with all-metal wing
Model 172: improved Model 170 with fixed tricycle landing gear; progressively upgraded with all-round vision cockpit, swept tail etc, named **Skyhawk**. Military use with USAF as T-41A
Model 172RG: Model 172 with retractable landing gear and 134-kW (180-hp) Lycoming O-360 engine; named **Cutlass RG**
Model 172Q: Model 172RG with fixed landing gear; named **Cutlass**
Model R172: Model 172 with 157-kW (210-hp) engine and improved trim sold to civil users as **Reims Rocket** or **Hawk XP** and to military users as **T-41A/B/C**
Model 175: Model 172 with geared Continental GO-300-E engine; later named **Skylark**
Model 177: developed Model 172 with cantilever wing and streamlined cabin area; de luxe version named **Cardinal**
Model 177RG: Model 177 with retractable tricycle landing gear; named **Cardinal RG**
Model 180: developed Model 170 with increased power and squared-off fin/rudder; latterly named **Skywagon 180**
Model 182: Model 180 with fixed tricycle landing gear; progressively upgraded with swept tail, all-round vision cockpit etc; named **Skylane**; also sold as **Model T182** with turbocharged engine
Model R182: Model 182 with retractable tricycle landing gear; named **Skylane RG**
Model A185F: Model 180 with increased power, enlarged vertical tail and six seats; named **Skywagon** (later **Skywagon 185**) or **Ag Carryall** in crop-spraying version
Model 188: low-wing single-seat crop-sprayer with 172-kW (230-hp) engine; named **Agwagon**
Model A188: Model 188 with 224-kW (300-hp) engine; latterly named **Ag Truck**
Model T188C: Model 188 with 231-kW (310-hp) turbocharged engine; named **Ag Husky**
Model 190: four/five seater developed from **Cessna Airmaster** with 179-kW (240-hp) Continental radial engine; introduced 1947
Model 195: Model 190 with 224-kW (300-hp) Jacobs radial engine
Model 205: Model 210 with fixed tricycle landing gear
Model U206G: Model 205 with increased power; supplied in de luxe or utility versions and with optional turbocharged engine, initially named **Super Skywagon** or **Super Skylane**, and latterly **Stationair 6**
Model 207: stretched version of Model 206 with seven (later eight) seats and optional turbocharged engine; named **Stationair 7** or (from 1980) **Stationair 8**
Model 208: 14-seat turboprop utility aircraft based on Stationair 8; named **Caravan 1**
Model 210: six-seat high-performance aircraft developed from Model 182 and fitted with retractable tricycle landing gears; named **Centurion**; optional turbocharged engine version is **T210 Turbo Centurion**
Model P210: pressurised version of Model 210; named **Pressurized Centurion**
Model 305A: two-seat observation aircraft developed from Model 170; named **Bird Dog** and designated **L-19** or **OE-1** (US Marines) and later **O-1**
Model 321: Model 305A with redesigned fuselage and Model 180-style tail with 194-kW (260-hp) engine; delivered to US Navy as **OE-2**

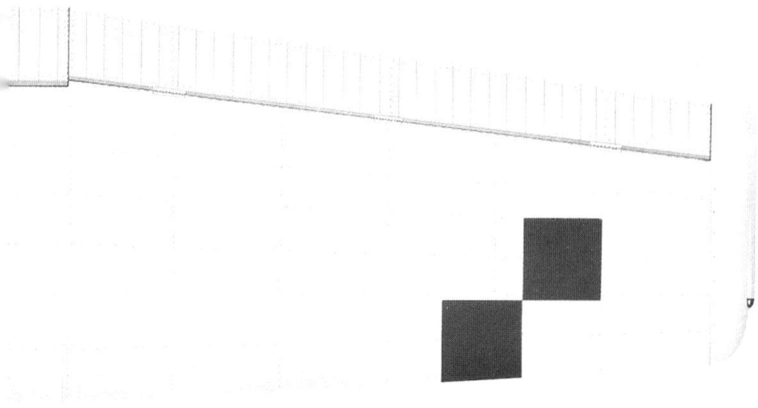

Beech Super King Air B200/350/Beech King Air C90A/B100

Specification

Beech Super King Air B200

Wingspan: 16.64 m (54 ft 6 in)
Length: 13.38 m (43 ft 9 in)
Height: 4.57 m (15 ft 0 in)
Wing area: 28.1 m^2 (303 sq ft)
Powerplant: two 633-kW (850-shp) Pratt & Whitney Canada PT6A-42 turboprops
Passenger capacity: up to 13 (Commuter model)
Empty weight: 3656 kg (8,060 lb)
Maximum take-off weight: 5670 kg (12,500 lb)
Maximum speed: 294 kt (544 km/h; 338 mph)
Cruising speed: 282 kt (523 km/h; 325 mph)
Service ceiling: 10668 m (35,000 ft)
Maximum range: 1,974 nm (3656 km/2,272 miles)

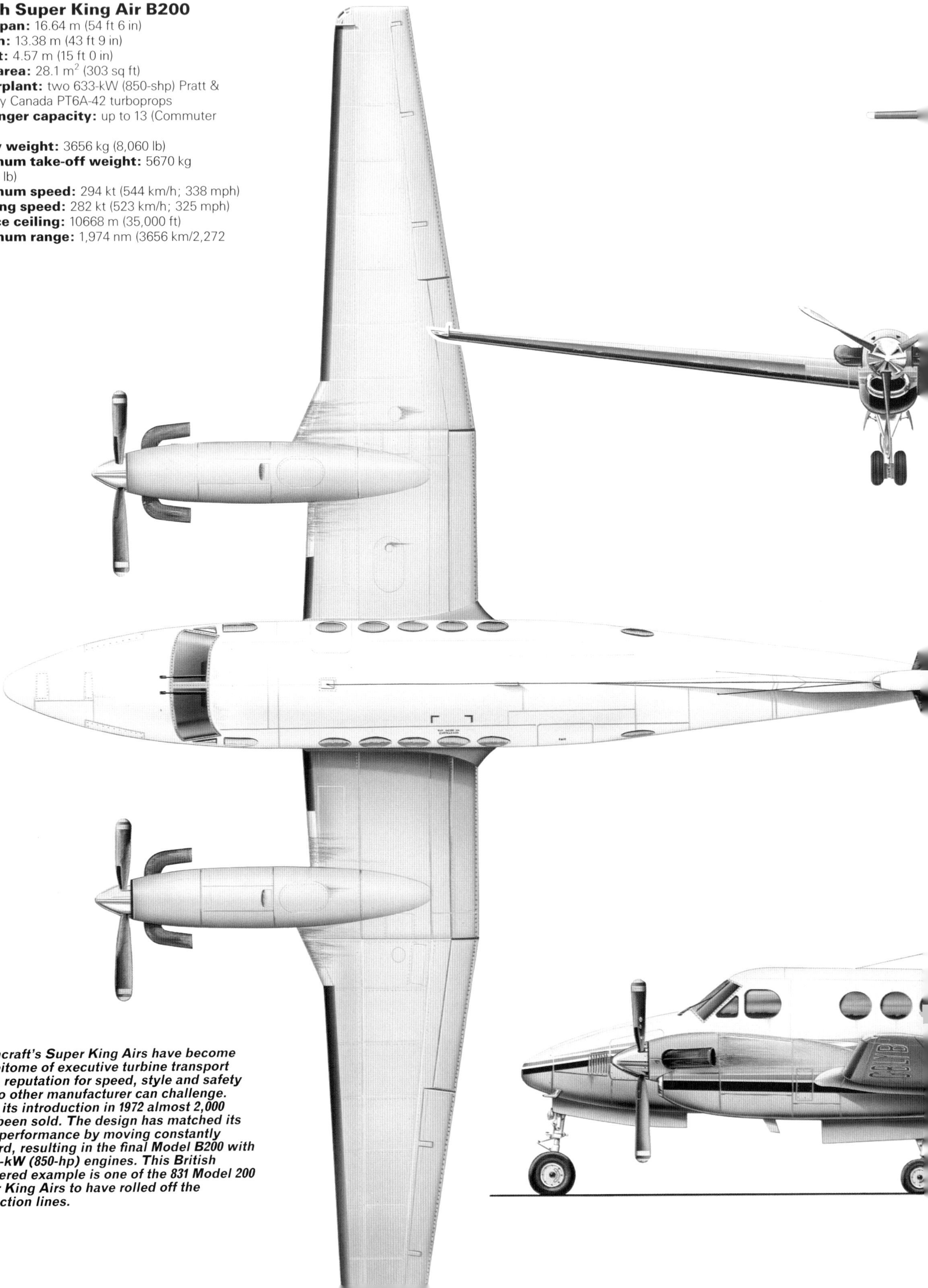

Beechcraft's Super King Airs have become the epitome of executive turbine transport with a reputation for speed, style and safety that no other manufacturer can challenge. Since its introduction in 1972 almost 2,000 have been sold. The design has matched its sales performance by moving constantly forward, resulting in the final Model B200 with its 134-kW (850-hp) engines. This British registered example is one of the 831 Model 200 Super King Airs to have rolled off the production lines.

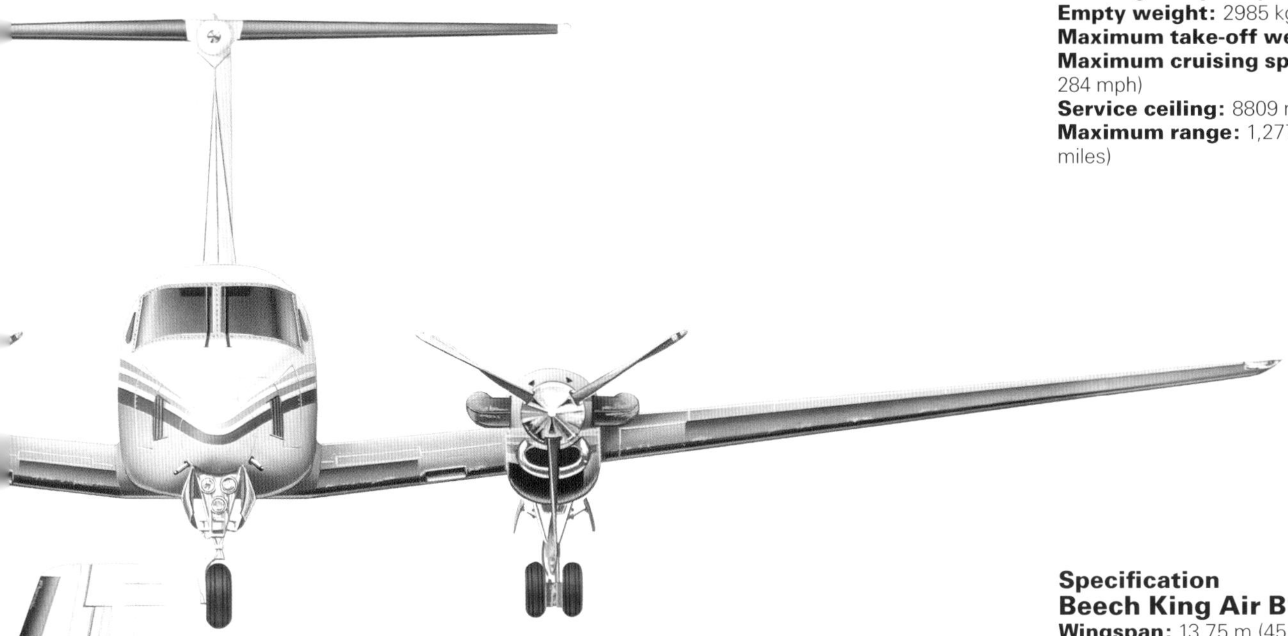

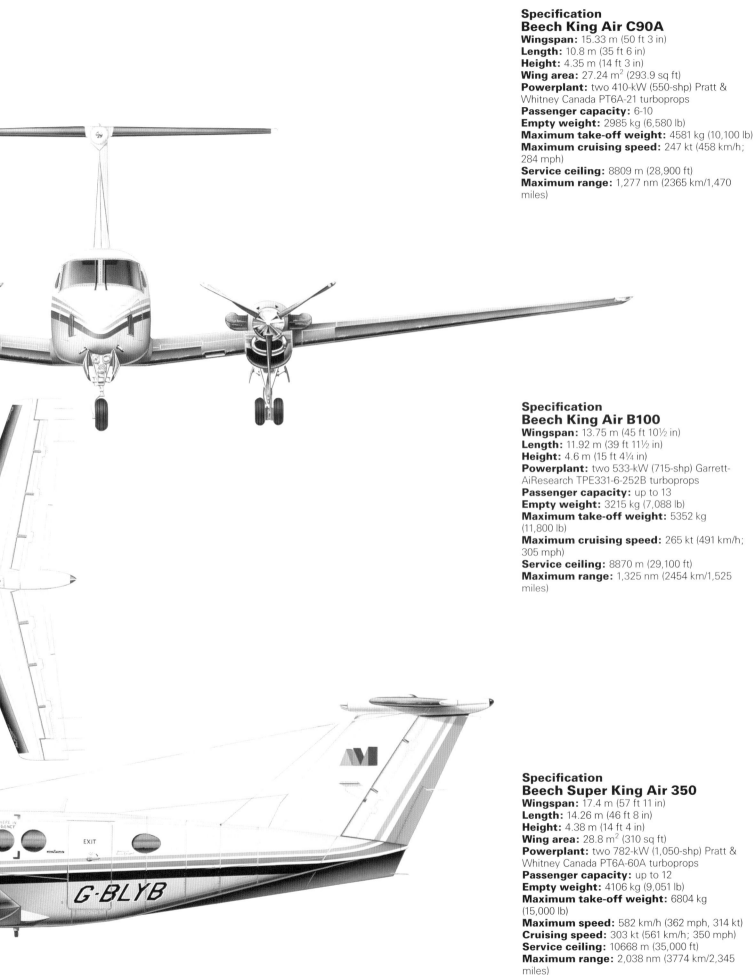

Specification
Beech King Air C90A
Wingspan: 15.33 m (50 ft 3 in)
Length: 10.8 m (35 ft 6 in)
Height: 4.35 m (14 ft 3 in)
Wing area: 27.24 m^2 (293.9 sq ft)
Powerplant: two 410-kW (550-shp) Pratt & Whitney Canada PT6A-21 turboprops
Passenger capacity: 6-10
Empty weight: 2985 kg (6,580 lb)
Maximum take-off weight: 4581 kg (10,100 lb)
Maximum cruising speed: 247 kt (458 km/h; 284 mph)
Service ceiling: 8809 m (28,900 ft)
Maximum range: 1,277 nm (2365 km/1,470 miles)

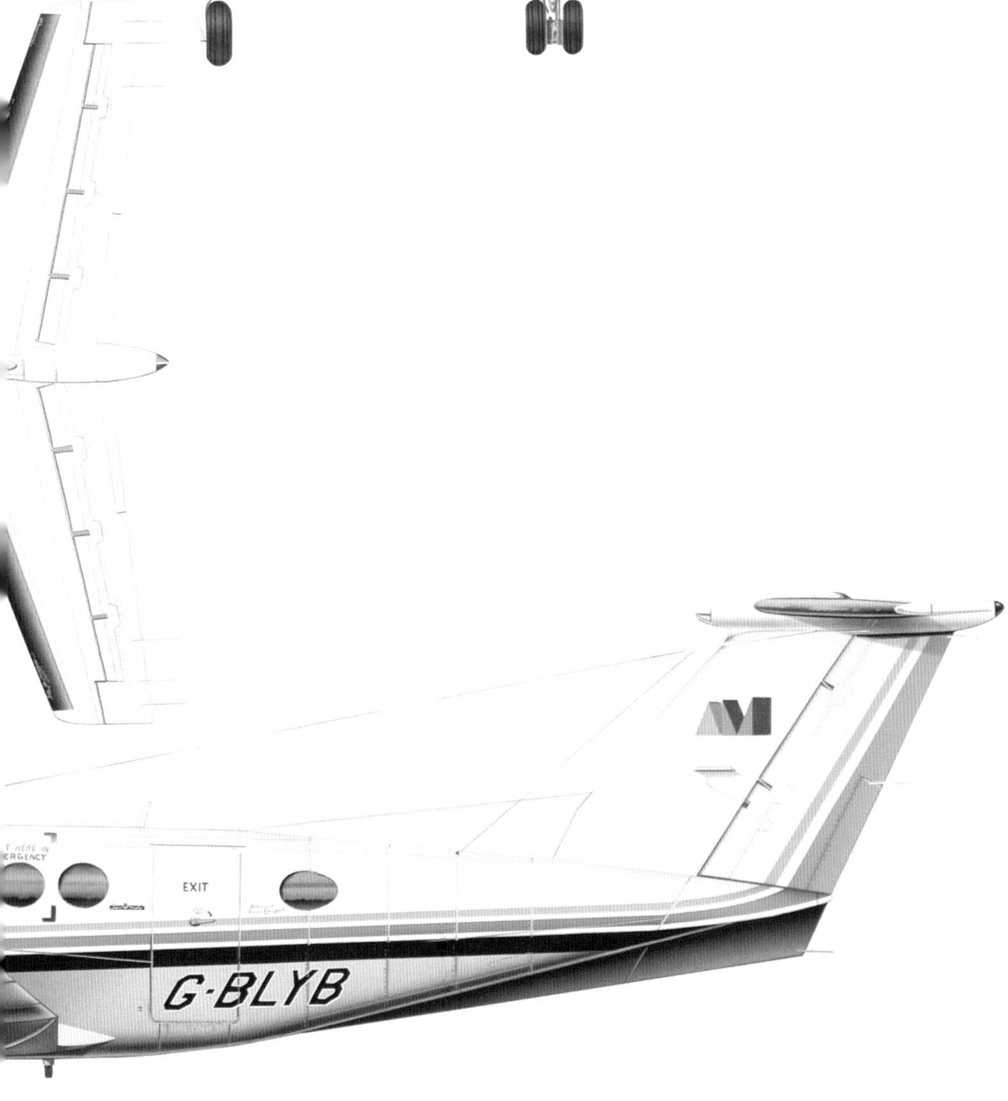

Specification
Beech King Air B100
Wingspan: 13.75 m (45 ft 10½ in)
Length: 11.92 m (39 ft 11½ in)
Height: 4.6 m (15 ft 4¼ in)
Powerplant: two 533-kW (715-shp) Garrett-AiResearch TPE331-6-252B turboprops
Passenger capacity: up to 13
Empty weight: 3215 kg (7,088 lb)
Maximum take-off weight: 5352 kg (11,800 lb)
Maximum cruising speed: 265 kt (491 km/h; 305 mph)
Service ceiling: 8870 m (29,100 ft)
Maximum range: 1,325 nm (2454 km/1,525 miles)

Specification
Beech Super King Air 350
Wingspan: 17.4 m (57 ft 11 in)
Length: 14.26 m (46 ft 8 in)
Height: 4.38 m (14 ft 4 in)
Wing area: 28.8 m^2 (310 sq ft)
Powerplant: two 782-kW (1,050-shp) Pratt & Whitney Canada PT6A-60A turboprops
Passenger capacity: up to 12
Empty weight: 4106 kg (9,051 lb)
Maximum take-off weight: 6804 kg (15,000 lb)
Maximum speed: 582 km/h (362 mph, 314 kt)
Cruising speed: 303 kt (561 km/h; 350 mph)
Service ceiling: 10668 m (35,000 ft)
Maximum range: 2,038 nm (3774 km/2,345 miles)

Tim Reggime

McDonnell Douglas DC-10-30

Specification
McDonnell Douglas DC-10-30
Type: high-capacity long-range commercial transport
Powerplant: three 23134-kg (51,000-lb) General Electric CF6-50C turbofans
Performance: maximum speed at 7620 m (25,000 ft) 982 km/h (610 mph); normal cruising speed 871 km/h (541 mph); maximum rate of climb (MTO weight) 884 m (2,900 ft) per minute; service ceiling 10180 m (33,400 ft); at 249475 kg (550,000 lb); range with maximum payload 7413 km (4,606 miles)
Weights: empty equipped 121198 kg (267,197 lb); maximum payload 48330 kg (106,550 lb); maximum take-off 259450 kg (572,000 lb)
Dimensions: span 50.41 m (165 ft 4 in); length 55.50 m (182 ft 1 in); height 17.70 m (58 ft 1 in)

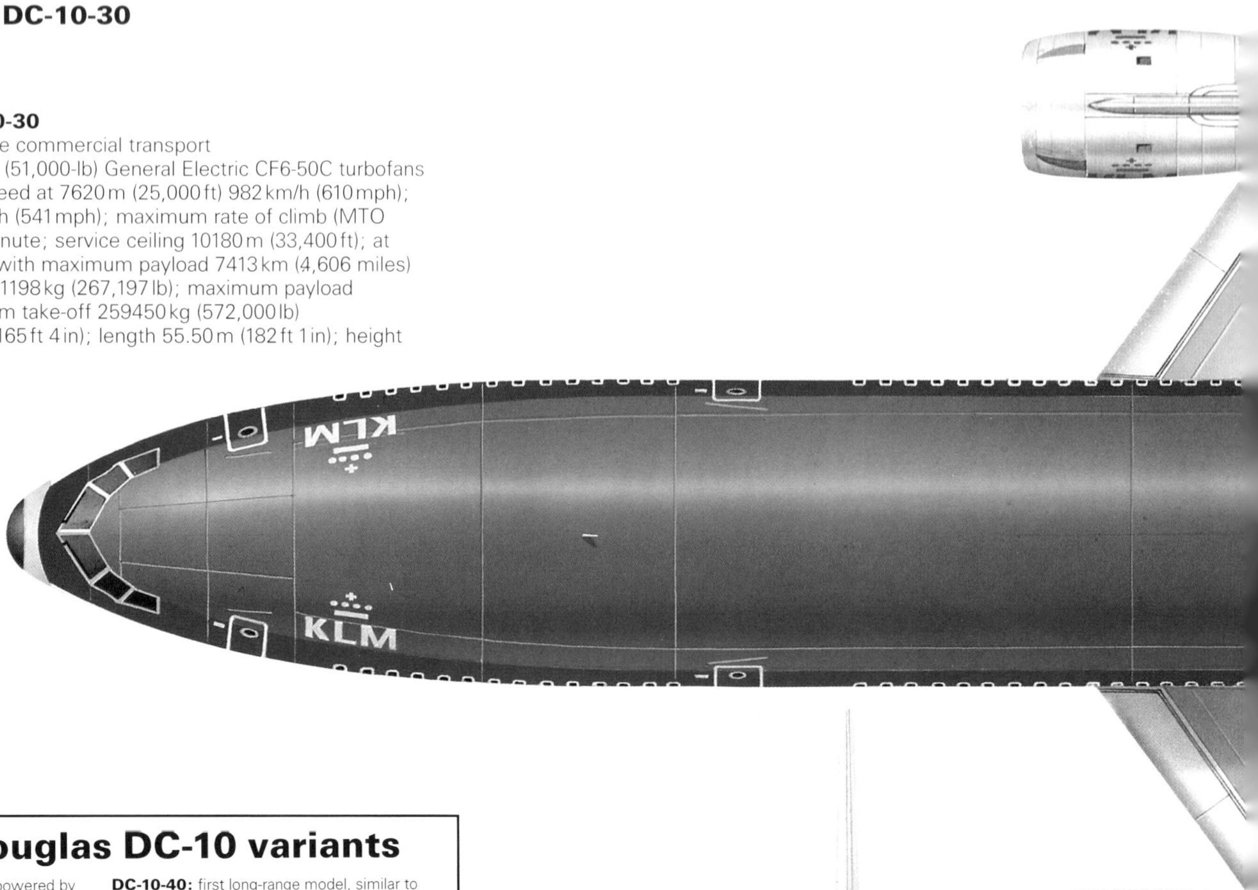

McDonnell Douglas DC-10 variants

DC-10-10: initial production version powered by 18144-kg (40,000-lb) thrust CF6-6 engines (later some fitted with 18598-kg/41,000-lb CF6-6D1); one fitted with drag-reducing winglets in 1981
DC-10-15: short-field version appearing at the end of the programme for Mexicana (5) and Aeromexico (2), a DC-10-10 airframe with 21092-kg (46,500-lb) thrust CF6-50C2F engines for use from hot/high airports
DC-10-30: standard long-range model, with various CF6 engines from 22226-kg (49,000-lb) thrust CF6-50A to 238140-kg (52,500-lb) thrust CF6-50C2; span increased by 3.05 m (10 ft), much greater fuel capacity, extra centreline landing gear
DC-10-30ER: extended-range model cleared to 263805 kg (580,000 lb) with additional fuel tank and 24494-kg (54,000-lb) thrust CF6-50C2B engines; used by Swissair and Finnair
DC-10-40: first long-range model, similar to later DC-10-30 but with Pratt & Whitney engines (see text for details); used by Northwest and Japan Air Lines
DC-10-10CF and **-30CF:** convertible passenger/freighter versions of DC-10-10 and DC-10-30 with increased maximum landing weight (and higher landing speed), heavy cargo floor with conveyors and loading system, large cargo door in left side, and provision for containers or pallets above floor and half-size containers or pallets at lower level
KC-10A Extender: US Air Force tanker/transport version of DC-10-30CF with greatly augmented fuel capacity, inflight-refuelling boom and hosereel for probe-equipped receiver aircraft. First flown 12 July 1980 and planned orders for 60 announced in 1982. All now in service with Strategic Air Command

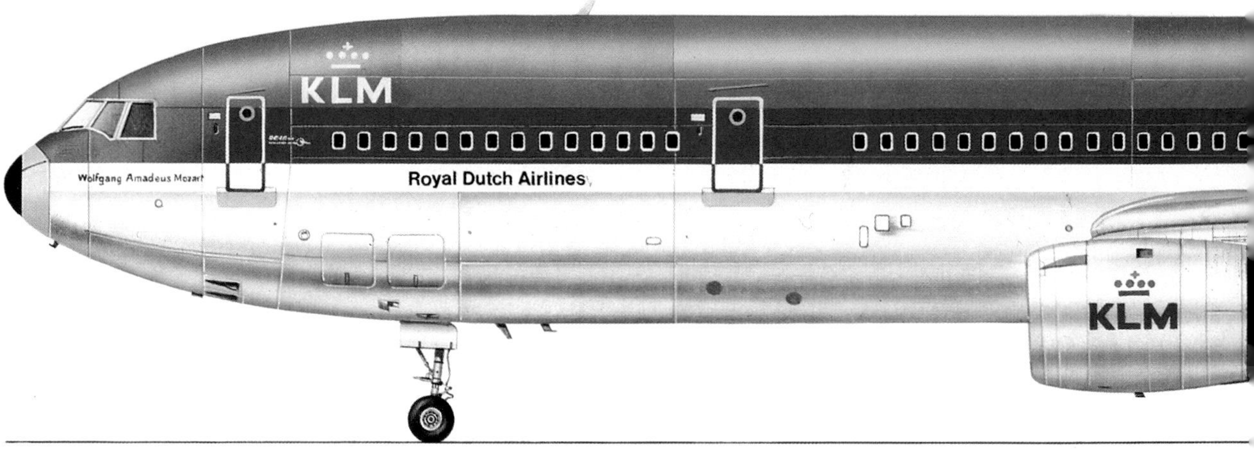

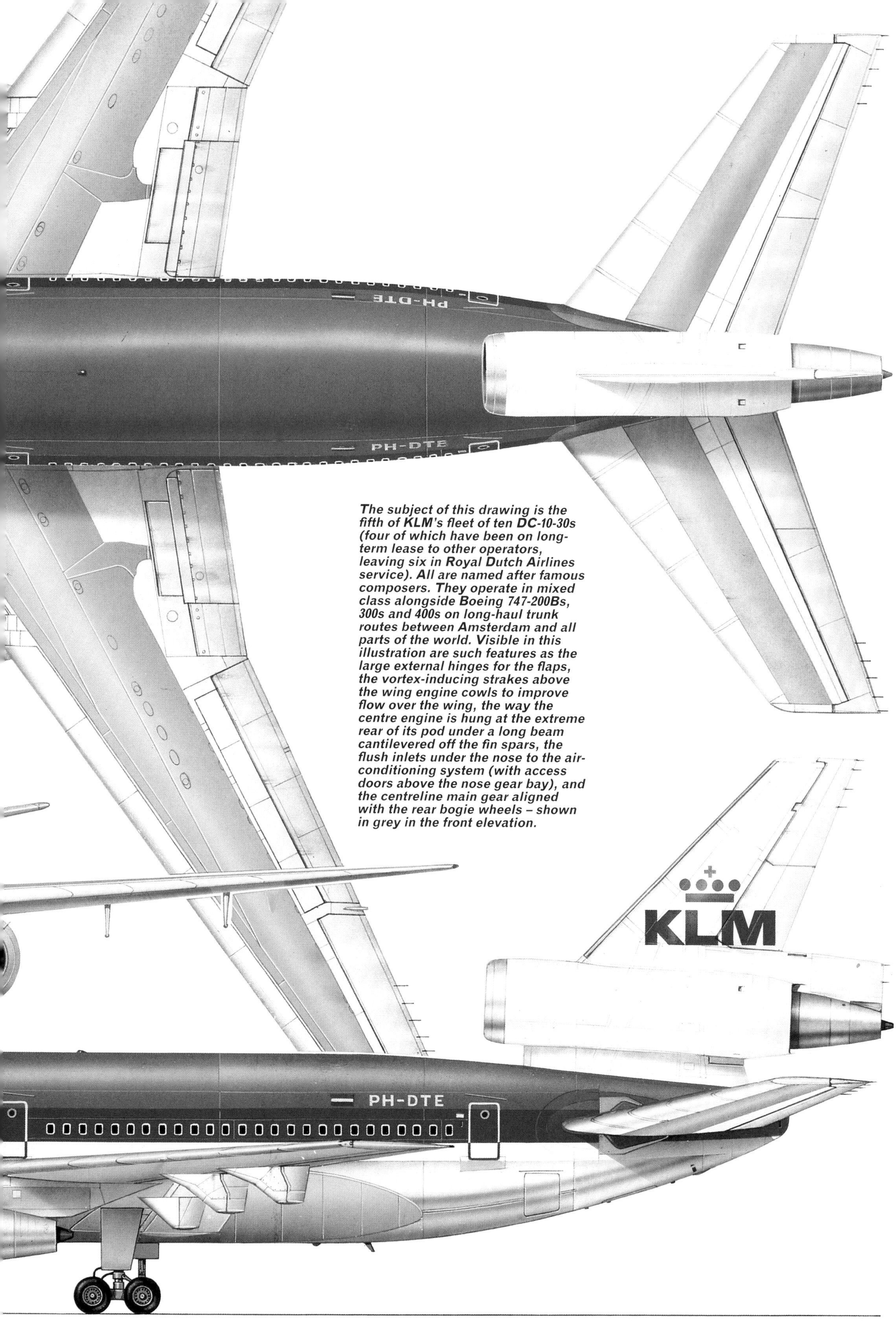

The subject of this drawing is the fifth of KLM's fleet of ten DC-10-30s (four of which have been on long-term lease to other operators, leaving six in Royal Dutch Airlines service). All are named after famous composers. They operate in mixed class alongside Boeing 747-200Bs, 300s and 400s on long-haul trunk routes between Amsterdam and all parts of the world. Visible in this illustration are such features as the large external hinges for the flaps, the vortex-inducing strakes above the wing engine cowls to improve flow over the wing, the way the centre engine is hung at the extreme rear of its pod under a long beam cantilevered off the fin spars, the flush inlets under the nose to the air-conditioning system (with access doors above the nose gear bay), and the centreline main gear aligned with the rear bogie wheels – shown in grey in the front elevation.

De Havilland Canada
DHC-6 Twin Otter 300

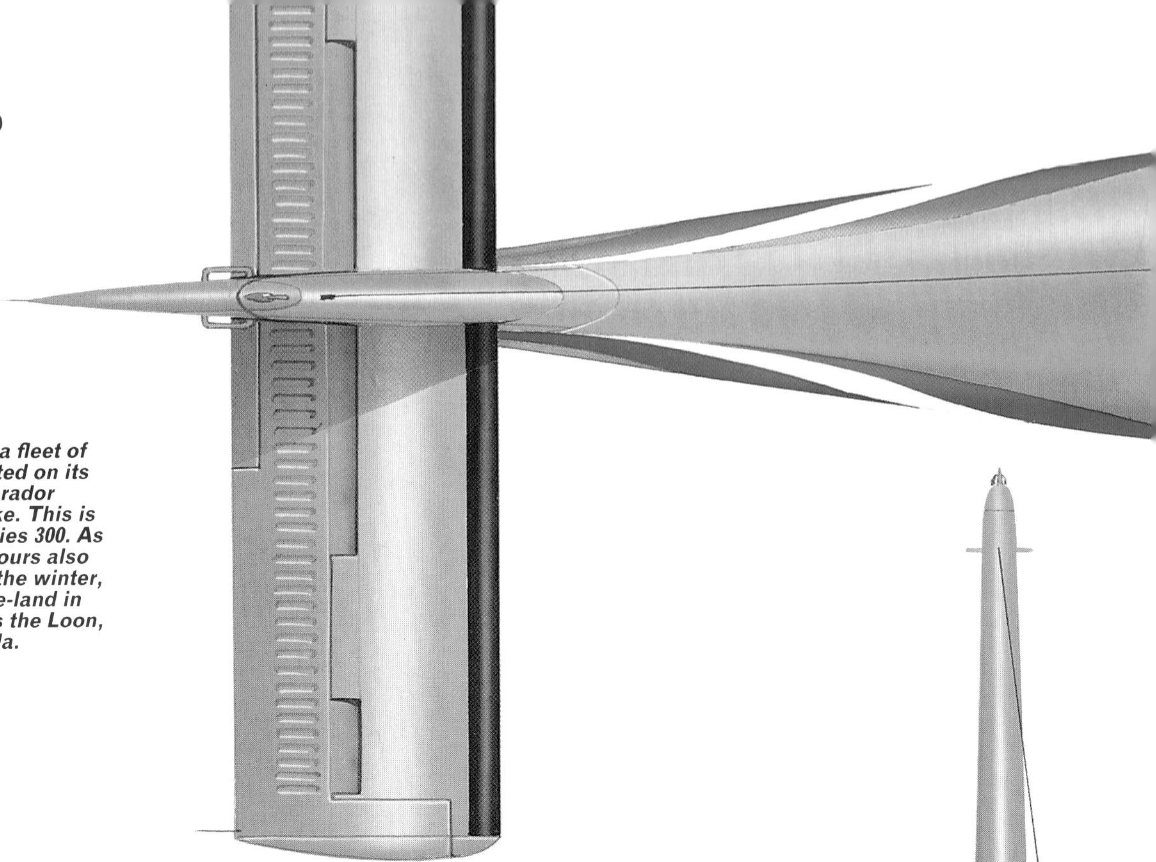

Based at North Bay, NorOntair has a fleet of Twin Otters and Dash Eights operated on its behalf by other airlines such as Labrador Airways, Air Dale and Bearskin Lake. This is one of its earlier Twin Otters, a Series 300. As well as eye-catching, the bright colours also serve as conspicuity marks during the winter, where the aircraft may have to force-land in the snow. The bird motif represents the Loon, a well-known bird of eastern Canada.

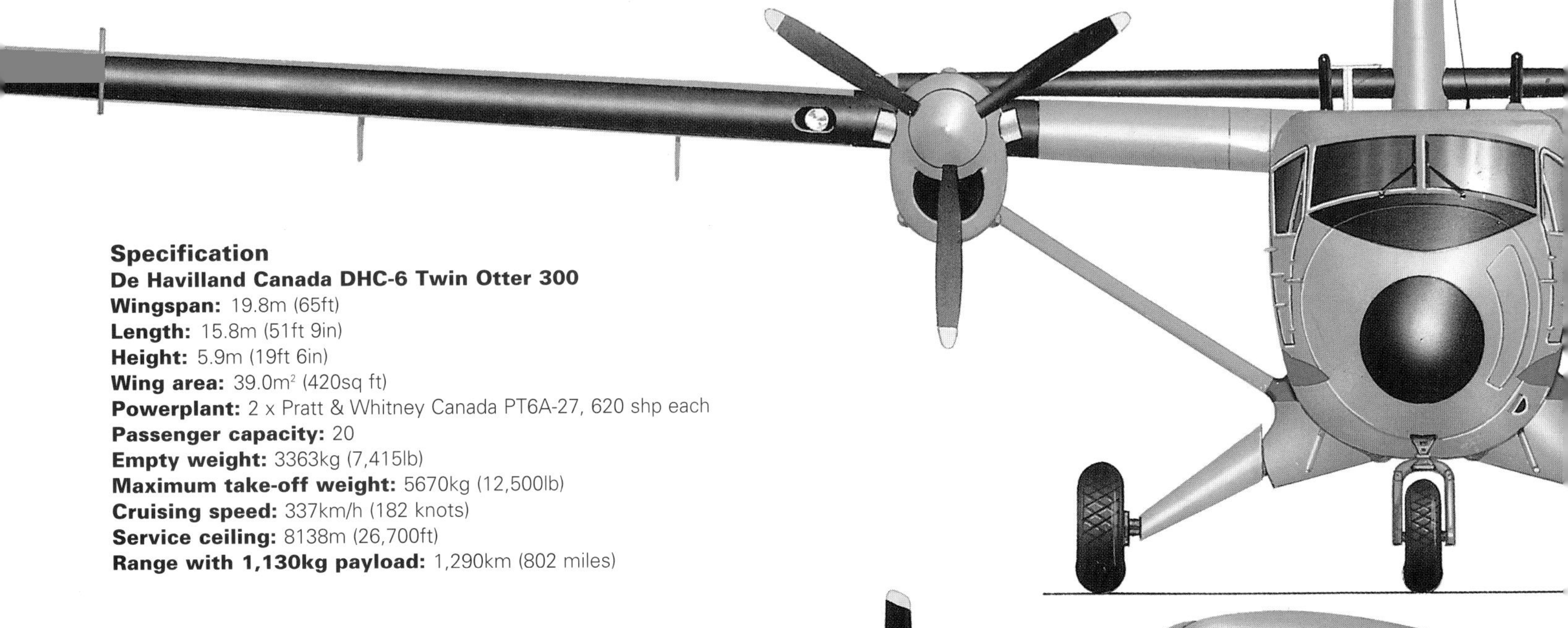

Specification
De Havilland Canada DHC-6 Twin Otter 300
Wingspan: 19.8m (65ft)
Length: 15.8m (51ft 9in)
Height: 5.9m (19ft 6in)
Wing area: 39.0m² (420sq ft)
Powerplant: 2 x Pratt & Whitney Canada PT6A-27, 620 shp each
Passenger capacity: 20
Empty weight: 3363kg (7,415lb)
Maximum take-off weight: 5670kg (12,500lb)
Cruising speed: 337km/h (182 knots)
Service ceiling: 8138m (26,700ft)
Range with 1,130kg payload: 1,290km (802 miles)

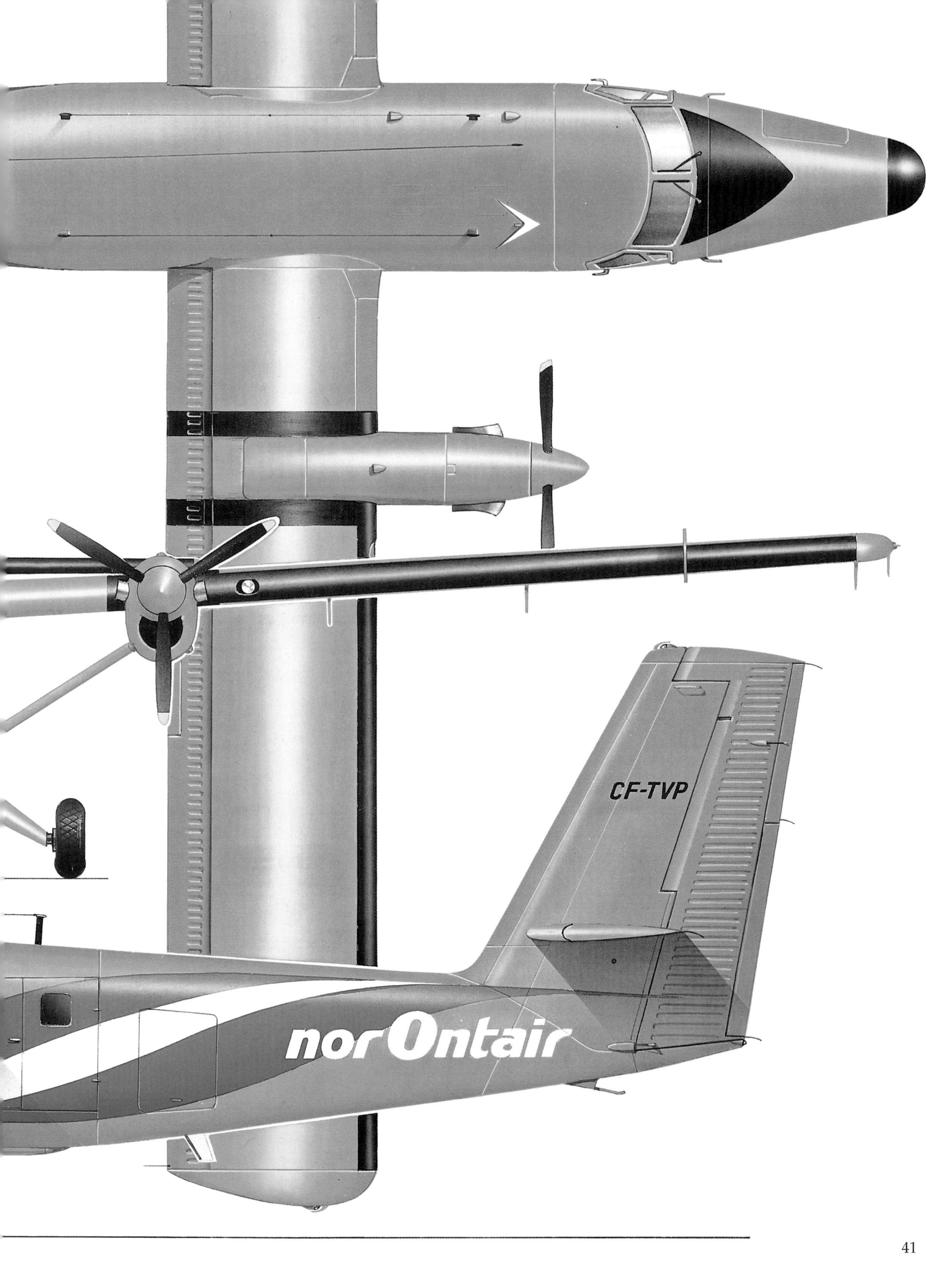
CF-TVP
norOntair

Tupolev Tu-144

Specification
Tupolev Tu-144 (early production aircraft)
Type: long-range supersonic transport
Powerplant: four Kuznetsov NK-144 turbofan, each rated at 127.5 kN (28,660 lb) thrust without afterburning and 171.6 km (38,580 lb) thrust with afterburning
Performance: maximum cruising speed Mach 2.35 (2500 km/h; 1,550 mph); normal cruising speed Mach 2.2 (2300 km/h; 1,430 mph); landing speed 280 km/h (174 mph); cruising altitude 16000-18000 m (52,500-59,000 ft); landing run 2500 m (8,530 ft); maximum range with 140 passengers at average speed of Mach 1.9 6500 km (4,030 miles)
Weights: operating empty 85000 kg (187,400 lb); maximum take-off 180,000 kg (396,830 lb); maximum fuel 9500 kg (209,440 lb); maximum payload 15000 kg (33,070 lb)
Dimensions: wing span 28.80 m (94 ft 6 in); length 65.70 m (215 ft 6½ in); height with wheels up 12.85 m (42 ft 2 in); wing area 438 m^2 (4,714.5 sq ft)

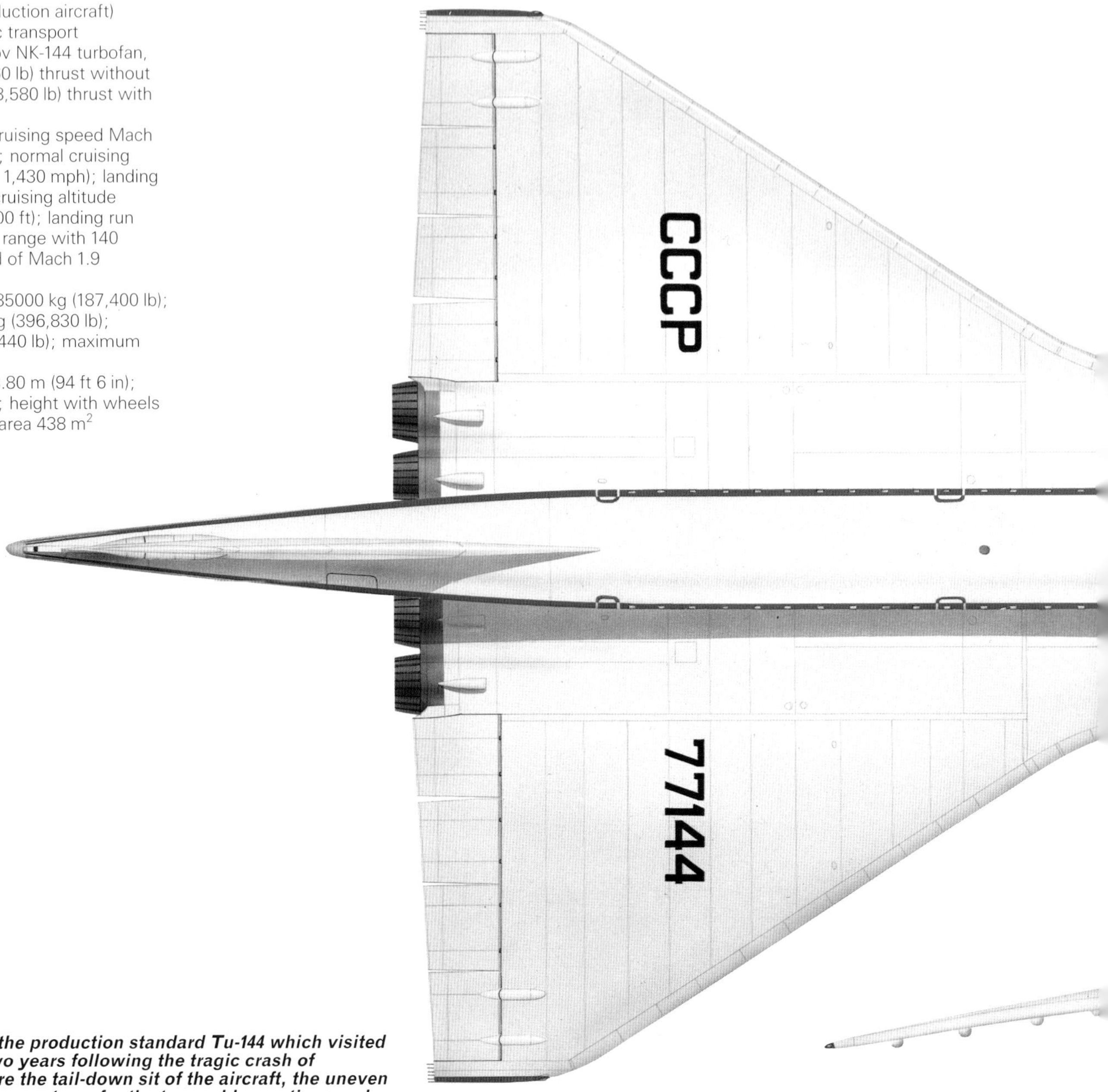

CCCP (USSR)-77144 was the production standard Tu-144 which visited the 1975 Paris air show, two years following the tragic crash of CCCP-77102. Noticeable are the tail-down sit of the aircraft, the uneven distribution of the actuating systems for the two rudder sections and the relatively-straight edges to the wing planform. The scrap view details the 12° movement of the drooping visor nose. The inscription on the nose of this Tupolev aircraft is Cyrillic for 'Tu-144' – surprisingly, no Russian name was applied.

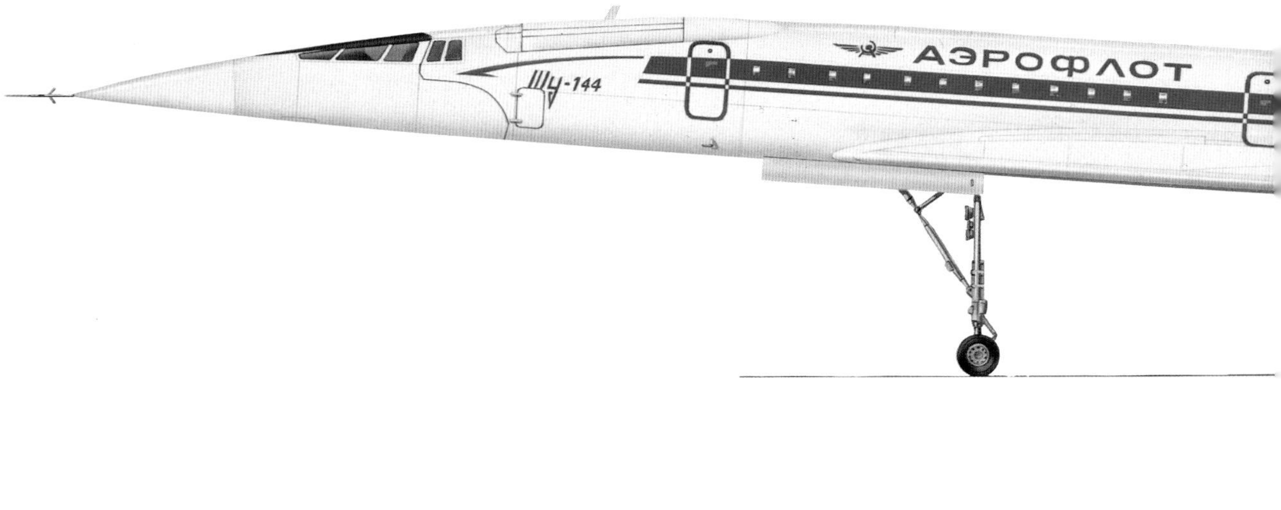

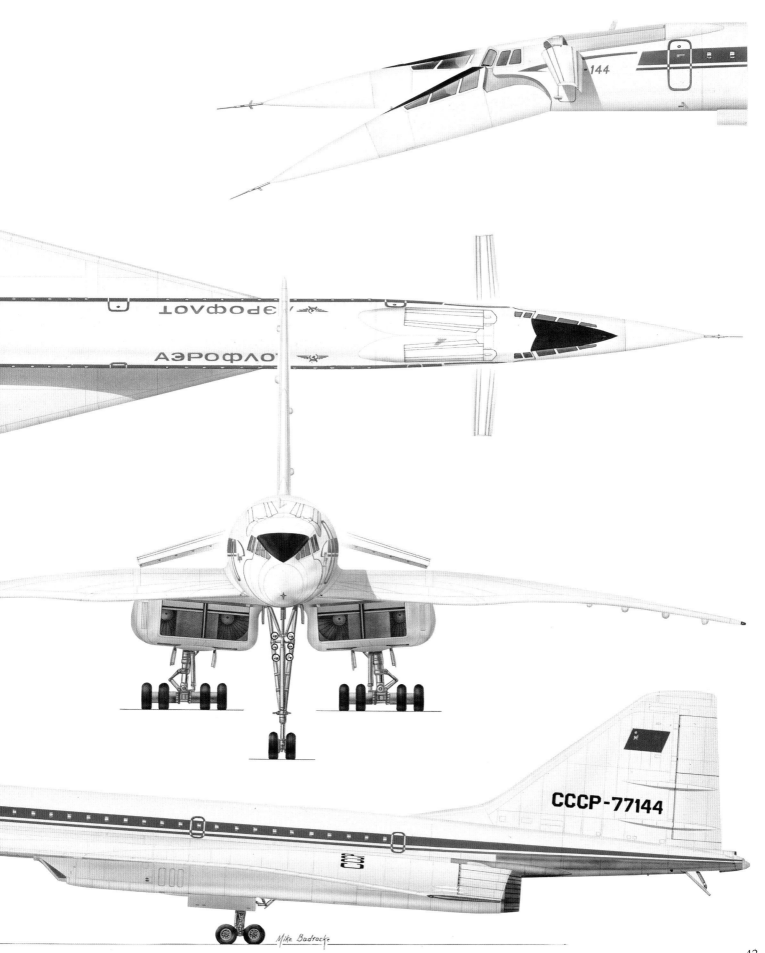

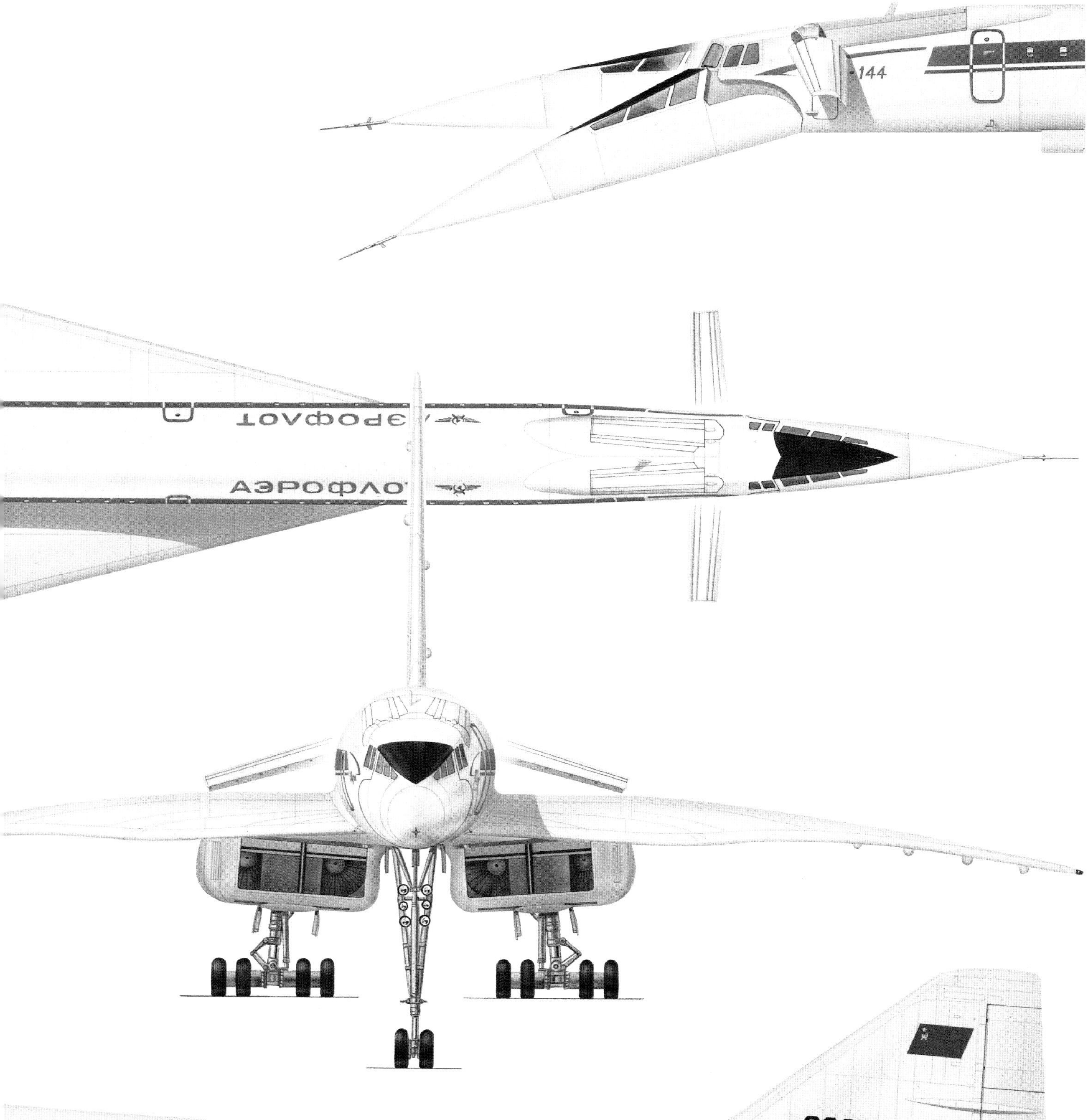
-144
АЭРОФЛОТ
СССР-77144
СССР
Mike Badrocke

АЭРОФЛОТ
ИЛ-76ТД

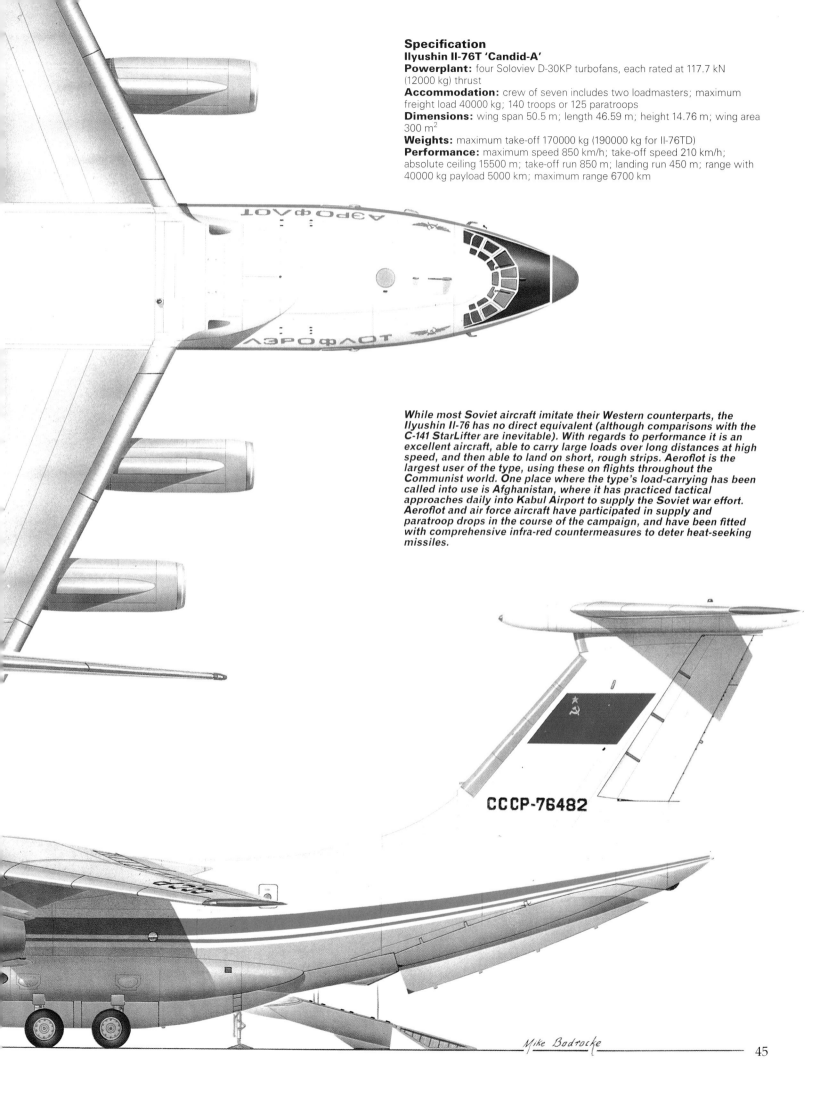

Specification

Ilyushin Il-76T 'Candid-A'

Powerplant: four Soloviev D-30KP turbofans, each rated at 117.7 kN (12000 kg) thrust

Accommodation: crew of seven includes two loadmasters; maximum freight load 40000 kg; 140 troops or 125 paratroops

Dimensions: wing span 50.5 m; length 46.59 m; height 14.76 m; wing area 300 m^2

Weights: maximum take-off 170000 kg (190000 kg for Il-76TD)

Performance: maximum speed 850 km/h; take-off speed 210 km/h; absolute ceiling 15500 m; take-off run 850 m; landing run 450 m; range with 40000 kg payload 5000 km; maximum range 6700 km

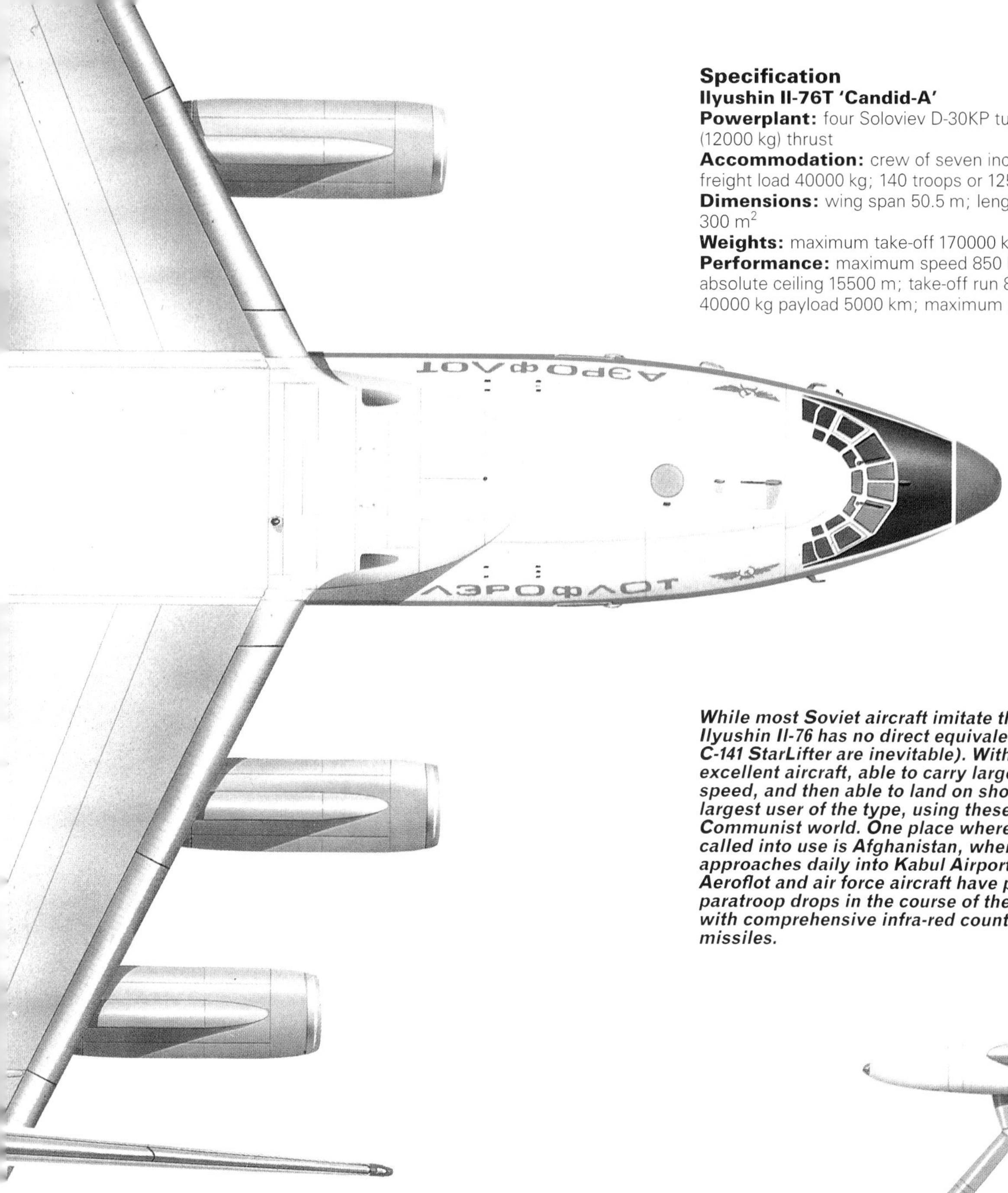

While most Soviet aircraft imitate their Western counterparts, the Ilyushin Il-76 has no direct equivalent (although comparisons with the C-141 StarLifter are inevitable). With regards to performance it is an excellent aircraft, able to carry large loads over long distances at high speed, and then able to land on short, rough strips. Aeroflot is the largest user of the type, using these on flights throughout the Communist world. One place where the type's load-carrying has been called into use is Afghanistan, where it has practiced tactical approaches daily into Kabul Airport to supply the Soviet war effort. Aeroflot and air force aircraft have participated in supply and paratroop drops in the course of the campaign, and have been fitted with comprehensive infra-red countermeasures to deter heat-seeking missiles.

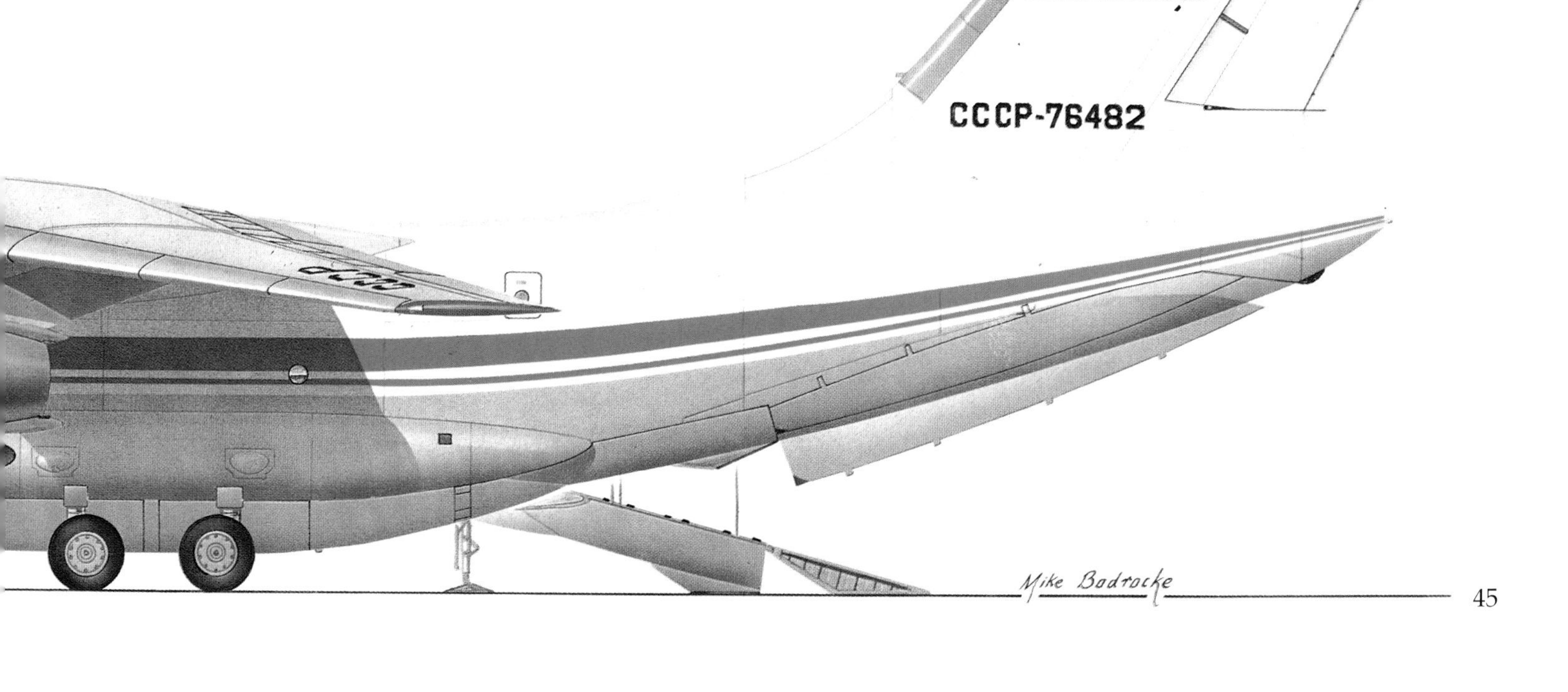

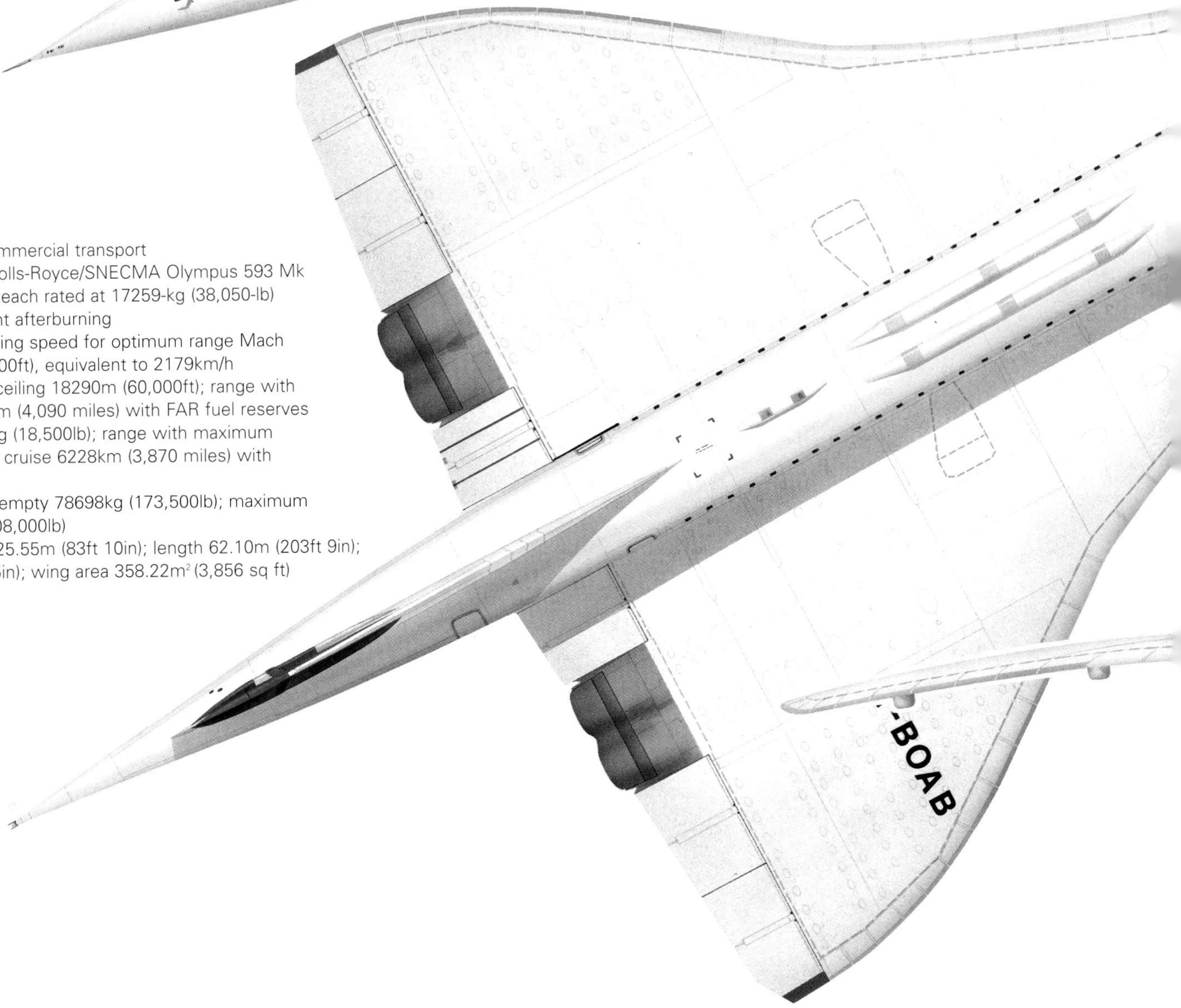

Specification

Concorde

Type: supersonic commercial transport

Powerplant: four Rolls-Royce/SNECMA Olympus 593 Mk 610 turbojet engines, each rated at 17259-kg (38,050-lb) thrust with 17 per cent afterburning

Performance: cruising speed for optimum range Mach 2.04 at 15635m (51,300ft), equivalent to 2179km/h (1,354 mph); service ceiling 18290m (60,000ft); range with maximum fuel 6582km (4,090 miles) with FAR fuel reserves and payload of 8845kg (18,500lb); range with maximum payload at Mach 2.02 cruise 6228km (3,870 miles) with FAR fuel reserves

Weights: operating empty 78698kg (173,500lb); maximum take-off 185066kg (408,000lb)

Dimensions: span 25.55m (83ft 10in); length 62.10m (203ft 9in); height 11.40m (37ft 5in); wing area 358.22m^2 (3,856 sq ft)

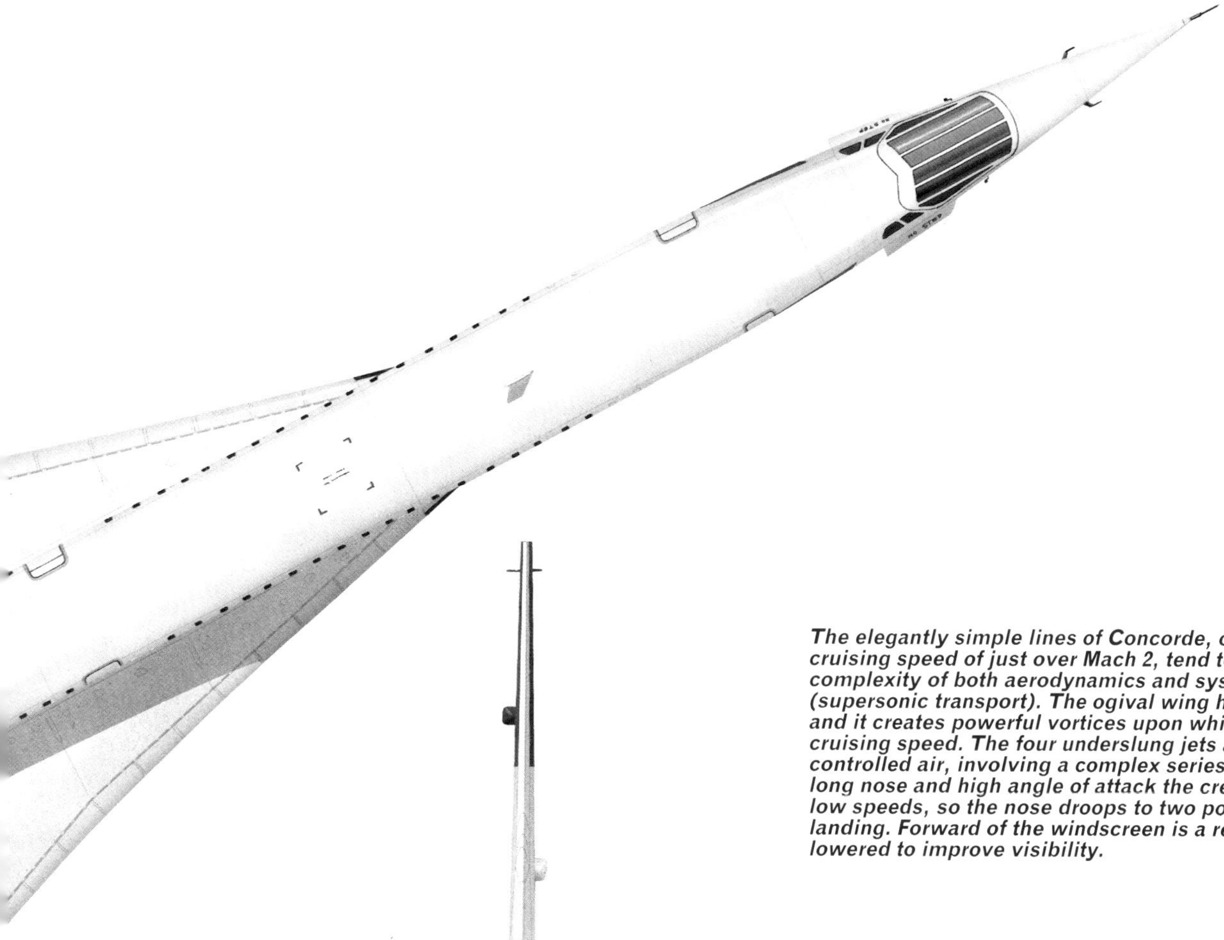

*The elegantly simple lines of Concorde, optimised for an economical cruising speed of just over Mach 2, tend to disguise the extreme complexity of both aerodynamics and systems of this pioneering **SST** (supersonic transport). The ogival wing has cambered leading edges, and it creates powerful vortices upon which the aircraft rides at cruising speed. The four underslung jets are fed with carefully-controlled air, involving a complex series of intake ramps. With its long nose and high angle of attack the crew have no forward vision at low speeds, so the nose droops to two positions for take-off and landing. Forward of the windscreen is a retractable 'visor' which is lowered to improve visibility.*

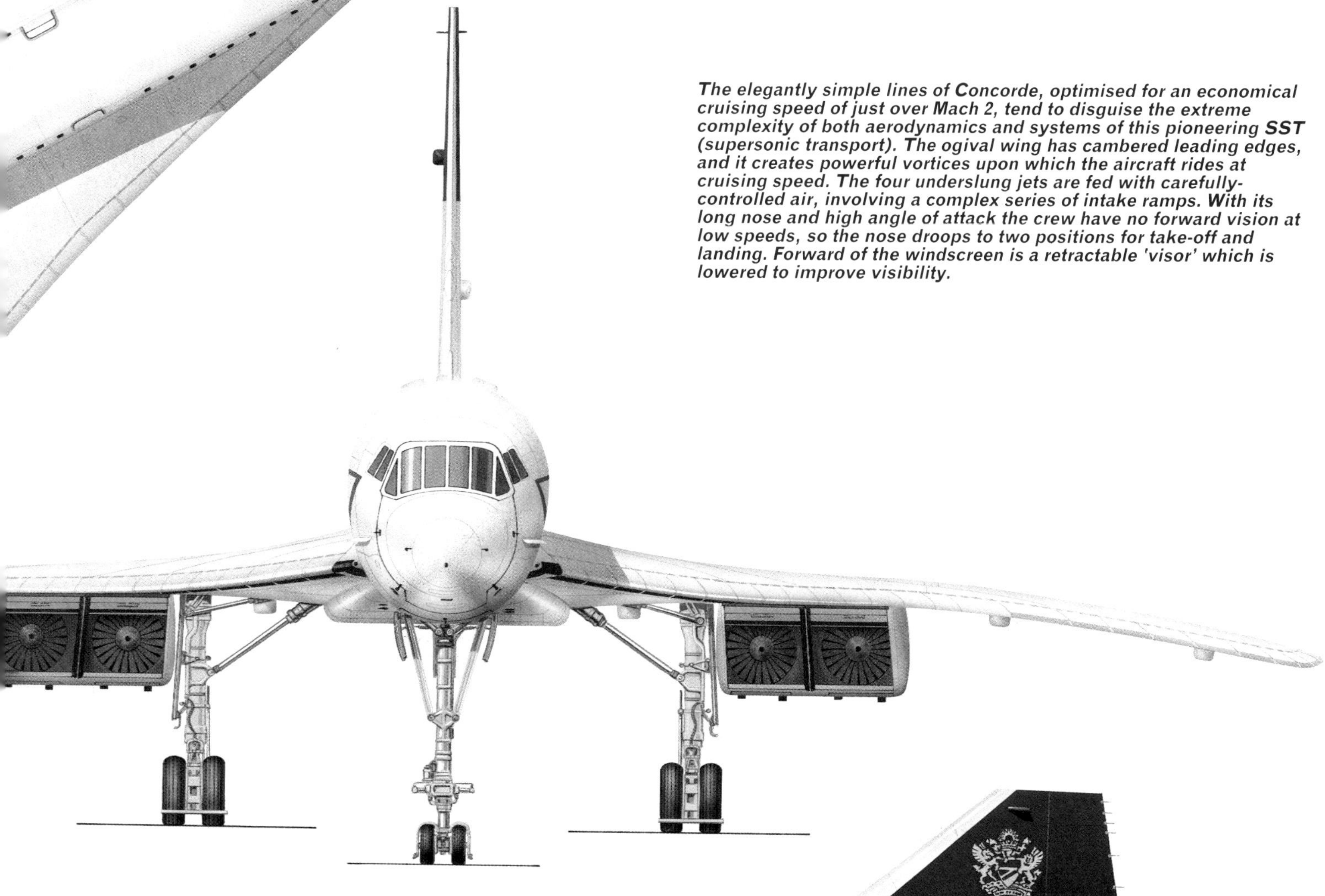

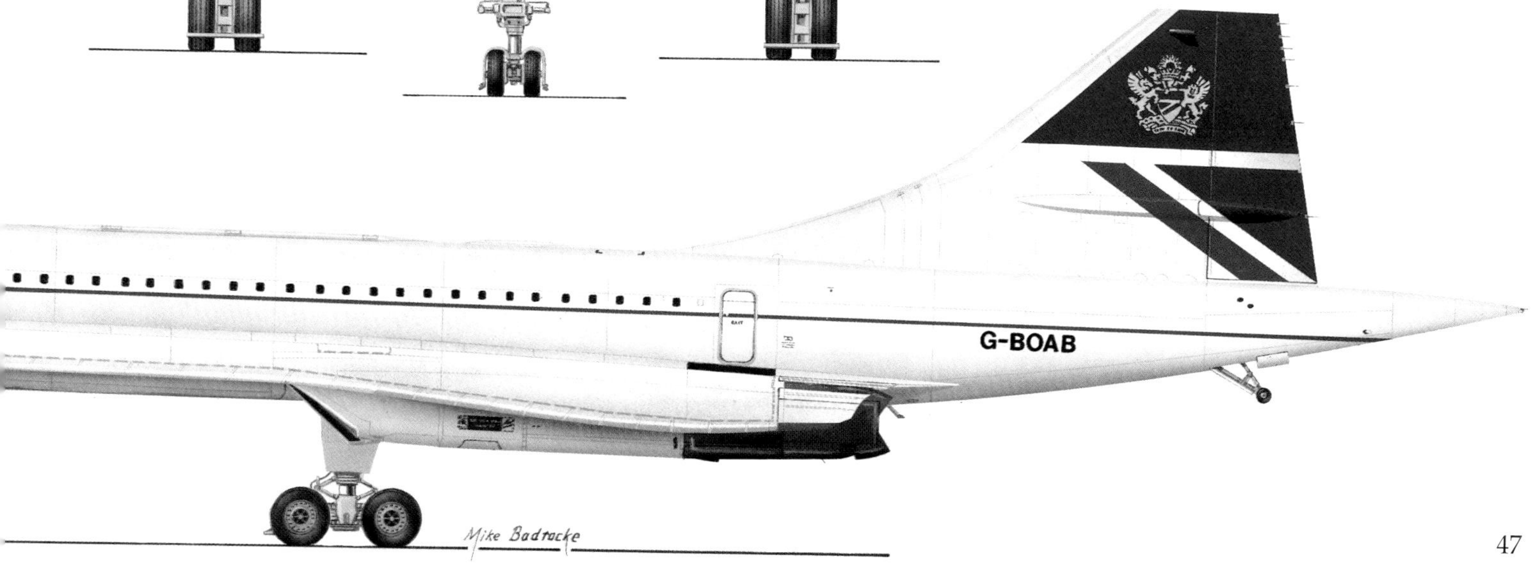

Fokker F28 Fellowship

Specification

Fokker F28 Fellowship Mk 3000 and Mk 4000
Type: short/medium range airliner
Powerplant: two Rolls-Royce RB183-2 Mk 555-15P turbofans, developing 44 kN (9,900 lb) thrust each
Performance: maximum cruising speed at 7000 m (23,000 ft) 843 km/h (523 mph); maximum cruising altitude 10675 m (35,000 ft); take-off length at sea level 1585 m (5,200 ft); range with normal load (Mk 4000) 2085 km (1,969 miles), (Mk 4000) 2085 km (1,295 miles)
Weights; operating empty (Mk 3000) 16965 kg (37,400 lb), (Mk 4000) 17645 kg (38,900 lb); maximum take-off 33110 kg (73,000 lb)
Dimensions: span 25.07 (82 ft 3 in); length (Mk 3000) 27.40 m (89 ft 10¾ in), (Mk 4000) 29.61 m (97 ft 1¾ in); height 8.47 m (27 ft 9½ in); wing area 79.00 m^2 (850 sq ft)
Accommodation: normal flight crew of two with optional third seat; (Mk 3000) up to 65 passengers in five-abreast seating, (Mk 4000) up to 85 passengers

Following the lead of contemporary airliners such as the One-Eleven and DC-9, Fokker adopted the rear-mounted engine configuration with T-tail for the F28. It had been developed in response to the sales success of the turboprop F27, and the desire by operators to have greater performance available. Its suitability to Third World and domestic operations was considerably enhanced by the adoption of powered ailerons, double-slotted Fowler flaps, lift dumpers and a split tailcone airbrake for excellent short-field performance. This aircraft is seen in the colours of West German carrier Aviaction.

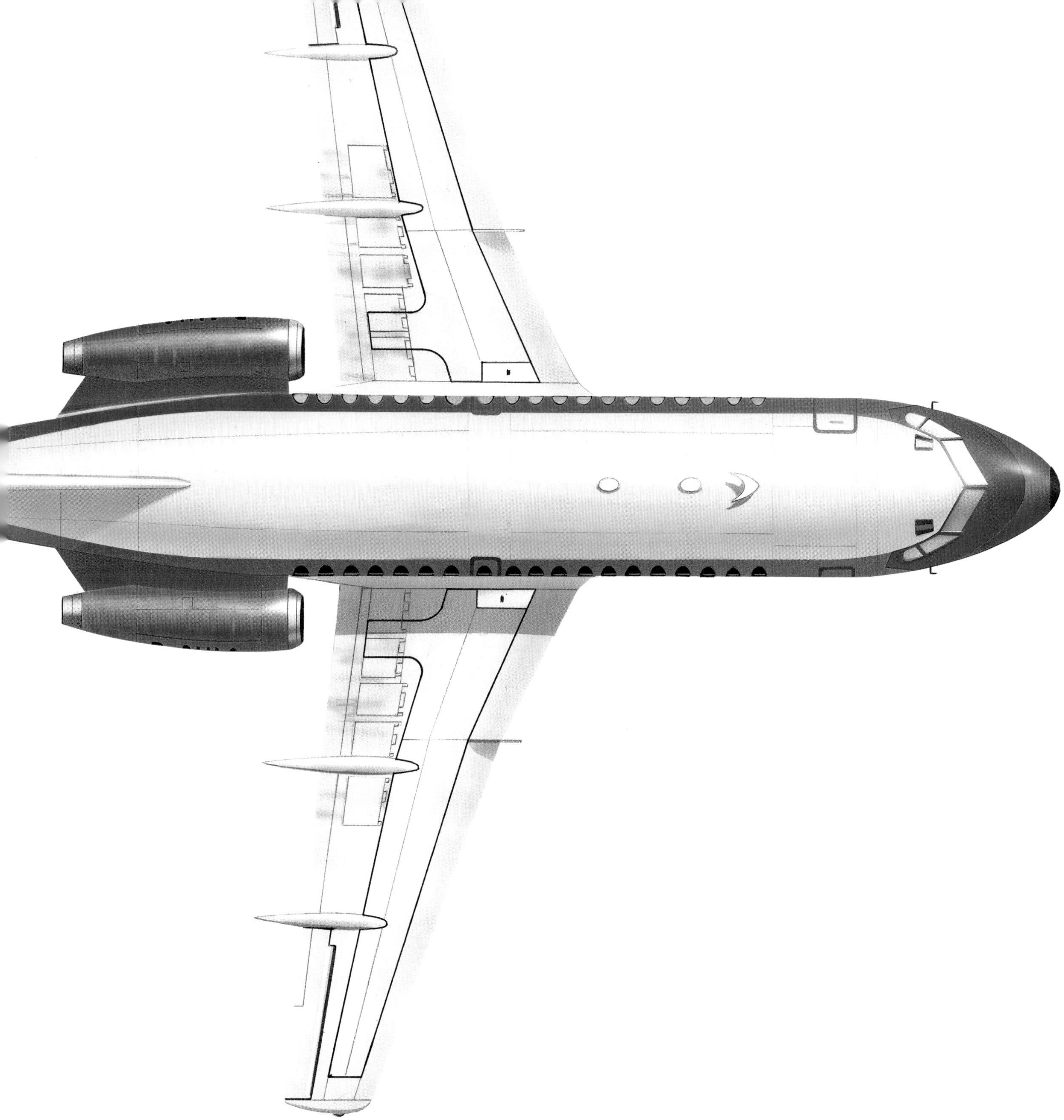

D-AHLA
AVIACTION

De Havilland Canada DHC-7

Dash-7 Series 100

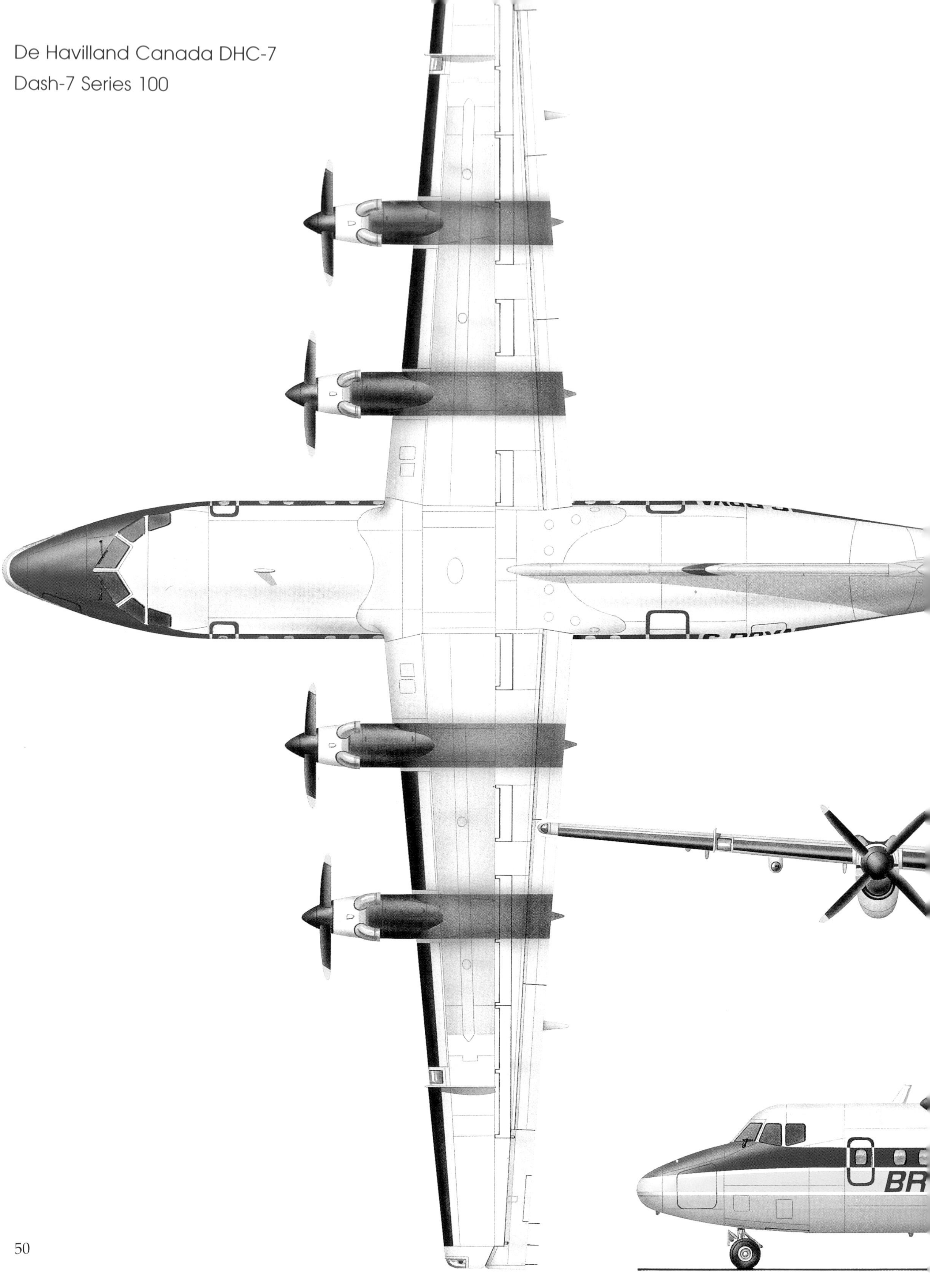

Variants

DHC-7 Dash-7: two pre-production aircraft built for testing programme and demonstrations
Dash-7 Series 100: production passenger-carrying model powered by four Pratt & Whitney PT6A-50 turboprop engines; accommodation for 50 passengers
Dash-7 Series 101: cargo/passenger-carrying model with large access door in forward port fuselage
Series 150: improved version introduced in 1986. Maximum take-off and landing weights are increased and there is an optional increase in fuel capacity
CC-132: military model operated by Canadian Armed Forces for VIP/transport duties; two built
DHC-7R: maritime surveillance version
DHC-7IR: ice reconnaissance version

Specification

de Havilland Canada DHC-7 Dash-7 Series 100
Type: 50/56-seat passenger or passenger/cargo transport
Powerplant: four 835-kW (1,120-shp) Pratt & Whitney Canada PT6A-50 turboprops fitted with four-blade Hamilton Standard 24 PF constant-speed propellers
Performance: maximum cruise speed at 2438 m (8,000 ft) at 18598 kg (41,000 lb) weight 431 km/h (268 mph); cruising speed at 4572 m (15,000 ft) with full IFR fuel reserves and 4309-kg (9,500-lb) payload of passengers and baggage/freight 421 km/h (263 mph); maximum fuel range with 2948-kg (6,500-lb) payload 2180 km (1,355 miles); FAR Part 25 take-off field length at 18598-kg (41,000-lb) weight at 25° flap setting 689 m (2,260 ft); FAR STOL landing field length at 19051-kg (42,000-lb) maximum landing weight 594 m (1,950 ft)
Weights: operational empty weight 12406 kg (27,350 lb); maximum take-off 19958 kg (44,000 lb); maximum payload 5284 kg (11,650 lb)
Dimensions: span 28.35 m (93 ft 0 in); length 24.59 m (80 ft 8 in); height 7.98 m (26 ft 2 in); wing area 79.9 m^2 (860 sq ft)
Accommodation: standard seating for 50 passengers in four-abreast arrangement with centre aisle or (high-density) 56 passengers; maximum two flight attendants and two flight crew

Brymon Airways now uses five Dash-7s and also investigated the viability of the Dash-8 as a convenient mid-capacity aircraft to fit in between the Dash-7 and the Twin Otter. The airline benefits from de Havilland Canada having taken a major shareholding in Brymon, and it is a valuable proving ground for the aircraft. The remarkable STOL performance of the Dash-7 has enabled Brymon Airways, in conjunction with the Mowlem construction group, to gain approval for the London Docklands airport project. In particular, the Dash-7 has proved to be very quiet.

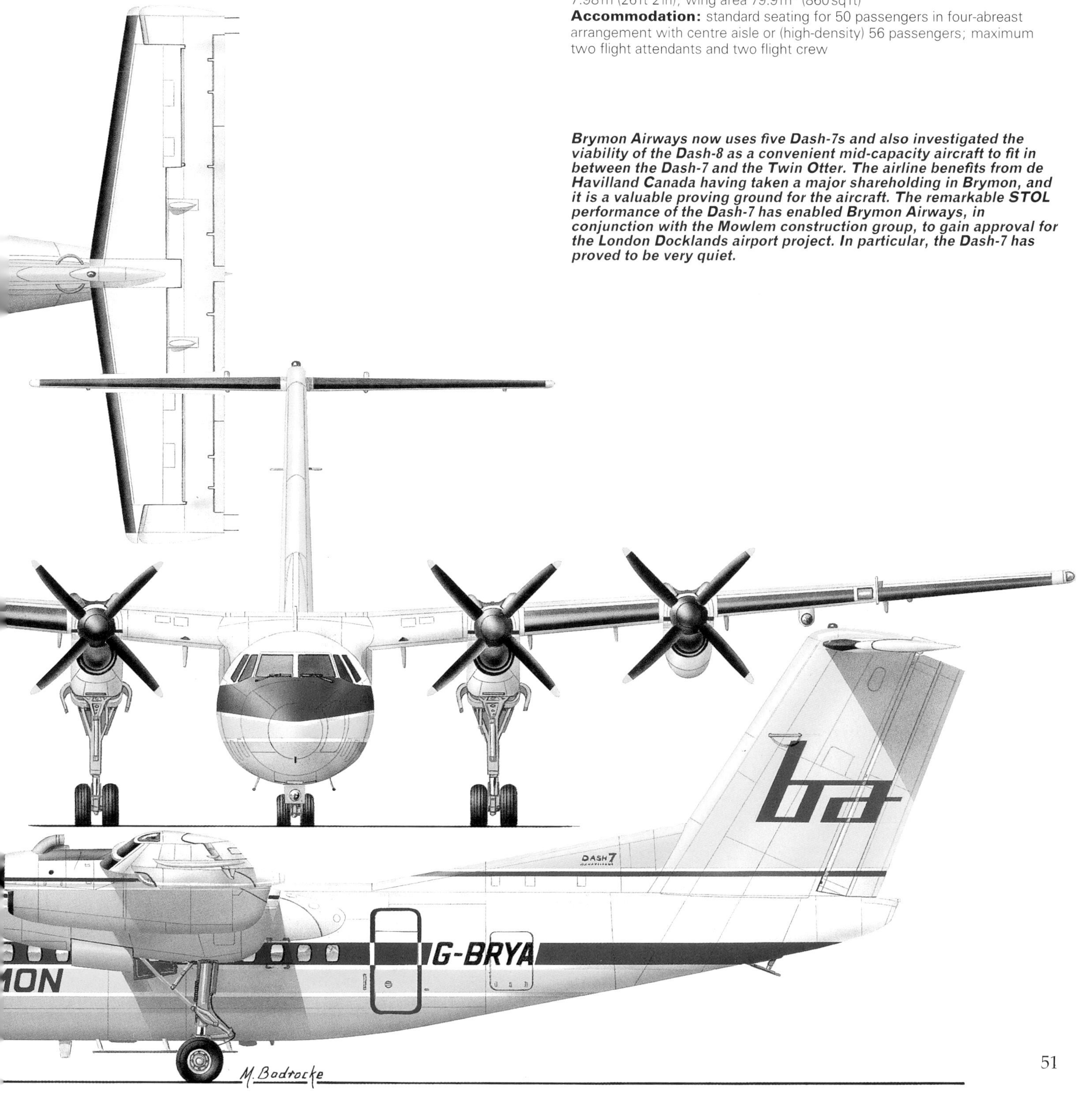

Piper PA-28 Cherokee 160/PA-28-181 Archer II/PA-28-236 Dakota

Specification
Piper PA-28 Cherokee 160
Wingspan: 9.14 m (30 ft 0 in)
Length: 7.10 m (23 ft 3½ in)
Height: 2.22 m (7 ft 3½ in)
Wing area: 14.86 m (160 sq ft)
Powerplant: one 119.2-kW (160-hp) Lycoming O-320-B2B
Cabin capacity: 4
Empty weight: 551 kg (1,215 lb)
Maximum take-off weight: 998 kg (2,200 lb)
Maximum speed: 222 km/h (138 mph)
Cruising speed: 201 km/h (125 mph)
Service ceiling: 4572 m (15,000 ft)
Maximum range: 1303 km/h (810 miles)

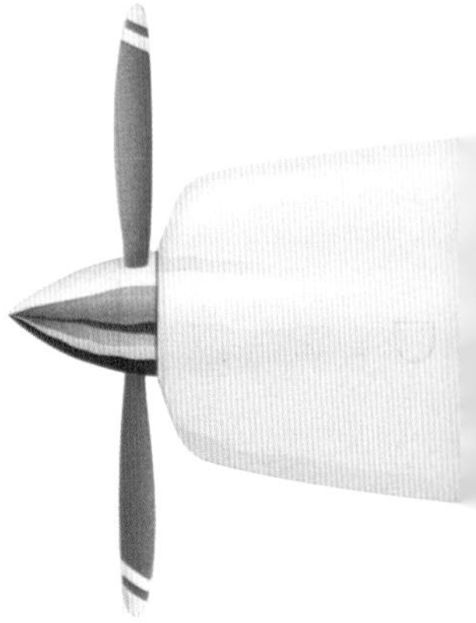

Specification
Piper PA-28-181 Archer II
Wingspan: 10.66 m (35 ft 0 in)
Length: 7.3 m (24 ft 0 in)
Height: 2.25 m (7 ft 4 in)
Wing area: 15.79 m (170 sq ft)
Powerplant: one 134.1-kW (180-hp) Lycoming O-360-A4M
Cabin capacity: 4
Empty weight: 630.5 kg (1,390 lb)
Maximum take-off weight: 1156 kg (2,550 lb)
Maximum speed: 243 km/h (151 mph)
Cruising speed: 236 km/h (147 mph)
Service ceiling: 4161 m (13,650 ft)
Maximum range: 1456 km/h (905 miles)

Specification
Piper PA-28-236 Dakota
Type: light tourer
Powerplant: one Textron Lycoming 0-540-J3A5D flat-six piston engine developing 175 kW (235 hp), driving a two-bladed constant-speed Hartzell propeller
Performance: maximum speed at sea level 274 km/h (170 mph); stalling speed, flaps down 120 km/h (75 mph); maximum rate of climb at sea level 338 m (1,110 ft) per minute; service ceiling 5335 m (17,500 ft); take-off run 270 m (886 ft); landing run 252 m (825 ft); range with maximum fuel and best cruising speed 1501 km (933 miles)
Weights: empty 730 kg (1,610 lb); maximum take-off 1361 kg (3,000 lb); standard fuel capacity 291.5 litres (64 Imp gal)
Dimensions: wing span 10.67 m (35 ft 0 in); length 7.54 m (24 ft 8¾ in); height 2.18 m (7 ft 2 in); tailplane span 3.92 m (12 ft 10½ in); wheel track 3.05 m (10 ft 0 in); wheelbase 1.98 m (6 ft 6 in); wing area 15.8 m^2 (170 sq ft)
Accommodation: four seats in pairs arrangement; entry door on starboard side; baggage compartment at rear of cabin with 0.74 m (26 cu ft) capacity

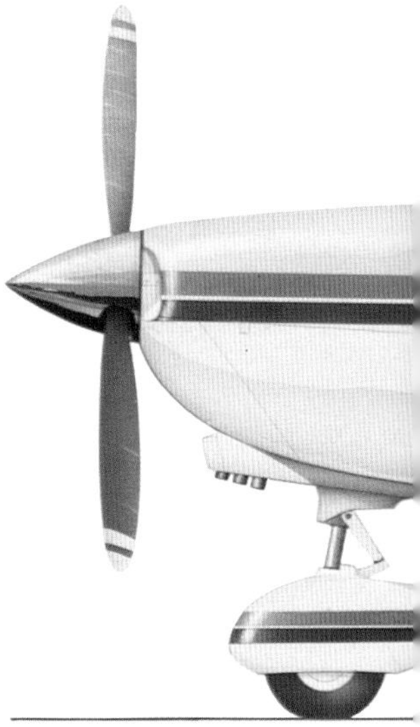

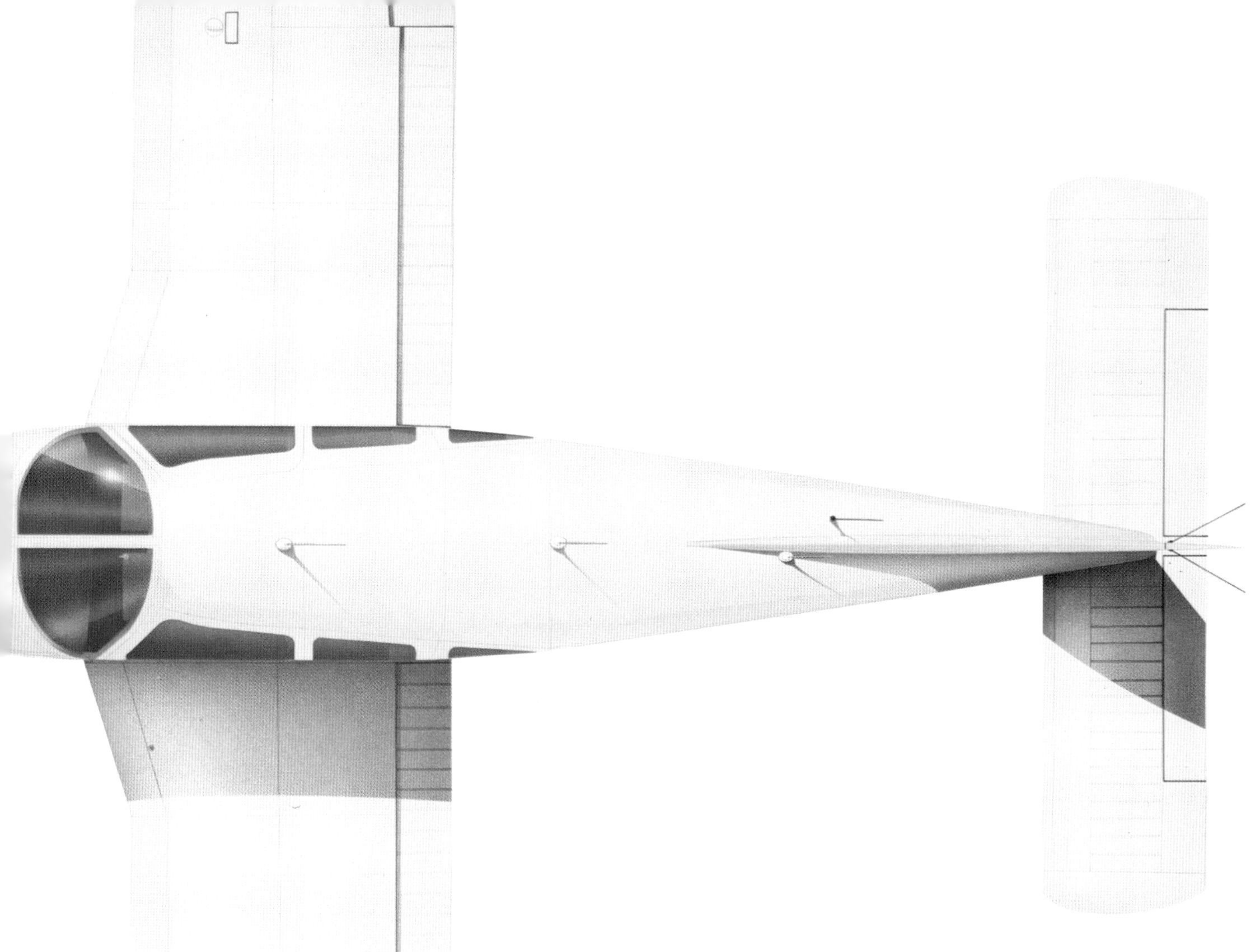

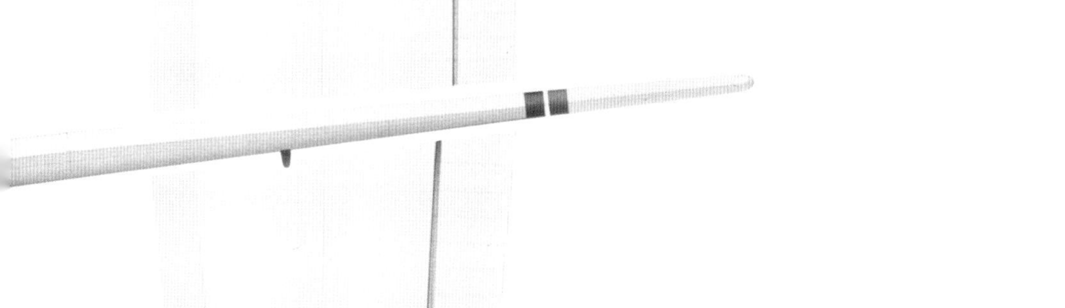

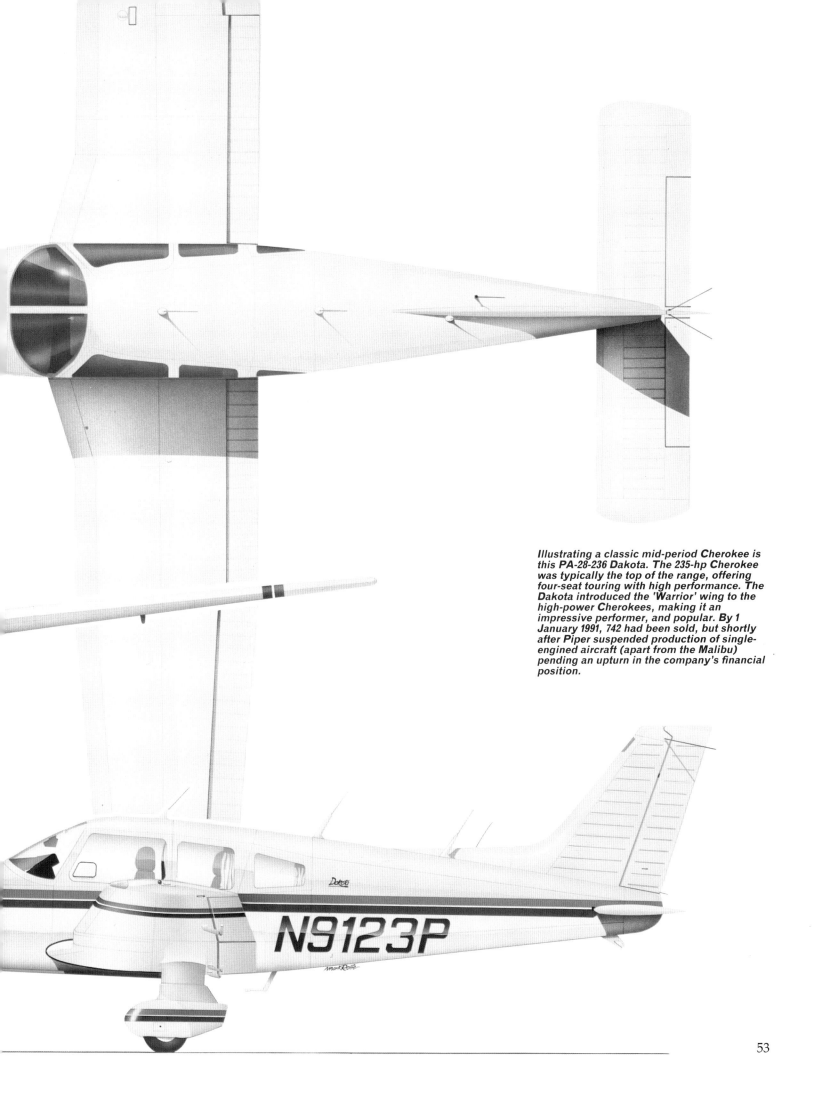

Illustrating a classic mid-period Cherokee is this PA-28-236 Dakota. The 235-hp Cherokee was typically the top of the range, offering four-seat touring with high performance. The Dakota introduced the 'Warrior' wing to the high-power Cherokees, making it an impressive performer, and popular. By 1 January 1991, 742 had been sold, but shortly after Piper suspended production of single-engined aircraft (apart from the Malibu) pending an upturn in the company's financial position.

Lockheed L-1011-500

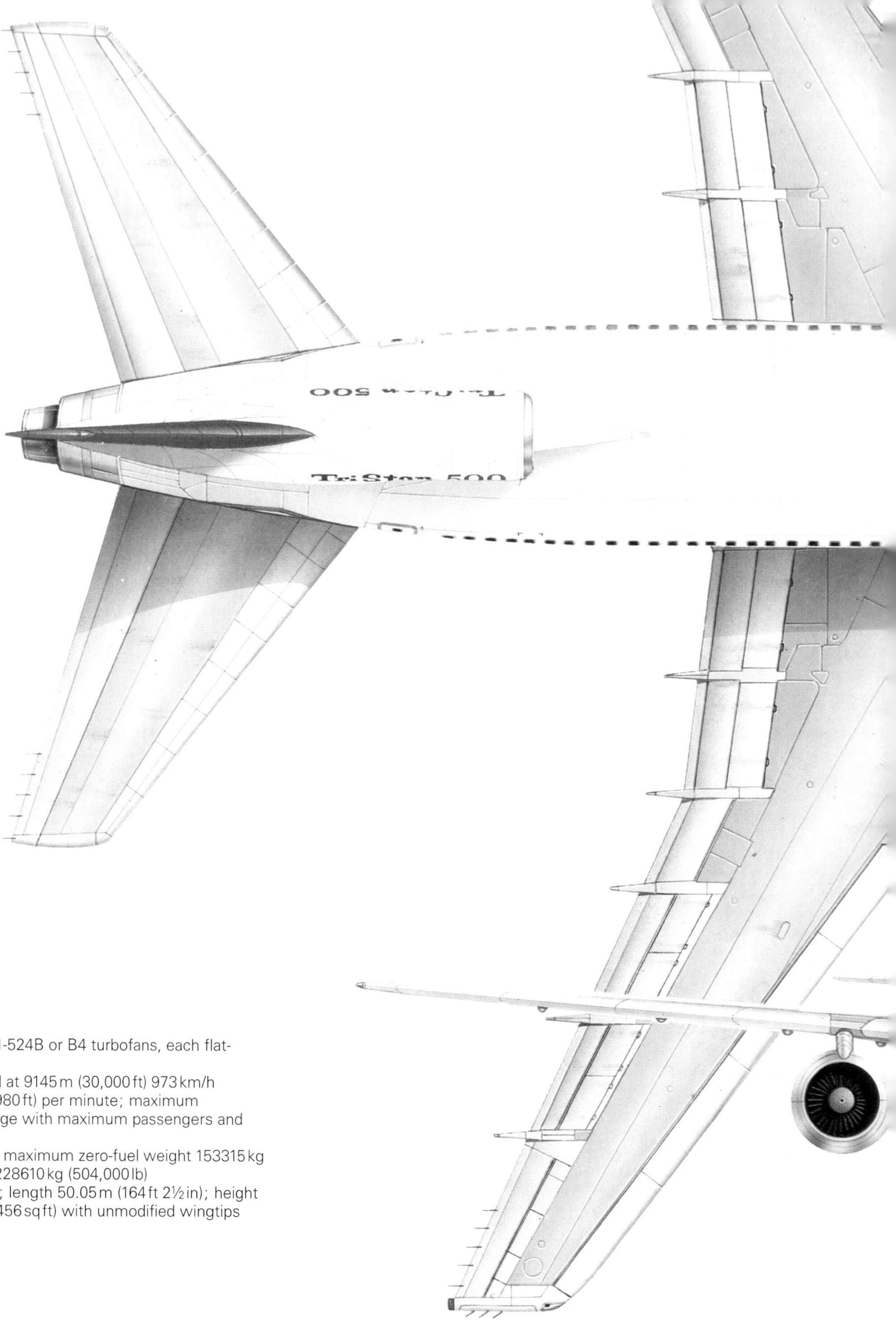

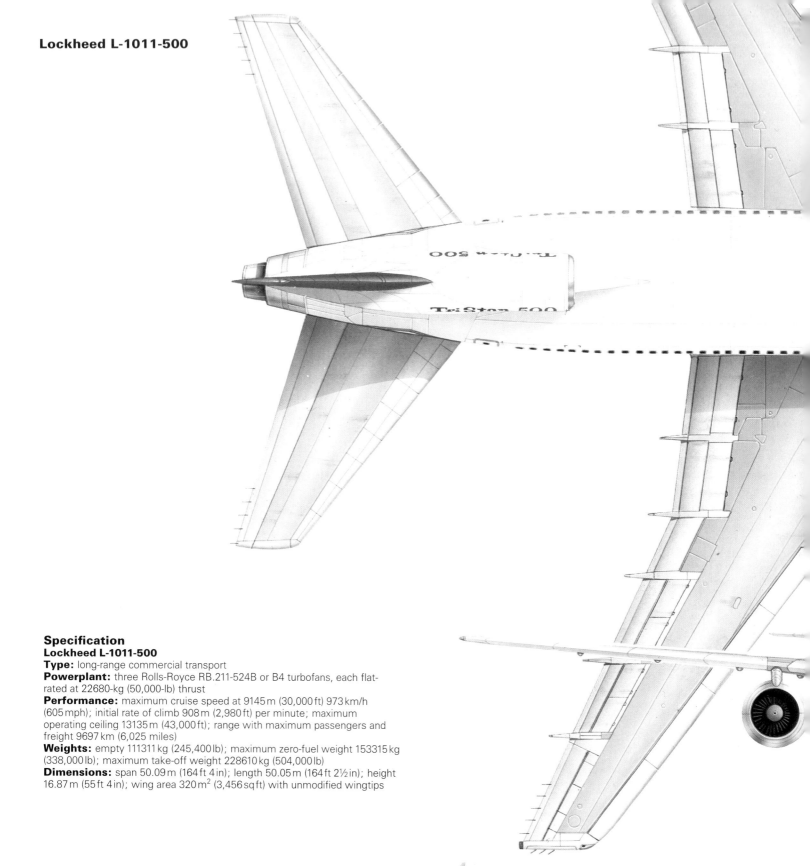

Specification

Lockheed L-1011-500

Type: long-range commercial transport
Powerplant: three Rolls-Royce RB.211-524B or B4 turbofans, each flat-rated at 22680-kg (50,000-lb) thrust
Performance: maximum cruise speed at 9145 m (30,000 ft) 973 km/h (605 mph); initial rate of climb 908 m (2,980 ft) per minute; maximum operating ceiling 13135 m (43,000 ft); range with maximum passengers and freight 9697 km (6,025 miles)
Weights: empty 111311 kg (245,400 lb); maximum zero-fuel weight 153315 kg (338,000 lb); maximum take-off weight 228610 kg (504,000 lb)
Dimensions: span 50.09 m (164 ft 4 in); length 50.05 m (164 ft 2½ in); height 16.87 m (55 ft 4 in); wing area 320 m^2 (3,456 sq ft) with unmodified wingtips

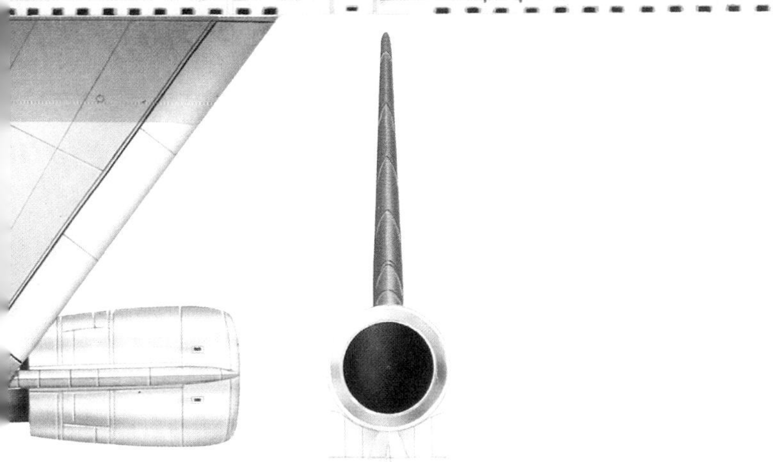

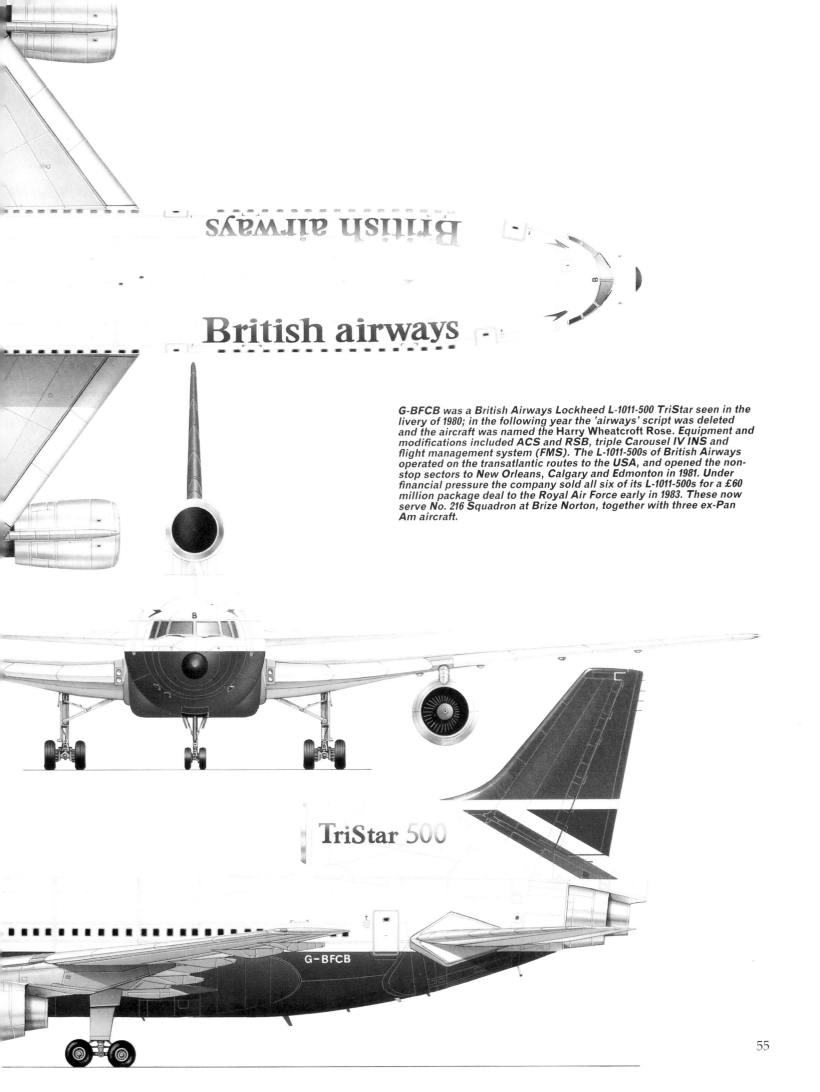

G-BFCB was a British Airways Lockheed L-1011-500 TriStar seen in the livery of 1980; in the following year the 'airways' script was deleted and the aircraft was named the Harry Wheatcroft Rose. Equipment and modifications included ACS and RSB, triple Carousel IV INS and flight management system (FMS). The L-1011-500s of British Airways operated on the transatlantic routes to the USA, and opened the non-stop sectors to New Orleans, Calgary and Edmonton in 1981. Under financial pressure the company sold all six of its L-1011-500s for a £60 million package deal to the Royal Air Force early in 1983. These now serve No. 216 Squadron at Brize Norton, together with three ex-Pan Am aircraft.

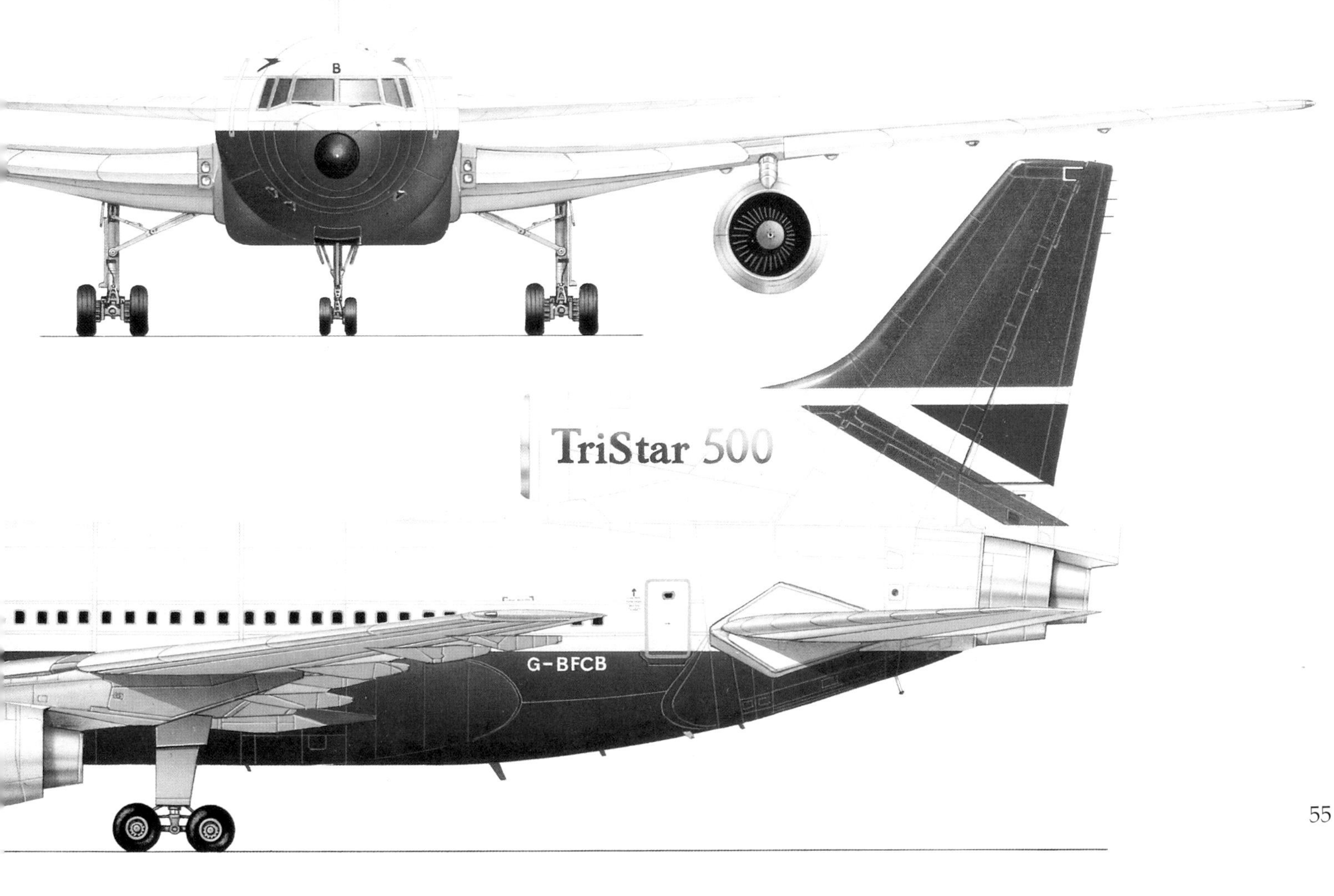

McDonnell Douglas DC-9 and MD-80 variants

DC-9-10: initial 80-seat version with derated 5557-kg (12,250-lb) thrust JT8D-5 engines; flown in February 1965 and entered service in December 1965; also produced in freighter (**DC-9-10F**) and convertible (**DC-9-10CF**) versions
DC-9-15: heavier, higher-powered version of DC-9-10, with 6350-kg (14,000-lb) thrust JT8D-1 engines; DC-9-10/15 deliveries totalled 137 aircraft; production completed
DC-9-20: version developed for SAS, with DC-9-30 wing, DC-9-40 powerplant and DC-9-10 fuselage; first deliveries December 1968; 10 built; production completed
DC-9-30: stretched 105-seat version, first delivered in January 1967, initially with 6350-kg (14,000-lb) JT8D-7 turbofans; later DC-9-30s offered with increased gross weights, auxiliary fuel in underfloor tanks and JT8D-15 engines of 7031-kg (15,500-lb) thrust; also produced as **DC-9-30F** freighter, **DC-9-30CF** convertible and **DC-9-30RC** quick-change variants; 620 of all types delivered 1967-82; production completed
C-9A Nightingale: medical evacuation version of DC-9-30CF, for US Air Force; 21 delivered 1968-73; production completed
C-9B Skytrain II: logistic support transport; 15 delivered to US Navy and two to government of Kuwait; production completed
VC-9C: three VIP transports for USAF, delivered in 1975
DC-9-40: 115-seat stretched version with JT8D-9 engines, developed for SAS and delivered in February 1968; 71 built; production completed
DC-9-50: stretched, 139-seat development of DC-9-30 with JT8D-15 or JT8D-17 engines; 99 delivered 1975-82; production completed
MD-80: originally designated **DC-9 Super 80**; highly modified, further stretched development of DC-9 with extended wing, new engines and many other changes; flown in October 1979, and certificated in August 1980
MD-81: original MD-80 version with 8392-kg (18,500-lb) JT8D-209 engines and 63504-kg (140,000-lb) gross weight; entered service in October 1980
MD-82: JT8D-217A engines rated at 9072-kg (20,000-lb) thrust; 66680-kg (147,000-lb) maximum take-off weight
MD-83: extended-range development with 9526-kg (21,000-lb) thrust JT8D-219 engines, 72576 kg (160,000 lb) gross weight and 1,100 US gal (4164 litres) of additional fuel
MD-87: short-fuselage version with maximum of 130 seats in single-class arrangement. JT8D-217C engines
MD-88: updated long-fuselage version with modern cockpit, flight management system. JT8D-219 engines
MD-90: proposed MD-80 family update, recent configurations offering propfan propulsion
P-9D: propfan-powered maritime surveillance proposal to replace P-3 Orion in US Navy service

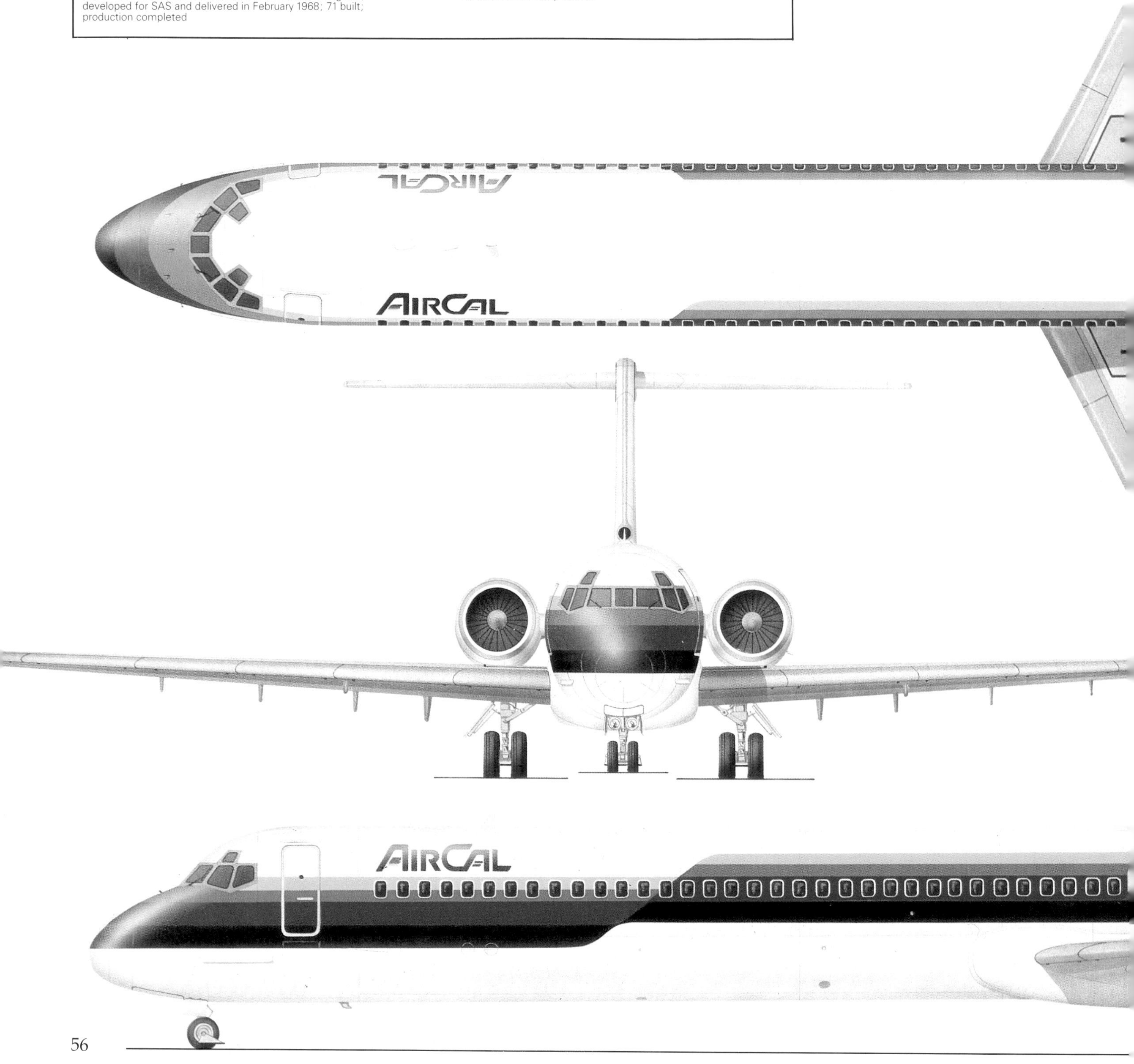

The final length version of the family is the MD-80, now available in varying range and equipment fits. AirCal was a major operator (now bought up by American Airlines), using its aircraft on the lucrative Californian corridor between Los Angeles and San Francisco.

Specification

McDonnell Douglas MD-82

Type: 172-seat short/medium-range airliner

Powerplant : two Pratt & Whitney JT8D-217A turbofans, each rated at 9072-kg (20,000-lb) thrust

Performance: maximum cruise speed Mach 0.8 (850 km/h/528 mph) at high altitude; range with 155 passengers 3000 km (1,800 miles); take-off field length 2175 m (7,140 ft); landing field length 1405 m (4,605 ft)

Weights: empty 36465 kg (80,392 lb); maximum take-off 66680 kg (147,000 lb)

Dimensions: span 32.87 m (107 ft 10 in); length overall 45.06 m (147 ft 10 in); height 9.04 m (29 ft 8 in); wing area 118.82 m^2 (1,279 sq ft)

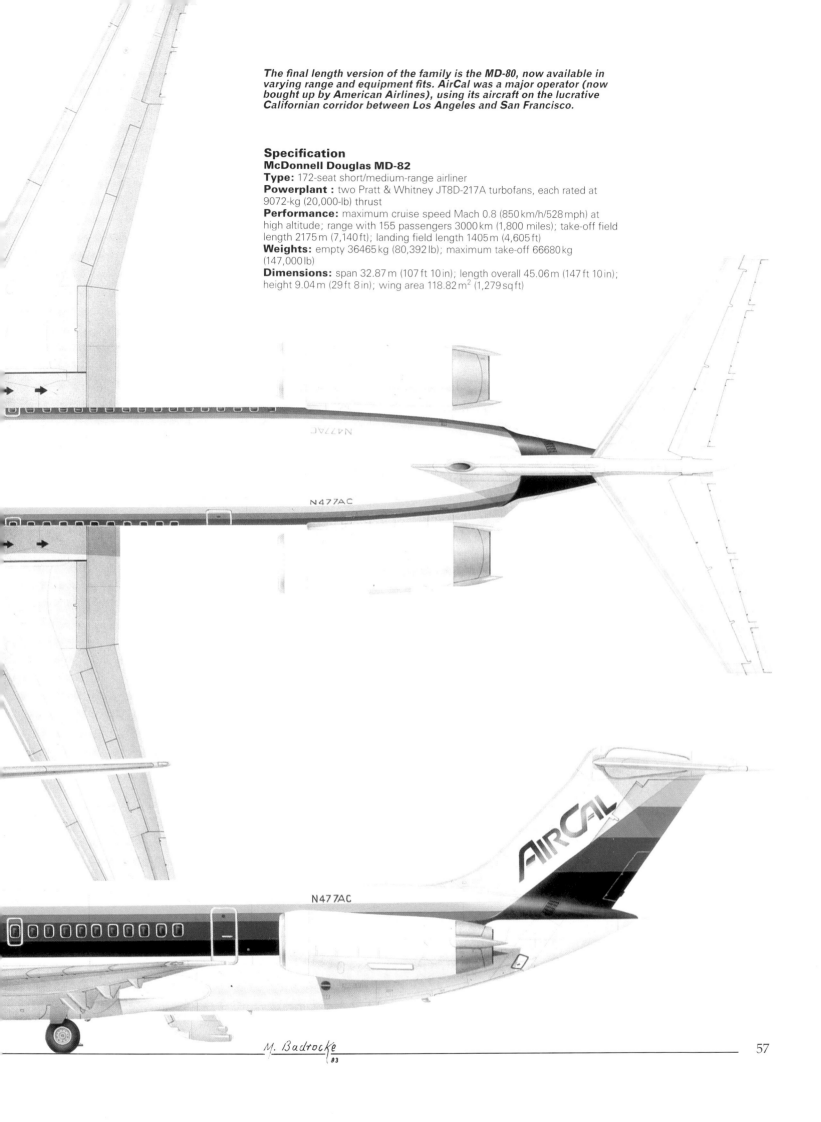

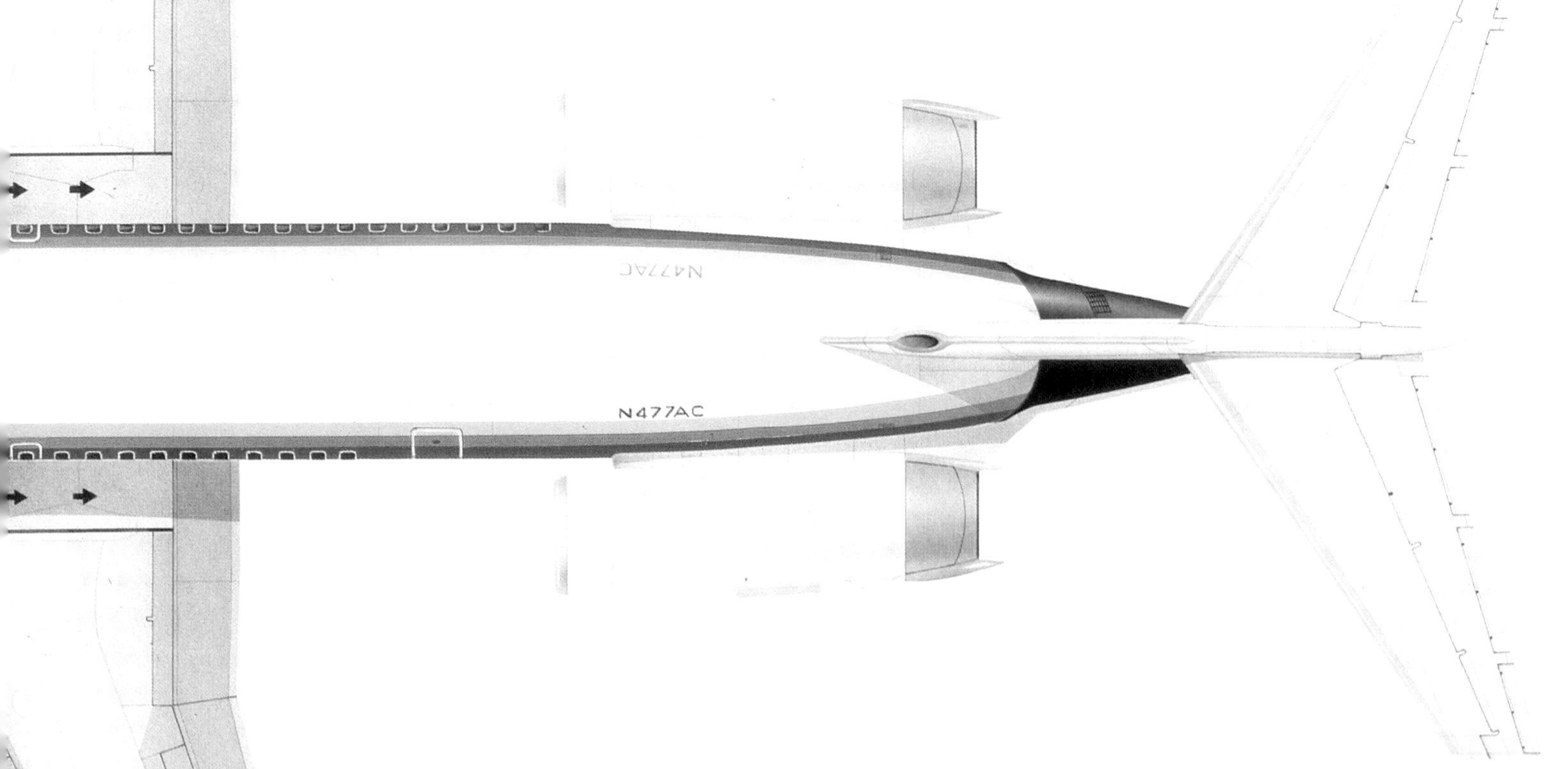

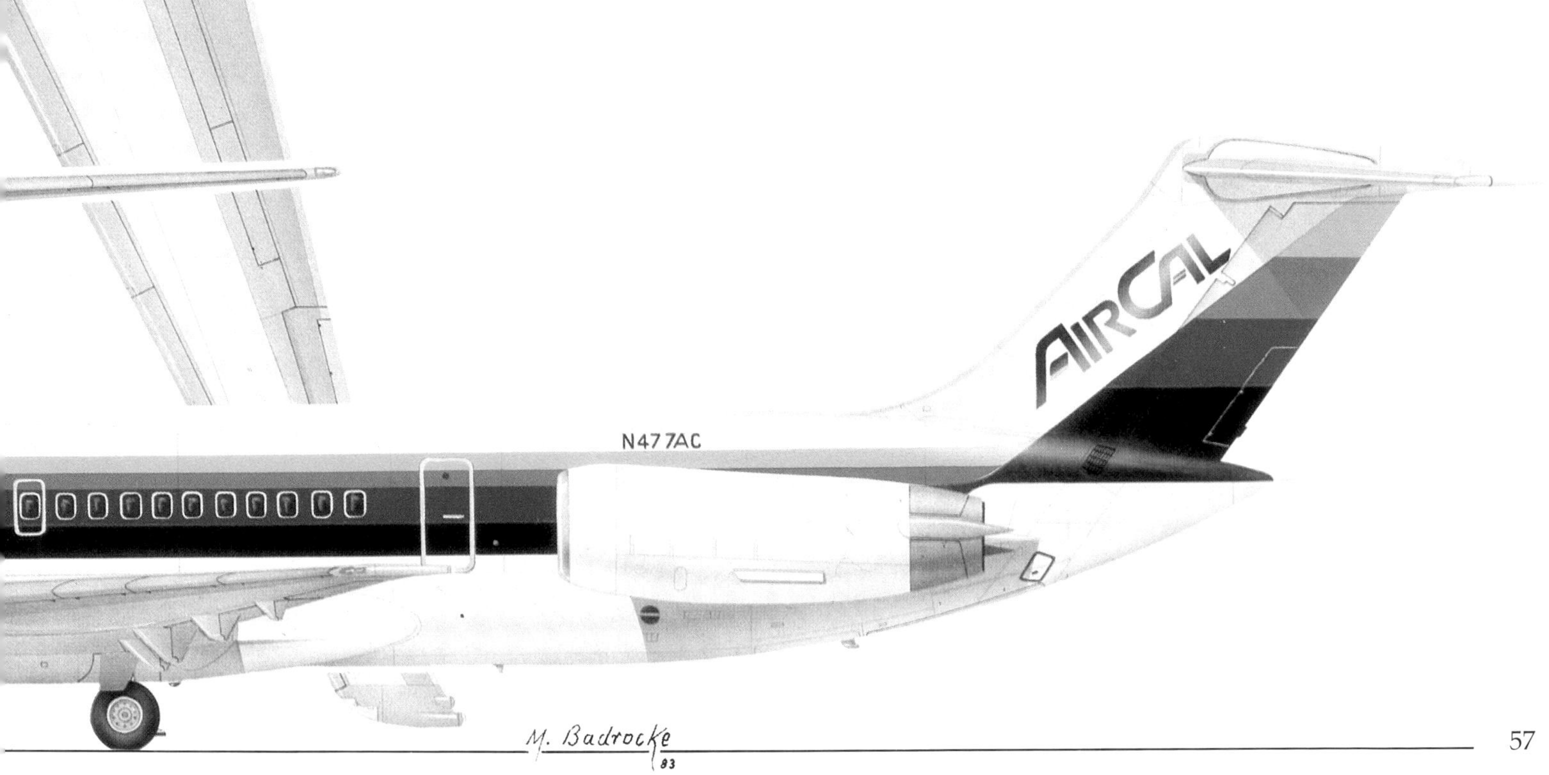

M. Badrocke 83

Rockwell Sabreliner 65

The Acopian Technical Company are the proud possessors of this, the 76th and final production Sabre 65, which they bought as new in the early 1980s. Only one Sabre 65 has been lost in an accident (at Toronto in January 1983) and, as comparatively recent aircraft, they have not gone the way of older Sabre 40s, several of which have been 'parted out' (broken-up) to provide spares. While this fate befalls increasing numbers of older business jets in general, any diminution in the Sabreliner population is counterbalanced somewhat by the return to civilian use of several of the former USAF aircraft stored at Davis-Monthan AFB.

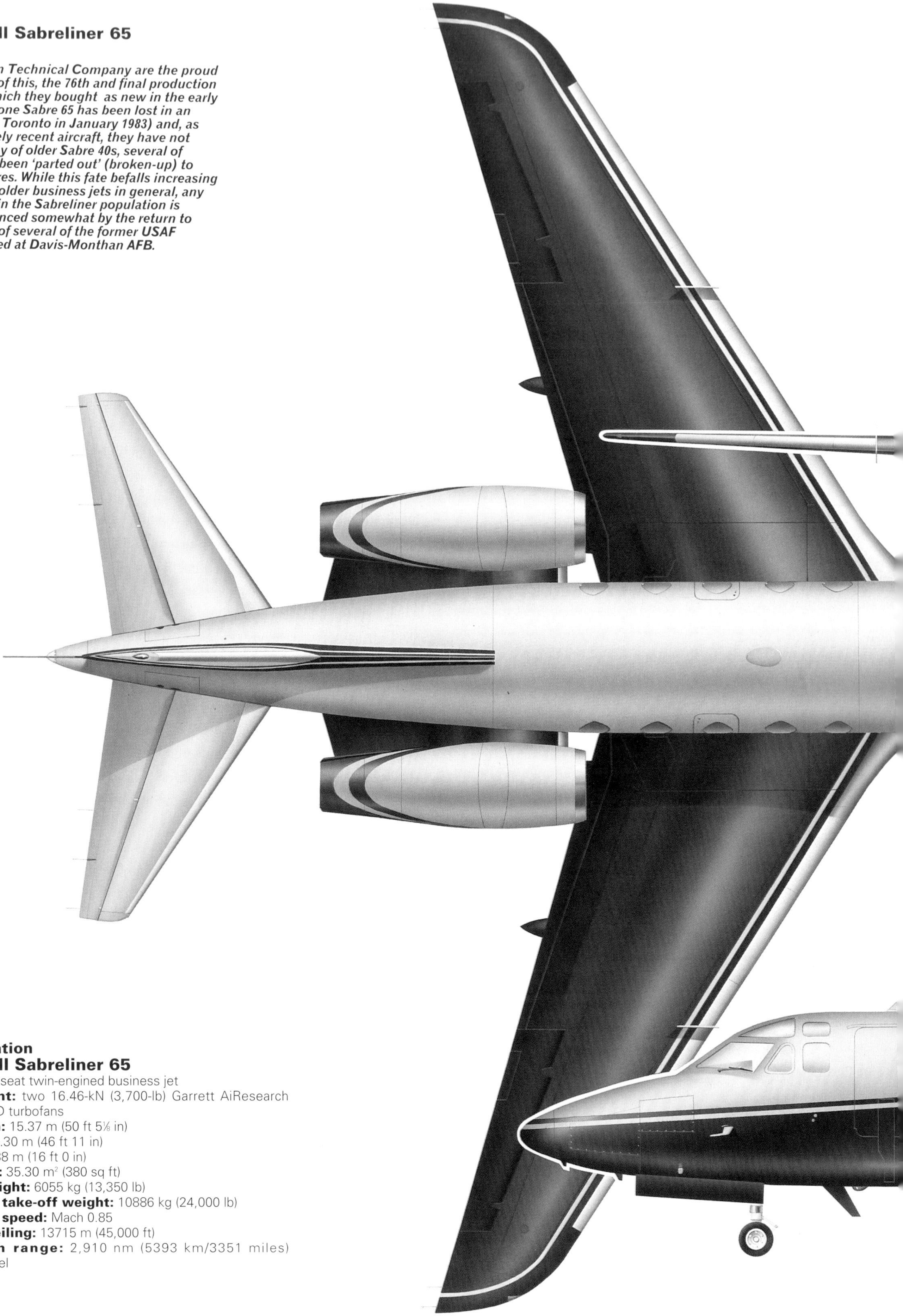

Specification
Rockwell Sabreliner 65
Type: 8-10 seat twin-engined business jet
Powerplant: two 16.46-kN (3,700-lb) Garrett AiResearch TFE731-3-1D turbofans
Wing span: 15.37 m (50 ft 5⅛ in)
Length: 14.30 m (46 ft 11 in)
Height: 4,88 m (16 ft 0 in)
Wing area: 35.30 m² (380 sq ft)
Empty weight: 6055 kg (13,350 lb)
Maximum take-off weight: 10886 kg (24,000 lb)
Maximum speed: Mach 0.85
Service ceiling: 13715 m (45,000 ft)
Maximum range: 2,910 nm (5393 km/3351 miles) with max fuel

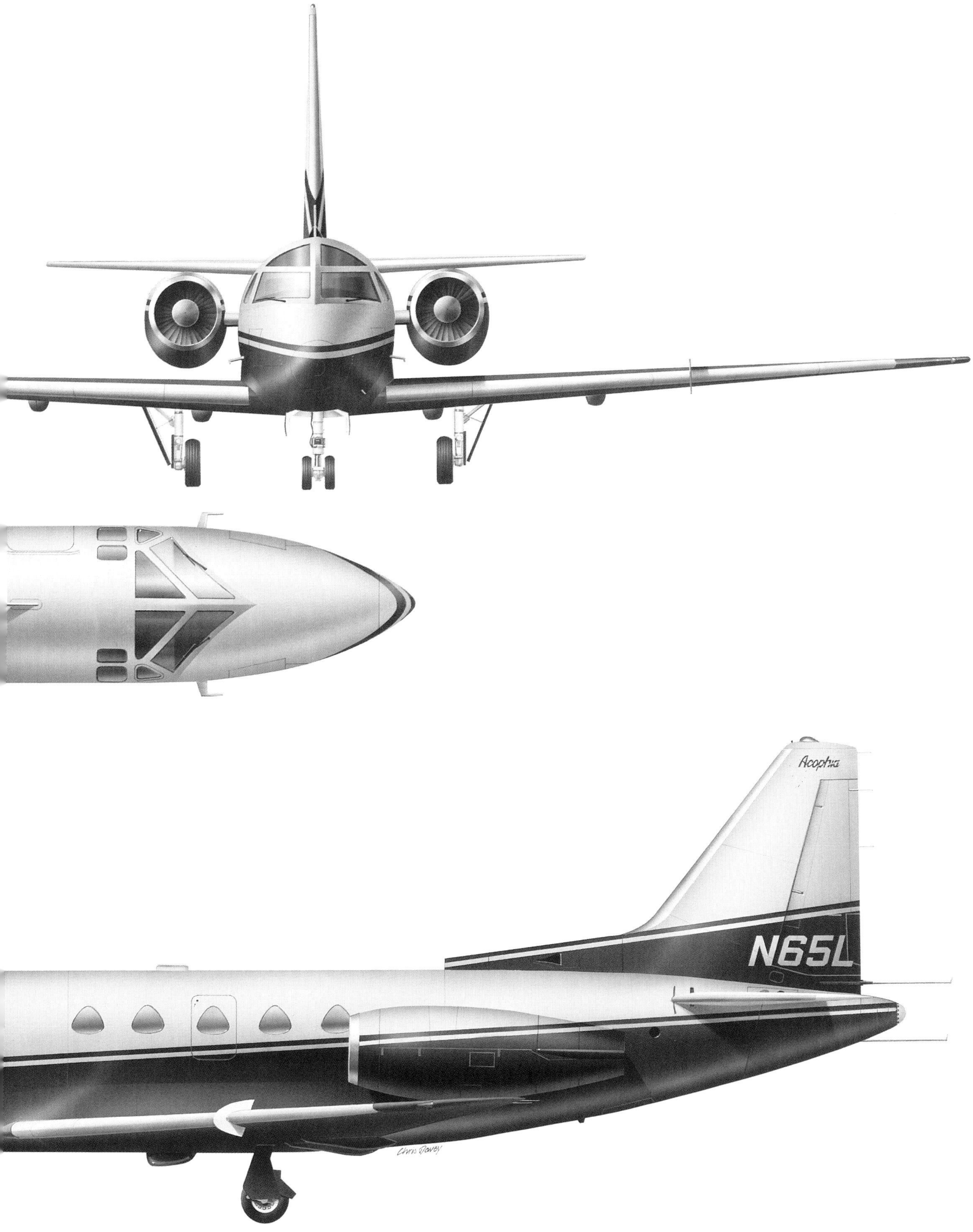
N65L

Fairchild/Swearingen SA 227AC Metro III

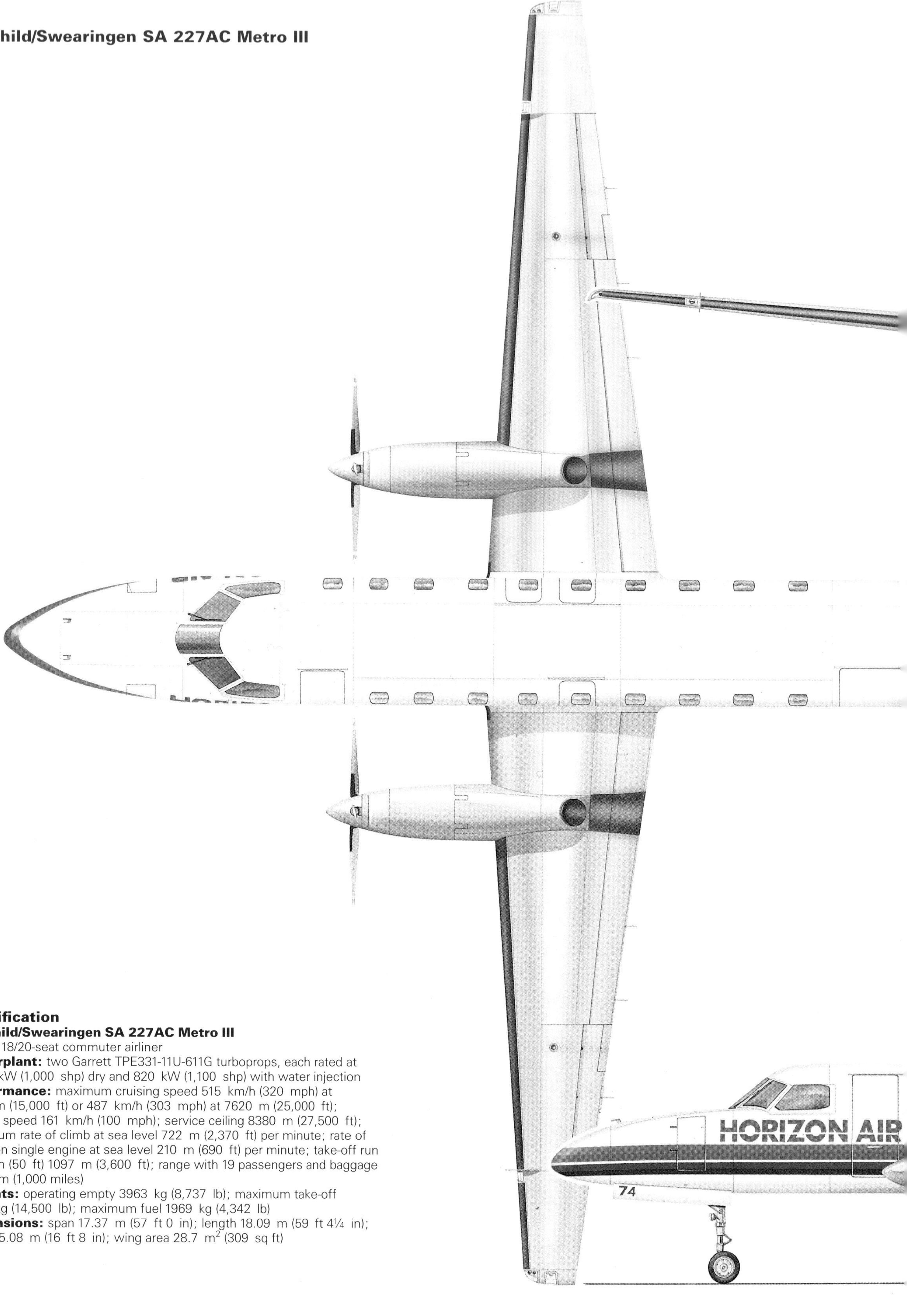

Specification

Fairchild/Swearingen SA 227AC Metro III
Type: 18/20-seat commuter airliner
Powerplant: two Garrett TPE331-11U-611G turboprops, each rated at 745.5 kW (1,000 shp) dry and 820 kW (1,100 shp) with water injection
Performance: maximum cruising speed 515 km/h (320 mph) at 4575 m (15,000 ft) or 487 km/h (303 mph) at 7620 m (25,000 ft); stalling speed 161 km/h (100 mph); service ceiling 8380 m (27,500 ft); maximum rate of climb at sea level 722 m (2,370 ft) per minute; rate of climb on single engine at sea level 210 m (690 ft) per minute; take-off run to 15 m (50 ft) 1097 m (3,600 ft); range with 19 passengers and baggage 1610 km (1,000 miles)
Weights: operating empty 3963 kg (8,737 lb); maximum take-off 6577 kg (14,500 lb); maximum fuel 1969 kg (4,342 lb)
Dimensions: span 17.37 m (57 ft 0 in); length 18.09 m (59 ft 4¼ in); height 5.08 m (16 ft 8 in); wing area 28.7 m^2 (309 sq ft)

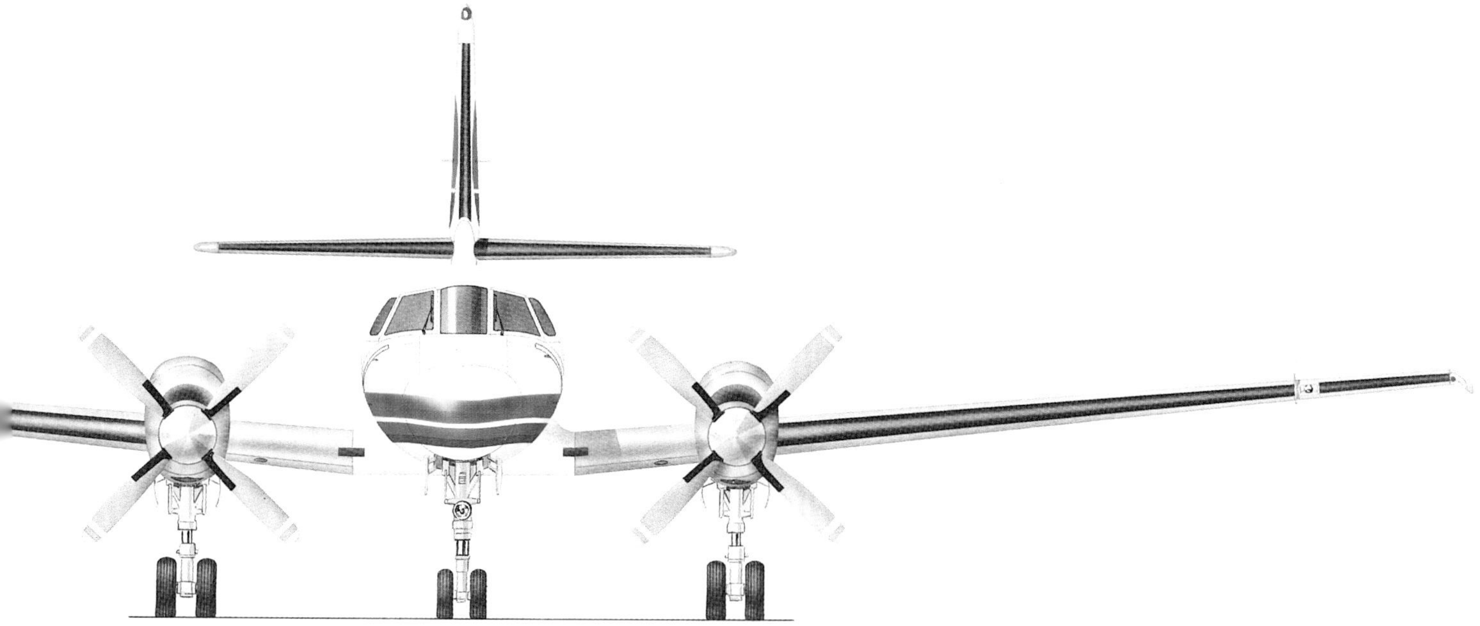

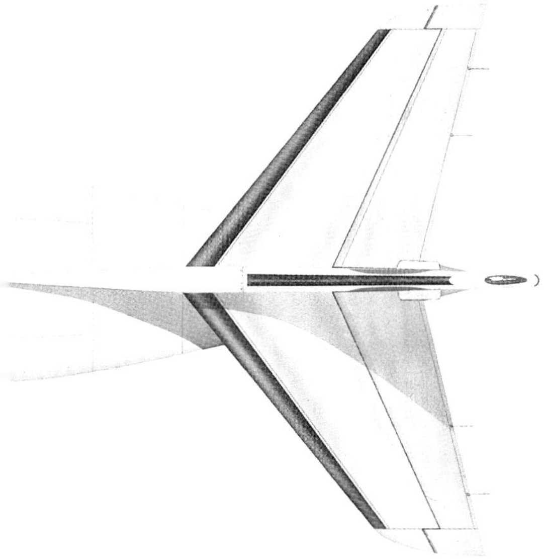

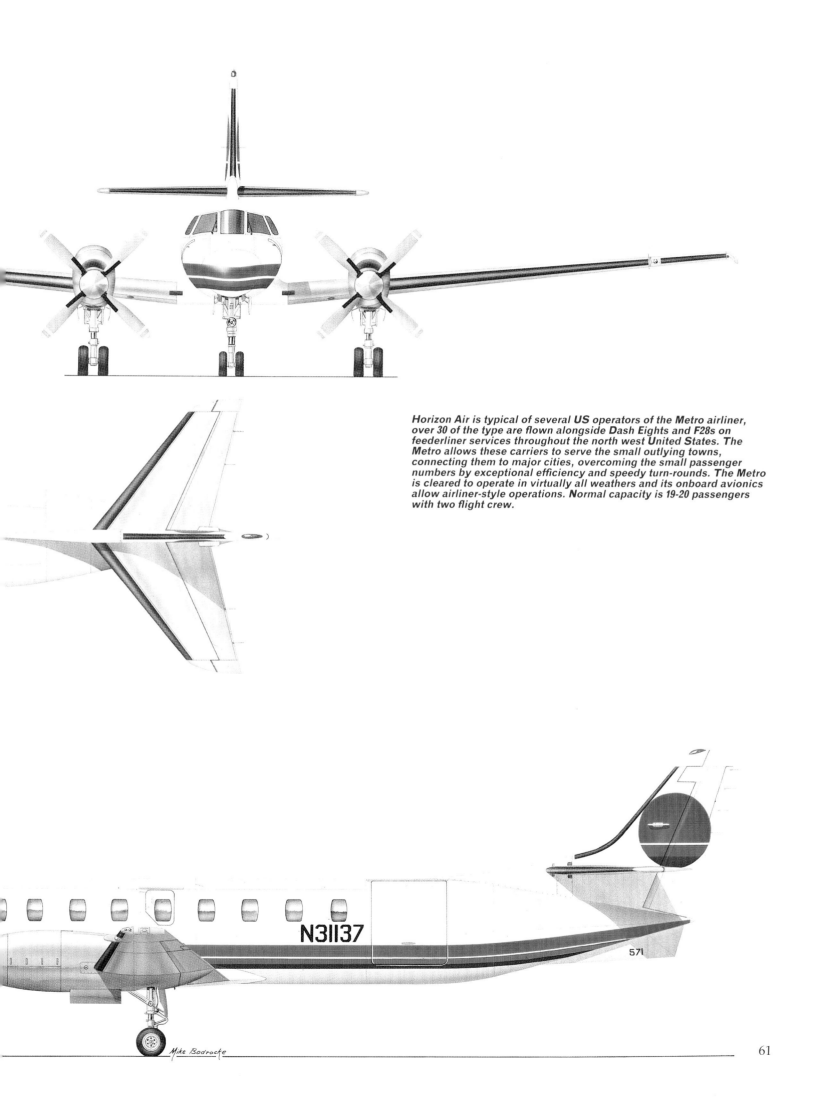

Horizon Air is typical of several US operators of the Metro airliner, over 30 of the type are flown alongside Dash Eights and F28s on feederliner services throughout the north west United States. The Metro allows these carriers to serve the small outlying towns, connecting them to major cities, overcoming the small passenger numbers by exceptional efficiency and speedy turn-rounds. The Metro is cleared to operate in virtually all weathers and its onboard avionics allow airliner-style operations. Normal capacity is 19-20 passengers with two flight crew.

Learjet Longhorn 55

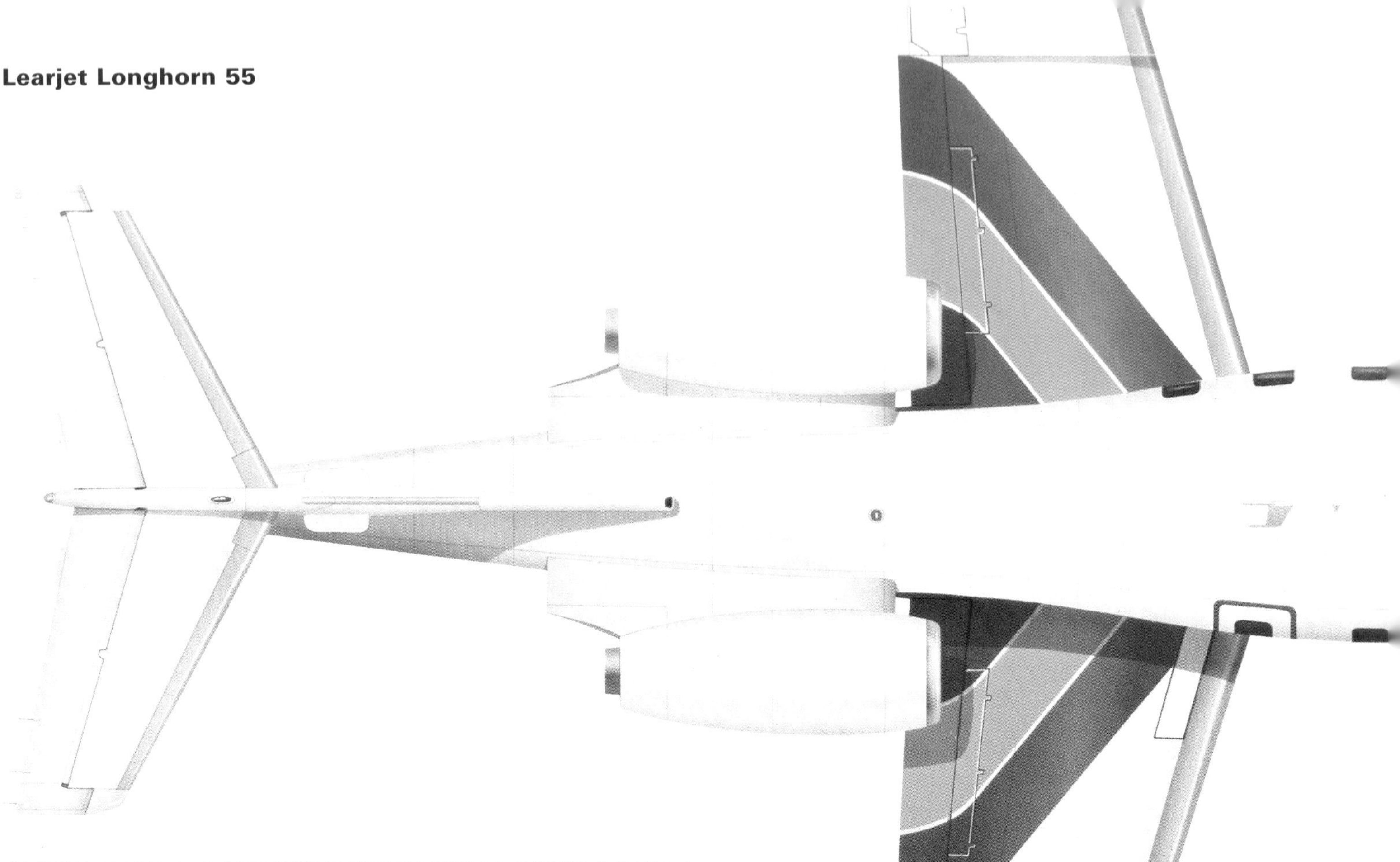

Gates Learjet variants

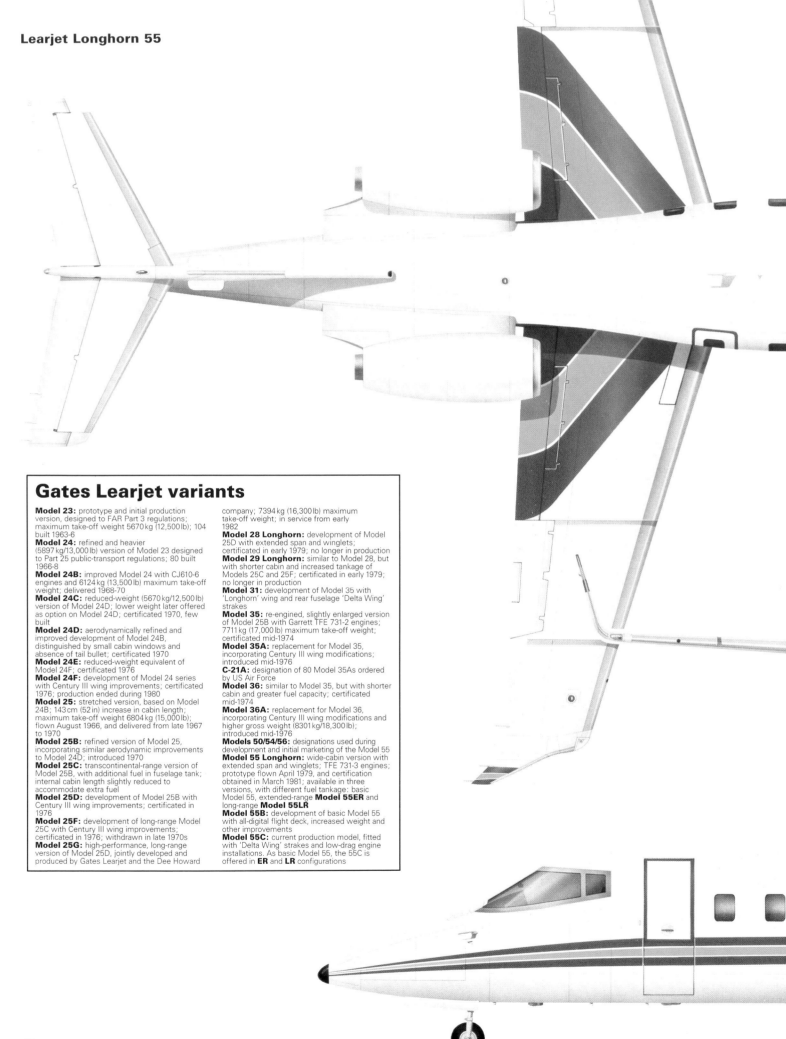

Model 23: prototype and initial production version, designed to FAR Part 3 regulations; maximum take-off weight 5670 kg (12,500 lb); 104 built 1963-6
Model 24: refined and heavier (5897 kg/13,000 lb) version of Model 23 designed to Part 25 public-transport regulations; 80 built 1966-8
Model 24B: improved Model 24 with CJ610-6 engines and 6124 kg (13,500 lb) maximum take-off weight; delivered 1968-70
Model 24C: reduced-weight (5670 kg/12,500 lb) version of Model 24D; lower weight later offered as option on Model 24D; certificated 1970, few built
Model 24D: aerodynamically refined and improved development of Model 24B, distinguished by small cabin windows and absence of tail bullet; certificated 1970
Model 24E: reduced-weight equivalent of Model 24F; certificated 1976
Model 24F: development of Model 24 series with Century III wing improvements; certificated 1976; production ended during 1980
Model 25: stretched version, based on Model 24B; 143 cm (52 in) increase in cabin length; maximum take-off weight 6804 kg (15,000 lb); flown August 1966, and delivered from late 1967 to 1970
Model 25B: refined version of Model 25, incorporating similar aerodynamic improvements to Model 24D; introduced 1970
Model 25C: transcontinental-range version of Model 25B, with additional fuel in fuselage tank; internal cabin length slightly reduced to accommodate extra fuel
Model 25D: development of Model 25B with Century III wing improvements; certificated in 1976
Model 25F: development of long-range Model 25C with Century III wing improvements; certificated in 1976; withdrawn in late 1970s
Model 25G: high-performance, long-range version of Model 25D, jointly developed and produced by Gates Learjet and the Dee Howard company; 7394 kg (16,300 lb) maximum take-off weight; in service from early 1982
Model 28 Longhorn: development of Model 25D with extended span and winglets; certificated in early 1979; no longer in production
Model 29 Longhorn: similar to Model 28, but with shorter cabin and increased tankage of Models 25C and 25F; certificated in early 1979; no longer in production
Model 31: development of Model 35 with 'Longhorn' wing and rear fuselage 'Delta Wing' strakes
Model 35: re-engined, slightly enlarged version of Model 25B with Garrett TFE 731-2 engines; 7711 kg (17,000 lb) maximum take-off weight; certificated mid-1974
Model 35A: replacement for Model 35, incorporating Century III wing modifications; introduced mid-1976
C-21A: designation of 80 Model 35As ordered by US Air Force
Model 36: similar to Model 35, but with shorter cabin and greater fuel capacity; certificated mid-1974
Model 36A: replacement for Model 36, incorporating Century III wing modifications and higher gross weight (8301 kg/18,300 lb); introduced mid-1976
Models 50/54/56: designations used during development and initial marketing of the Model 55
Model 55 Longhorn: wide-cabin version with extended span and winglets; TFE 731-3 engines; prototype flown April 1979, and certification obtained in March 1981; available in three versions, with different fuel tankage: basic Model 55, extended-range **Model 55ER** and long-range **Model 55LR**
Model 55B: development of basic Model 55 with all-digital flight deck, increased weight and other improvements
Model 55C: current production model, fitted with 'Delta Wing' strakes and low-drag engine installations. As basic Model 55, the 55C is offered in **ER** and **LR** configurations

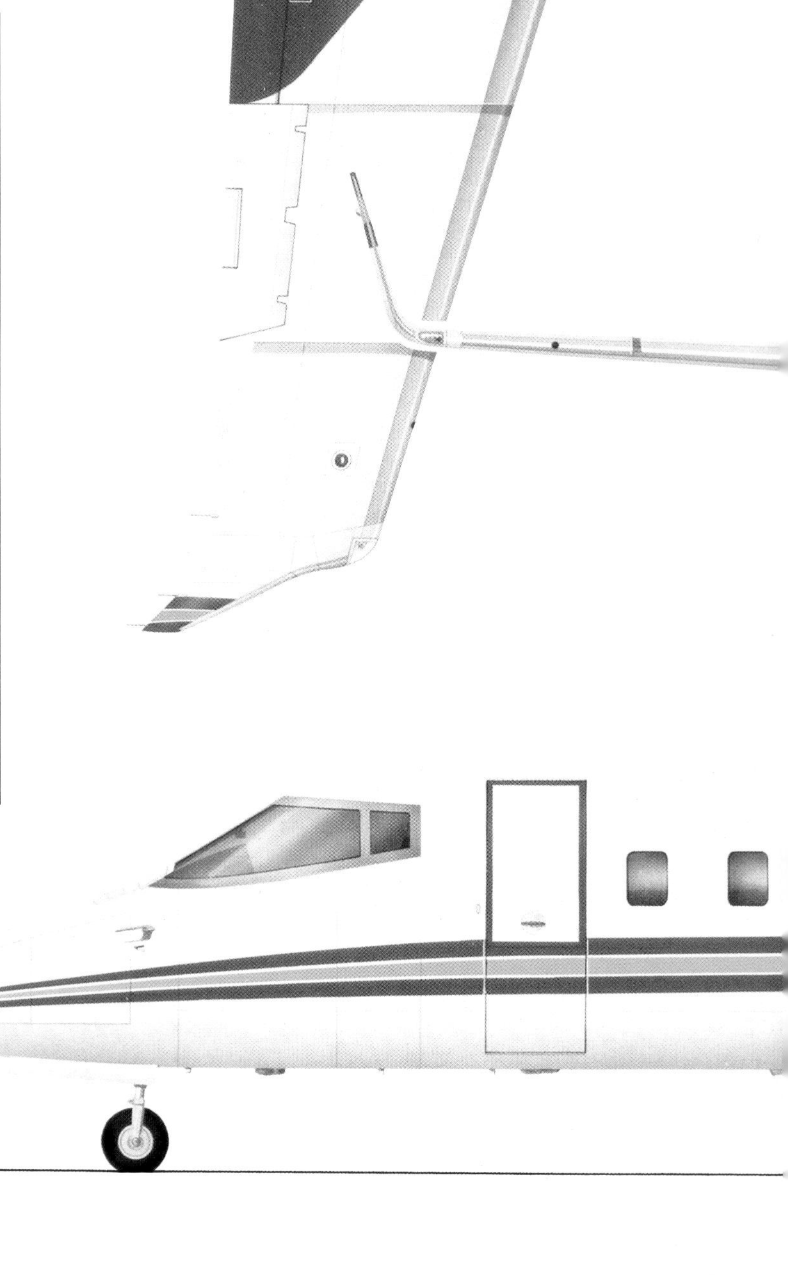

The newest and biggest Learjet is the Longhorn 55. Nearly twice the weight of the original Model 23, it is nevertheless a derivative of the 'narrow-body' 20/30 Learjets. The wider cabin tapers into the original centre-section, and the wing is based on that of the earlier aircraft, with span extensions outboard of the ailerons and drag-reducing winglets.

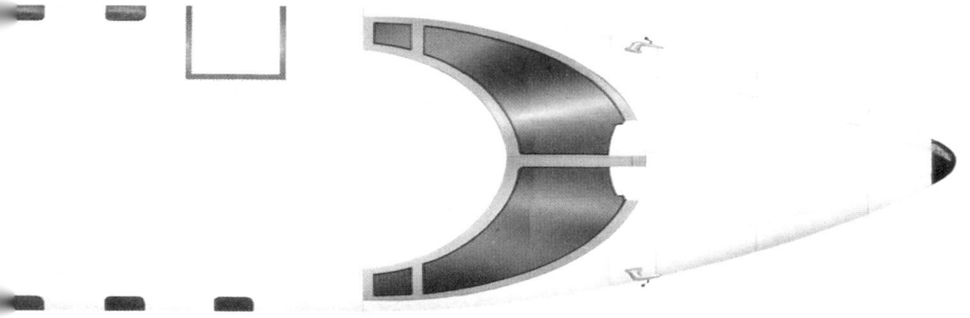

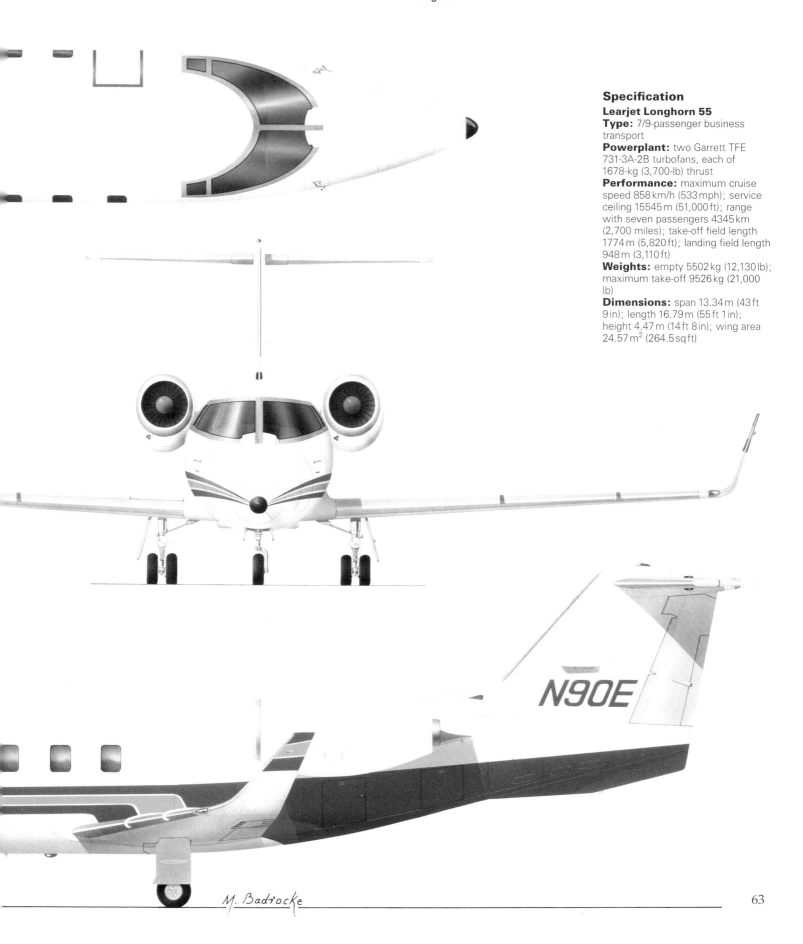

Specification

Learjet Longhorn 55

Type: 7/9-passenger business transport

Powerplant: two Garrett TFE 731-3A-2B turbofans, each of 1678-kg (3,700-lb) thrust

Performance: maximum cruise speed 858 km/h (533 mph); service ceiling 15545 m (51,000 ft); range with seven passengers 4345 km (2,700 miles); take-off field length 1774 m (5,820 ft); landing field length 948 m (3,110 ft)

Weights: empty 5502 kg (12,130 lb); maximum take-off 9526 kg (21,000 lb)

Dimensions: span 13.34 m (43 ft 9 in); length 16.79 m (55 ft 1 in); height 4.47 m (14 ft 8 in); wing area 24.57 m^2 (264.5 sq ft)

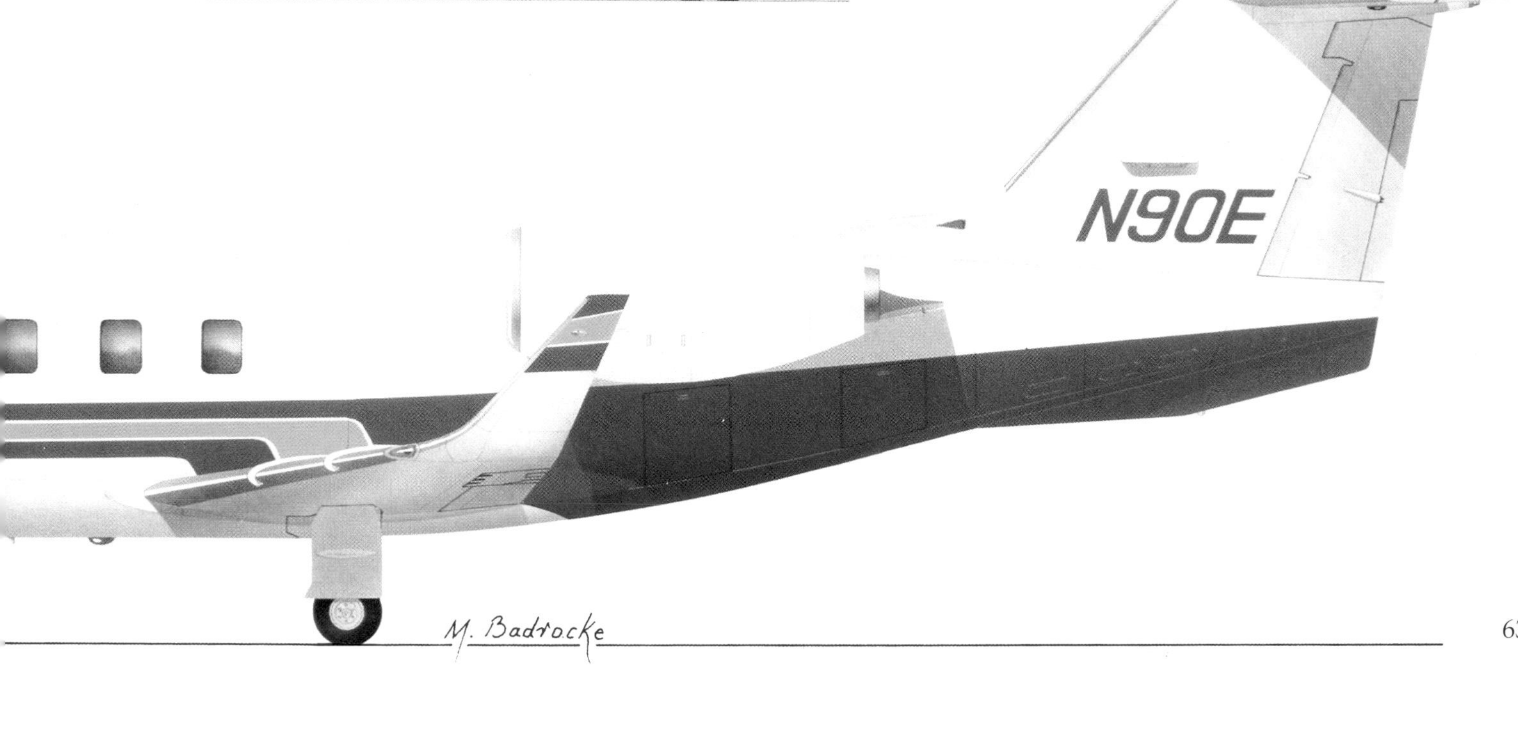

Specification
Shorts 360-100

Type: commuter transport and light freighter
Powerplant: two Pratt & Whitney Canada PT6A-65R turboprop engines rated at 875 kW (1,173 shp) continuous power and 990 kW (1,327 shp) maximum
Performance: maximum cruising speed 393 km/h (244 mph); take-off distance 1220 m (4,000 ft); landing distance 1450 m (4,760 ft); range with maximum fuel 1697 km (1,055 miles), with maximum passenger load 806 km (501 miles)
Weights: operating empty passenger configuration 7666 kg (16,900 lb), freighter configuration 7183 kg (15,835 lb); maximum take-off 11793 kg (26,000 lb); maximum payload passenger configuration 3184 kg (7,020 lb), freighter configuration 3765 kg (8,300 lb)
Dimensions: wing span 22.81 m (74 ft 10 in); length 21.59 m (70 ft 10 in); height 7.21 m (23 ft 8 in); tailplane span 7.19 m (23 ft 7 in); wing area 42.1 m^2 (453 sq ft)
Accommodation: flight crew of two pilots, with one cabin attendant; passenger configuration for 36 seats in 12 rows of three; freighter configuration offers 41.06 m^3 (1,450 cu ft) capacity in main cabin, plus baggage compartments in nose and rear fuselage

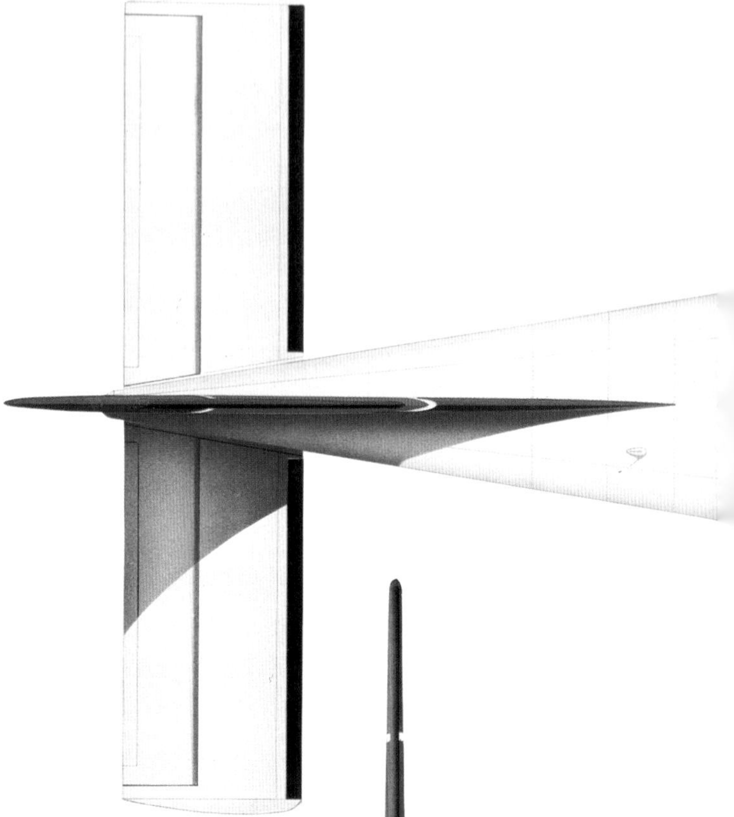

Specification
Shorts 360-300

Wingspan: 22.8 m (74 ft 9½ in)
Length: 21.6 m (70 ft 10 in)
Height: 7.3 m (23 ft 10¼ in)
Wing area: 12.9 m^2 (454 sq ft)
Powerplant: two 1061-kW (1,424-shp) Pratt & Whitney Canada PT6A-67R turboprops
Passenger capacity: 36-39
Empty weight: 7870 kg (17,350 lb)
Maximum take-off weight: 12293 kg (27,100 lb)
Cruising speed: 216 kt (400 km/h; 249 mph)
Maximum range: 861 nm (1595 km; 991 miles)
Range with maximum payload: 225 nm (417 km; 259 miles)

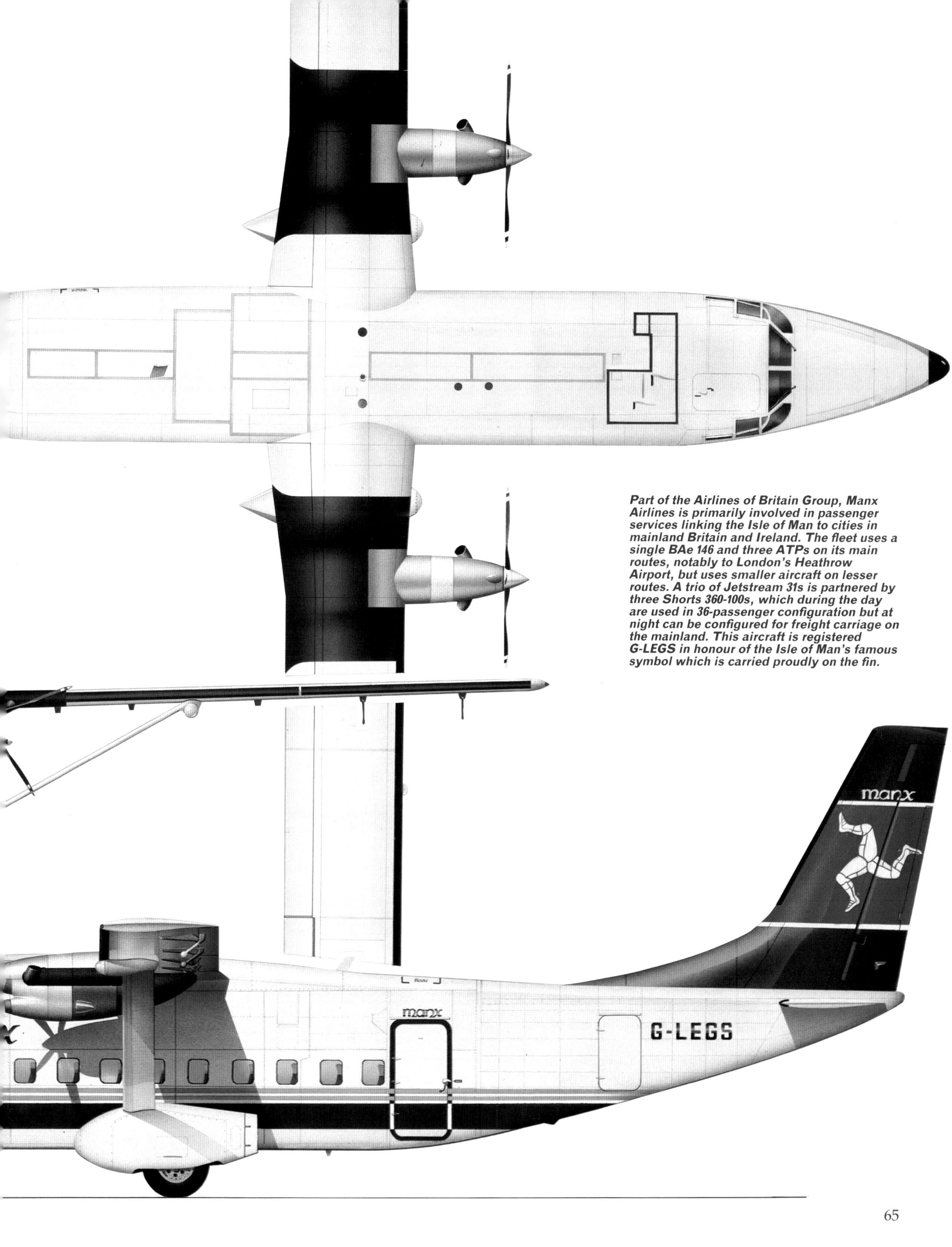

Part of the Airlines of Britain Group, Manx Airlines is primarily involved in passenger services linking the Isle of Man to cities in mainland Britain and Ireland. The fleet uses a single BAe 146 and three ATPs on its main routes, notably to London's Heathrow Airport, but uses smaller aircraft on lesser routes. A trio of Jetstream 31s is partnered by three Shorts 360-100s, which during the day are used in 36-passenger configuration but at night can be configured for freight carriage on the mainland. This aircraft is registered G-LEGS in honour of the Isle of Man's famous symbol which is carried proudly on the fin.

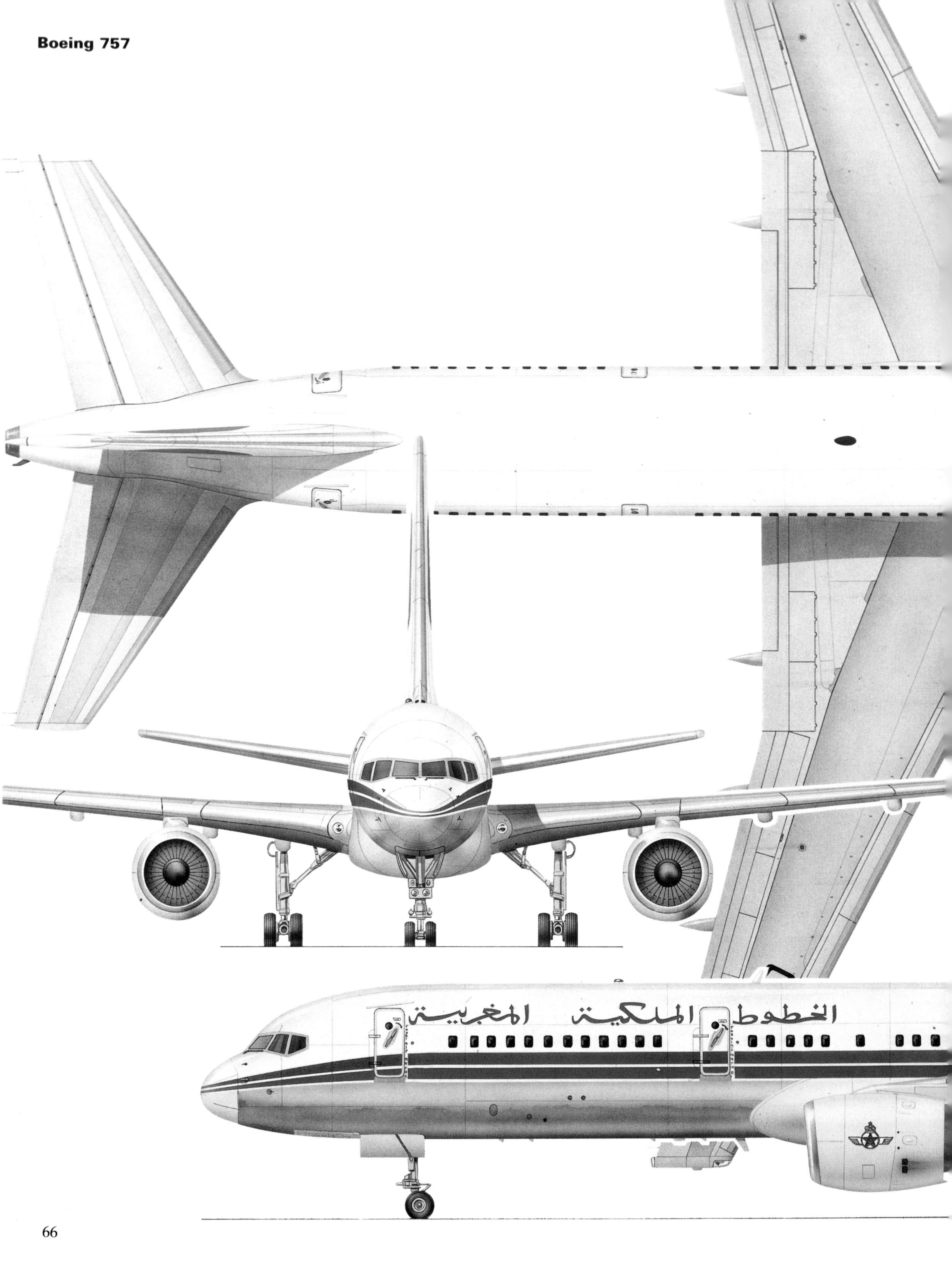
الخطوط الملكية المغربية

Boeing intended the Model 757 to be a replacement for the 727 and tri-jet, and as a partial replacement for the elderly 707. Consequently, several of the customers were operators of these aircraft. Royal Air Maroc retains the 707 and 727 in its inventory (as well as 737 and 747), these being augmented by a pair of Model 757-2B6s. These were delivered in 1986, powered by Pratt & Whitney PW2037 turbofans. The 757's cockpit is based on that of the larger 767, allowing great interoperability between the two types. Crews find minimal differences between flying the pair.

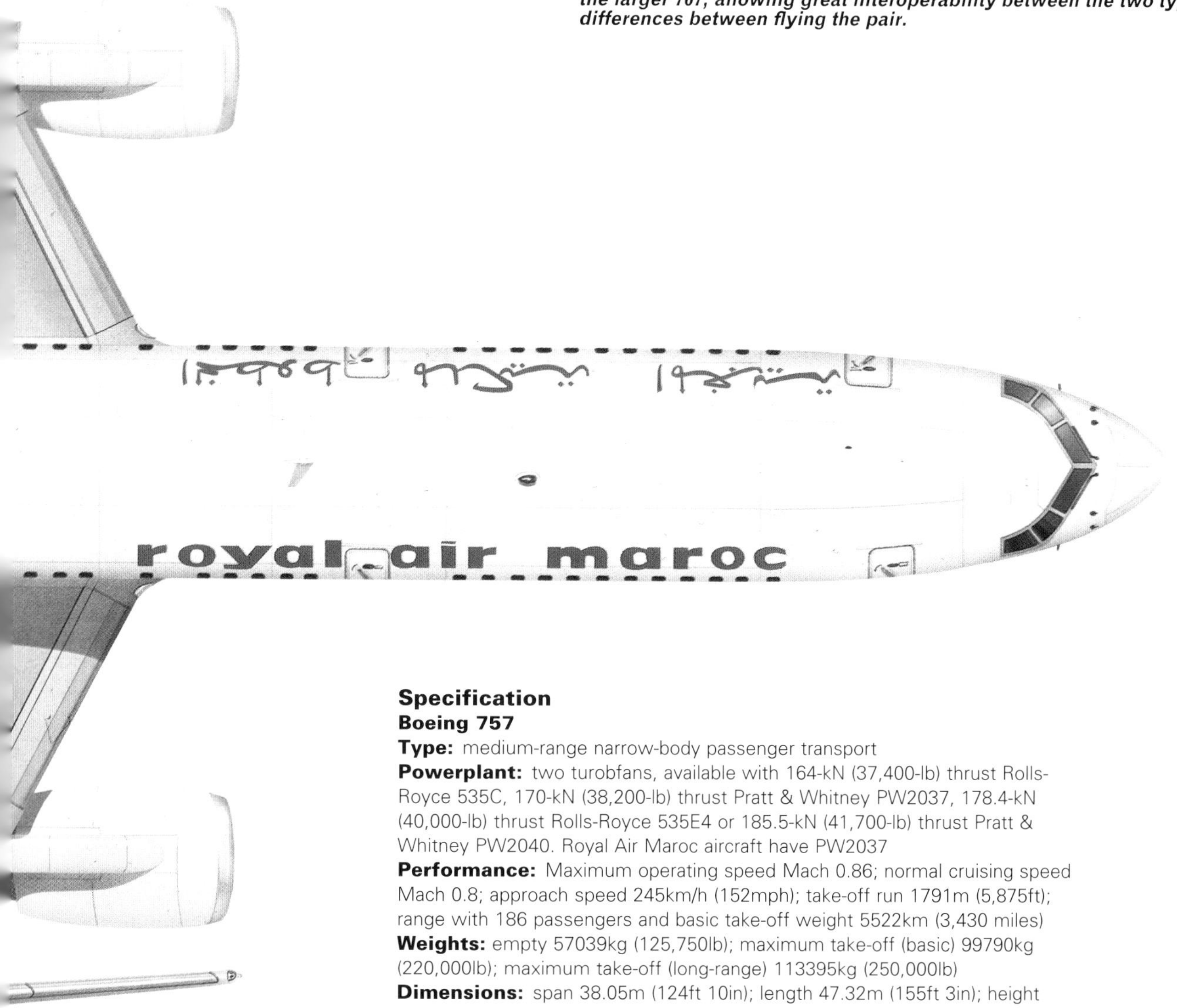

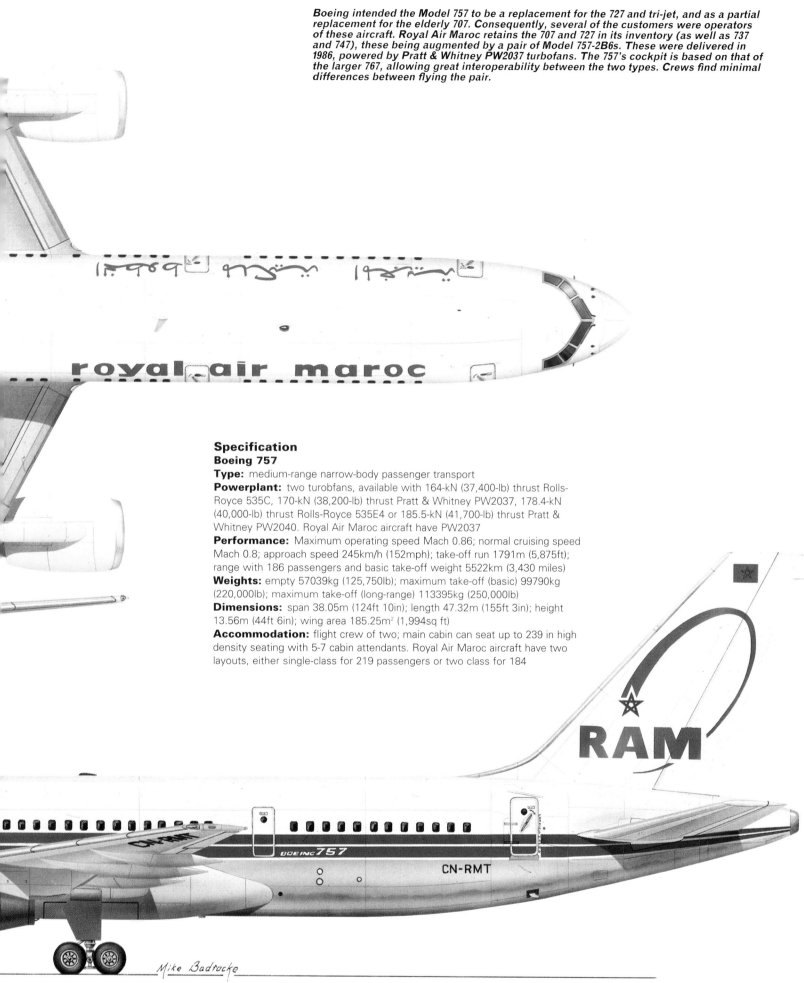

Specification

Boeing 757

Type: medium-range narrow-body passenger transport

Powerplant: two turobfans, available with 164-kN (37,400-lb) thrust Rolls-Royce 535C, 170-kN (38,200-lb) thrust Pratt & Whitney PW2037, 178.4-kN (40,000-lb) thrust Rolls-Royce 535E4 or 185.5-kN (41,700-lb) thrust Pratt & Whitney PW2040. Royal Air Maroc aircraft have PW2037

Performance: Maximum operating speed Mach 0.86; normal cruising speed Mach 0.8; approach speed 245km/h (152mph); take-off run 1791m (5,875ft); range with 186 passengers and basic take-off weight 5522km (3,430 miles)

Weights: empty 57039kg (125,750lb); maximum take-off (basic) 99790kg (220,000lb); maximum take-off (long-range) 113395kg (250,000lb)

Dimensions: span 38.05m (124ft 10in); length 47.32m (155ft 3in); height 13.56m (44ft 6in); wing area 185.25m^2 (1,994sq ft)

Accommodation: flight crew of two; main cabin can seat up to 239 in high density seating with 5-7 cabin attendants. Royal Air Maroc aircraft have two layouts, either single-class for 219 passengers or two class for 184

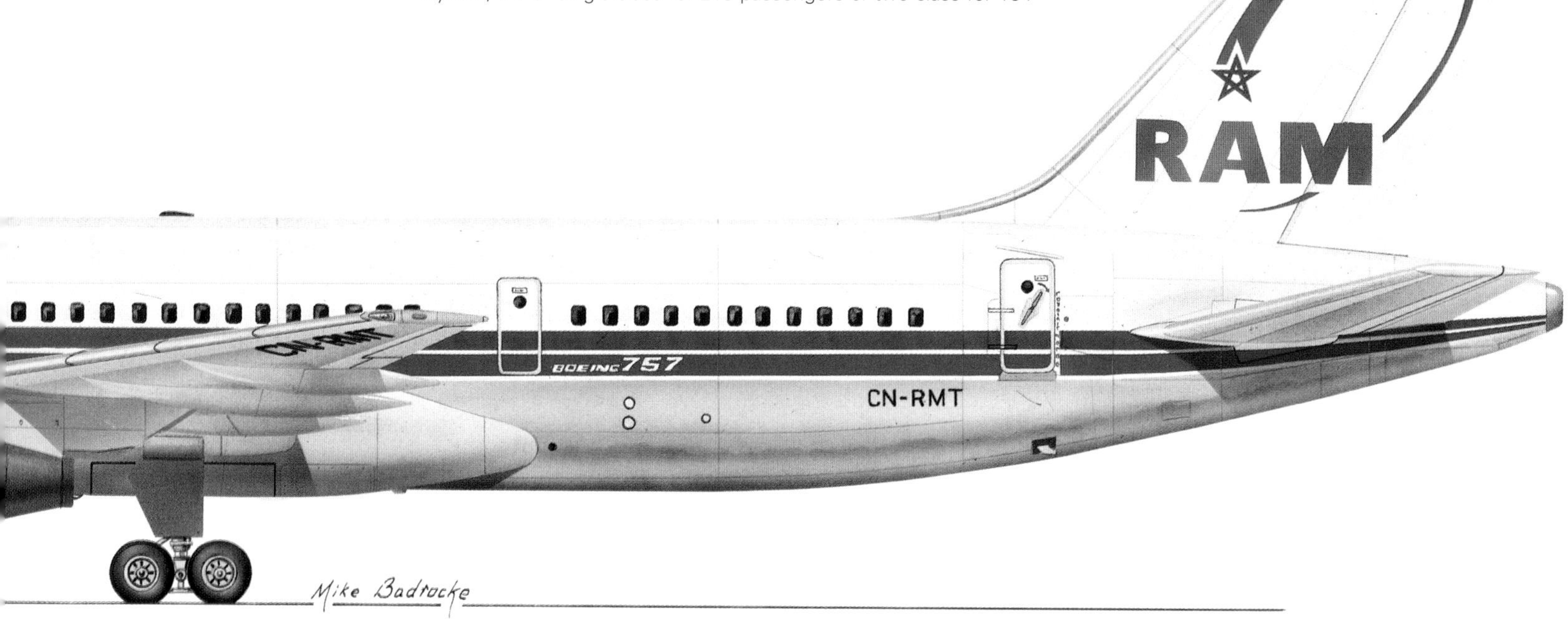

Canadair Challenger 600/601-3A

Specification
Canadair Challenger 600
Wingspan: 18.8 m (61 ft 10 in)
Length: 21 m (68 ft 5 in)
Height: 6.1 m (20 ft 8 in)
Wing area: 41.8 m^2 (450 sq ft)
Powerplant: two 33.4-kN (7,500-lb st) Avco Lycoming ALF 502L-2 turbofans
Passenger capacity: up to 19
Empty weight: 8491 kg (18,720 lb)
Maximum take-off weight: 18325 kg (40,400 lb)
Maximum speed: 450 kt (Mach 0.78) (833 km/h; 518 mph)
Cruising speed: 402 kt (Mach 0.70) (744 km/h; 462 mph)
Service ceiling: 13716 m (45,000 ft)
Maximum range: 2,800 nm (4506 km; 2,435 miles) with IFR reserves

Specification
Canadair Challenger 601-3A
Wingspan: 19.6 m (64 ft 4 in)
Length: 20.9 m (68 ft 5 in)
Height: 6.3 m (20 ft 8 in)
Wing area: 48.3 m^2 (520 sq ft)
Powerplant: two 40.66-kN (9,140-lb st) General Electric CF34-3A turbofans
Passenger capacity: up to 19
Empty weight: 9292 kg (20,485 lb)
Maximum take-off weight: 19550 kg (43,100 lb)
Maximum speed: 476 kt (882 km/h; 548 mph)
Cruising speed: 459 kt (850 km/h; 528 mph)
Service ceiling: 12497 m (41,000 ft)
Maximum range: 3,430 nm (6352 km; 2,982 miles) with IFR reserves

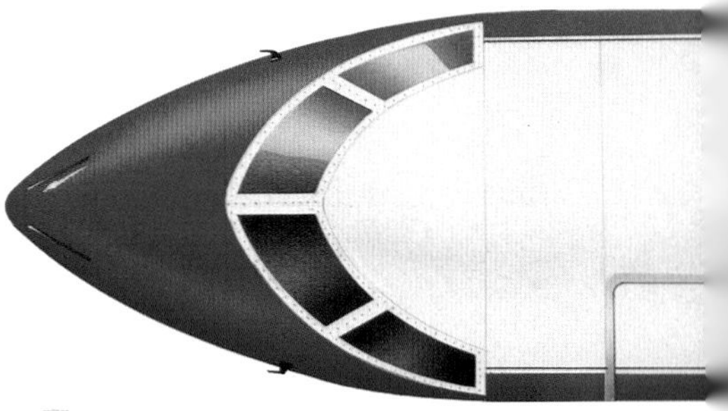

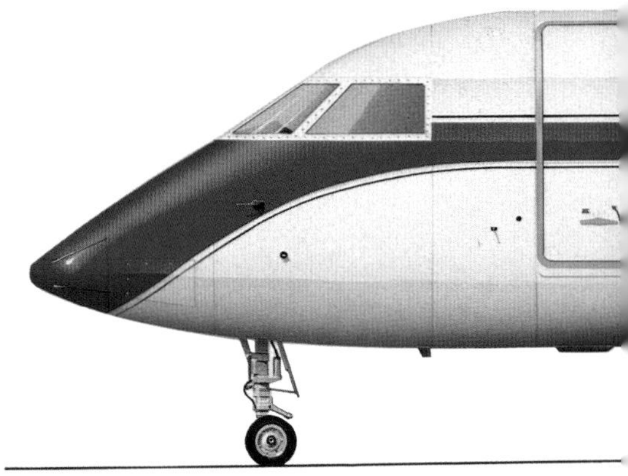

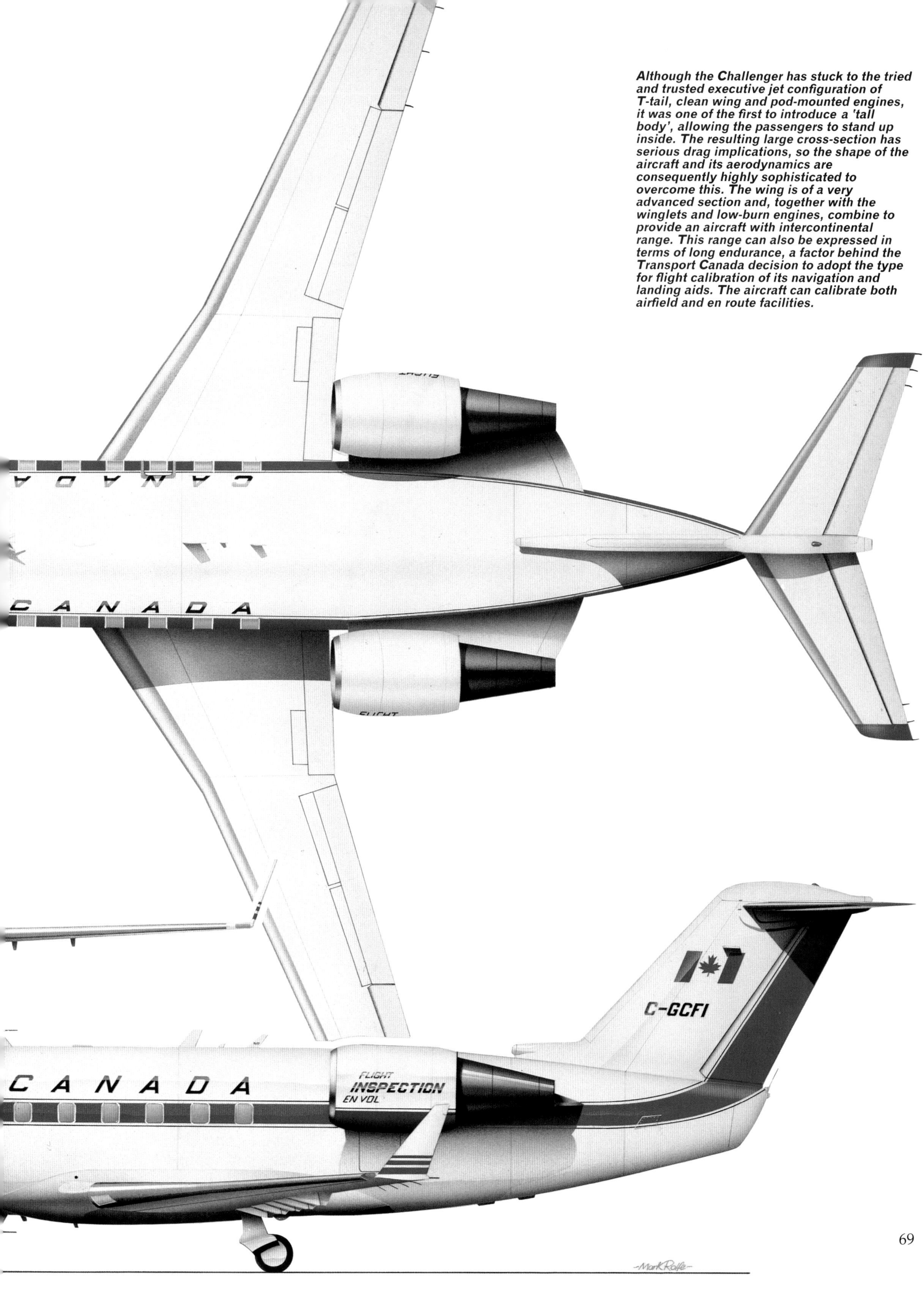

Although the Challenger has stuck to the tried and trusted executive jet configuration of T-tail, clean wing and pod-mounted engines, it was one of the first to introduce a 'tall body', allowing the passengers to stand up inside. The resulting large cross-section has serious drag implications, so the shape of the aircraft and its aerodynamics are consequently highly sophisticated to overcome this. The wing is of a very advanced section and, together with the winglets and low-burn engines, combine to provide an aircraft with intercontinental range. This range can also be expressed in terms of long endurance, a factor behind the Transport Canada decision to adopt the type for flight calibration of its navigation and landing aids. The aircraft can calibrate both airfield and en route facilities.

Piper PA-42-720 Cheyenne IIIA

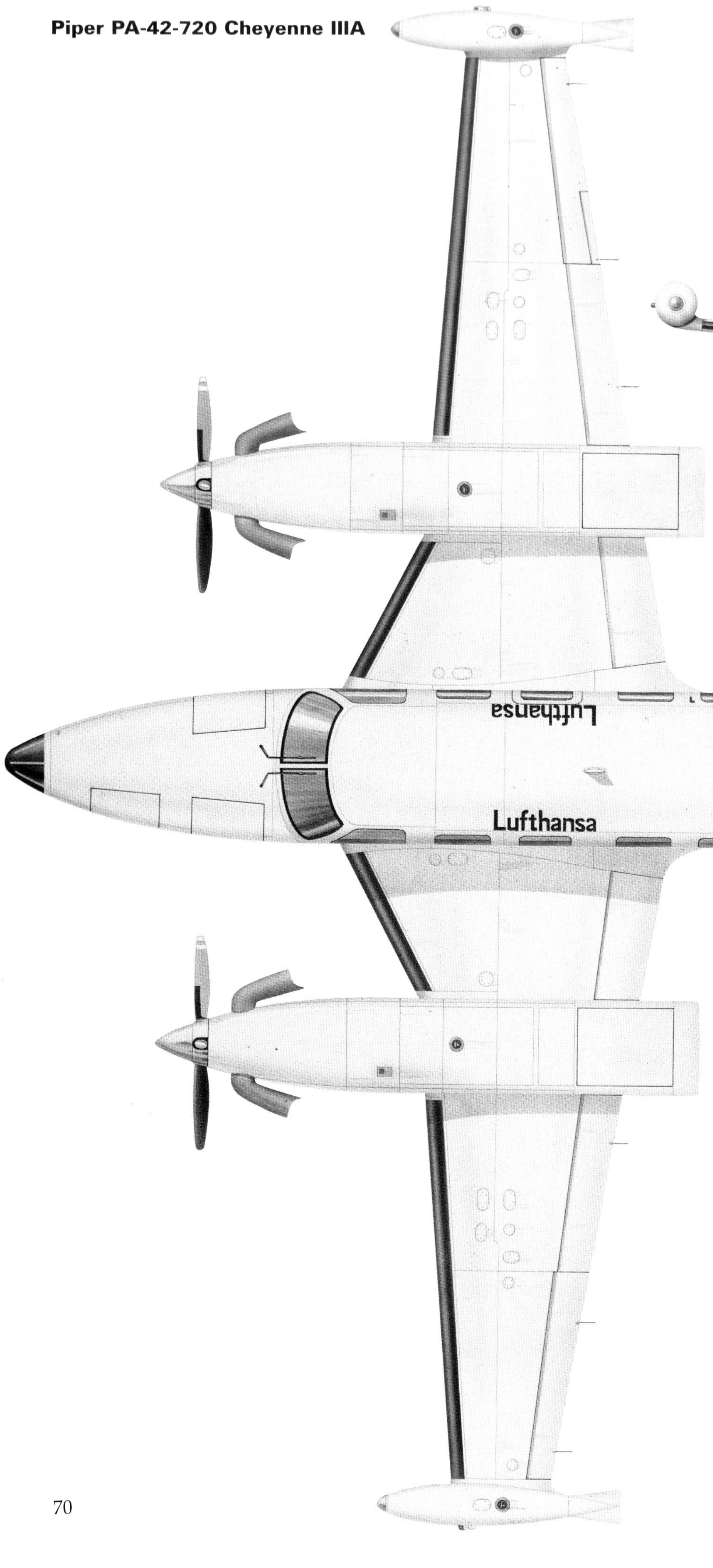

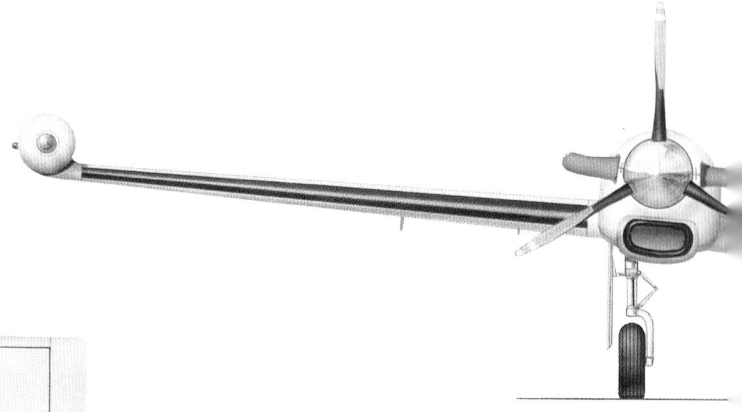

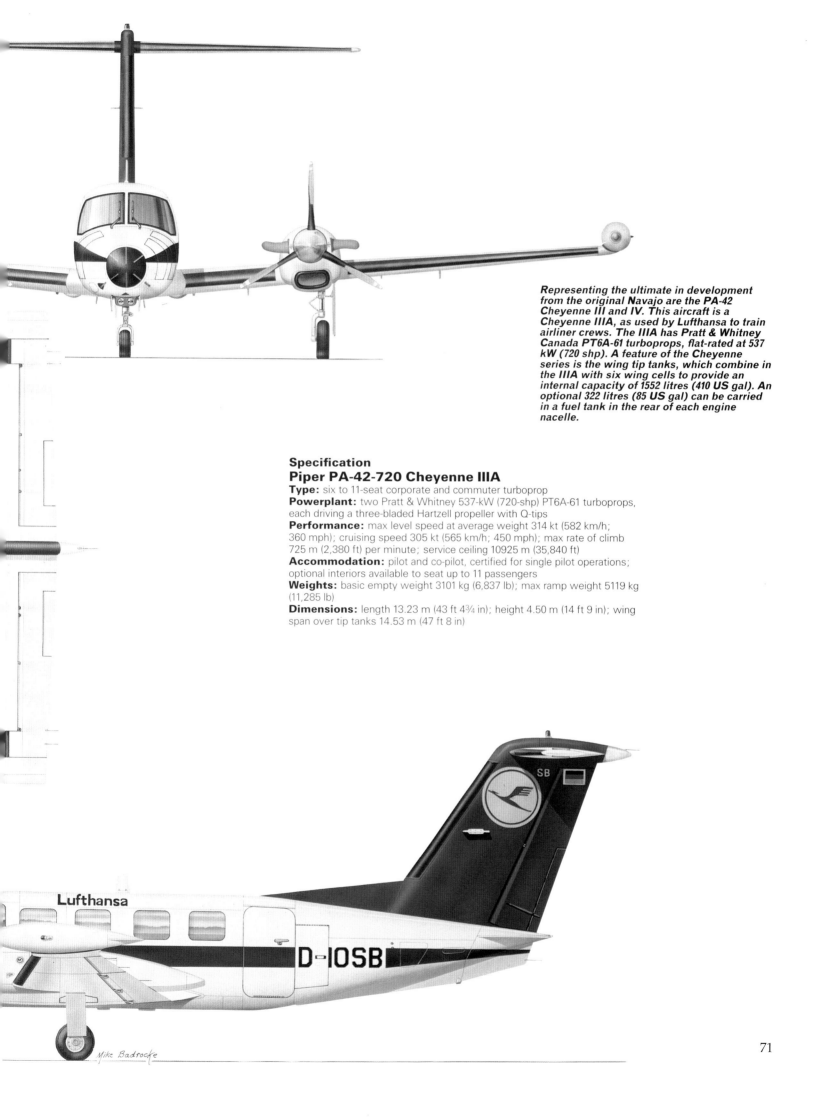

*Representing the ultimate in development from the original **Navajo** are the **PA-42 Cheyenne III** and **IV**. This aircraft is a **Cheyenne IIIA**, as used by **Lufthansa** to train airliner crews. The **IIIA** has **Pratt & Whitney Canada PT6A-61** turboprops, flat-rated at 537 kW (720 shp). A feature of the **Cheyenne** series is the wing tip tanks, which combine in the **IIIA** with six wing cells to provide an internal capacity of 1552 litres (410 US gal). An optional 322 litres (85 US gal) can be carried in a fuel tank in the rear of each engine nacelle.*

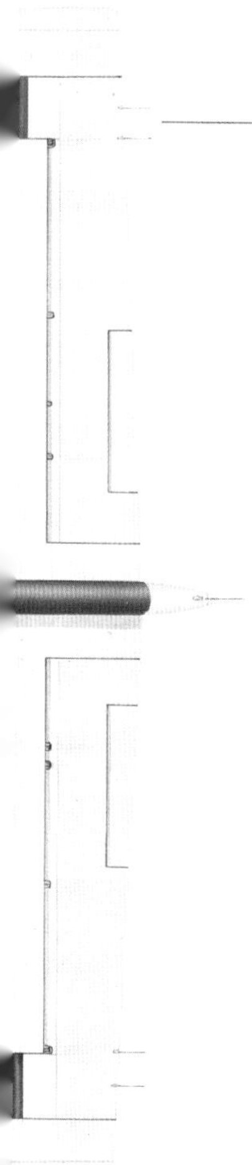

Specification
Piper PA-42-720 Cheyenne IIIA

Type: six to 11-seat corporate and commuter turboprop
Powerplant: two Pratt & Whitney 537-kW (720-shp) PT6A-61 turboprops, each driving a three-bladed Hartzell propeller with Q-tips
Performance: max level speed at average weight 314 kt (582 km/h; 360 mph); cruising speed 305 kt (565 km/h; 450 mph); max rate of climb 725 m (2,380 ft) per minute; service ceiling 10925 m (35,840 ft)
Accommodation: pilot and co-pilot, certified for single pilot operations; optional interiors available to seat up to 11 passengers
Weights: basic empty weight 3101 kg (6,837 lb); max ramp weight 5119 kg (11,285 lb)
Dimensions: length 13.23 m (43 ft 4¾ in); height 4.50 m (14 ft 9 in); wing span over tip tanks 14.53 m (47 ft 8 in)

Cessna Model 500 Citation I/650 Citation III

Specification
Cessna Model 500 Citation I

Wing span: 14.35 m (47 ft 1 in)
Length: 13.35 m (43 ft 8 in)
Height: 4.39 m (14 ft 4 in)
Wing area: 25.8 m^2 (278.5 sq ft)
Powerplant: two 9.79-kN (2,200-lb) Pratt & Whitney Canada JT15D-1B turbofans
Passenger capacity: six to eight
Empty weight: 3003 kg (6,620 lb)
Maximum take-off weight: 5376 kg (11,850 lb)
Maximum speed: Mach 0.705
Cruising speed: 357 kt (410 km/h; 255 mph) at 10668 m (35,000 ft)
Operational ceiling: 12496 m (41,000 ft)
Range with maximum fuel: 1,330 nm (2463 km/1,530 miles)

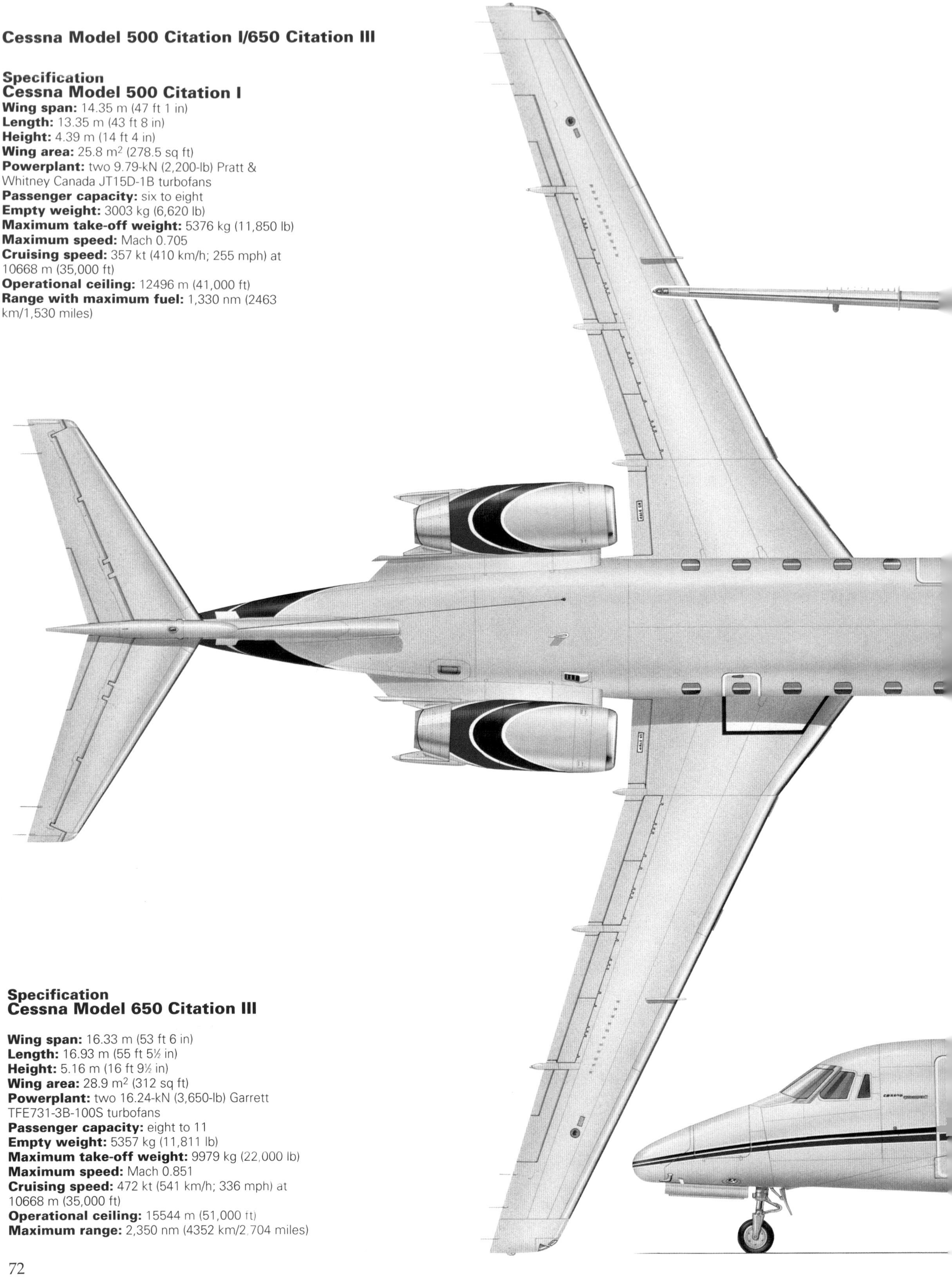

Specification
Cessna Model 650 Citation III

Wing span: 16.33 m (53 ft 6 in)
Length: 16.93 m (55 ft 5½ in)
Height: 5.16 m (16 ft 9½ in)
Wing area: 28.9 m^2 (312 sq ft)
Powerplant: two 16.24-kN (3,650-lb) Garrett TFE731-3B-100S turbofans
Passenger capacity: eight to 11
Empty weight: 5357 kg (11,811 lb)
Maximum take-off weight: 9979 kg (22,000 lb)
Maximum speed: Mach 0.851
Cruising speed: 472 kt (541 km/h; 336 mph) at 10668 m (35,000 ft)
Operational ceiling: 15544 m (51,000 ft)
Maximum range: 2,350 nm (4352 km/2,704 miles)

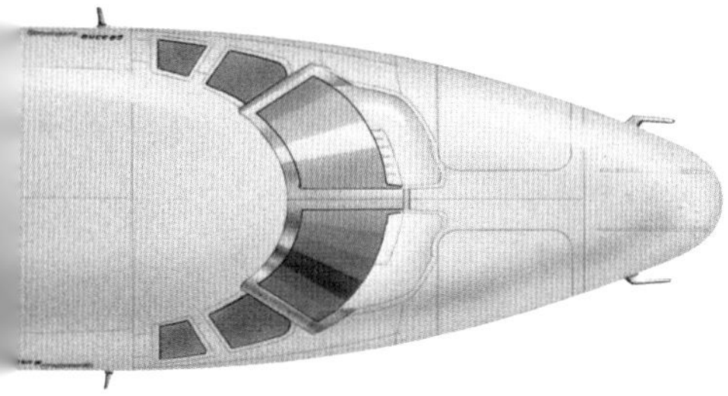

The late 1970s and early 1980s were lean times for business aviation. Born in 1979, the Citation III was the first of the Cessna jets to provide a truly intercontinental range but, like its contemporary the Gates 55 Longhorn, sales did not match those of its siblings. Both aircraft were powered by a pair of Garrett TFE731 engines and both represented a major new design departure by their parent companies. They were also arguably the most attractive of their stable's designs, but a generally poor economic climate put paid to Cessna's production run after only 189 had left the factory line. The majority of these went to existing Citation customers in the United States, who were trading up their existing aircraft. The effort expended on the Model 650 was not wasted, as the type went on to become the basis for Cessna's new designs for the 1990s.

Tupolev Tu-154M

Specification

Tupolev Tu-154M
Type: medium-range narrow-body transport
Powerplant: three 104-kN (23,380-lb) thrust Soloviev D-30KU-154-II turbofans
Performance: maximum cruising speed 950 km/h (590 mph); maximum cruising altitude 11900 m (39,000 ft); take-off and landing field length 2500 m (8,200 ft); range with maximum payload 3900 km (2,425 miles); range with maximum fuel and 5450-kg (12,015-lb) payload 6600 km (4,100 miles)
Weights: operating empty 55300 kg (121,915 lb); maximum take-off 100000 kg (220,460 lb); maximum payload 18000 kg (39,680 lb)
Dimensions: span 37.55 m (123 ft 2½ in); length 47.9 m (157 ft 1½ in); height 11.4 m (37 ft 5 in); wing area 201.45 m^2 (2,169 sq ft)
Accommodation: flight crew of three (two pilots and flight engineer); six-abreast seating for up to 180 passengers in high-density arrangement; up to five cabin staff; Balkan aircraft configured for either 151 passengers in single-class accommodation or eight first-class, 38 business-class and 105 economy-class seats.

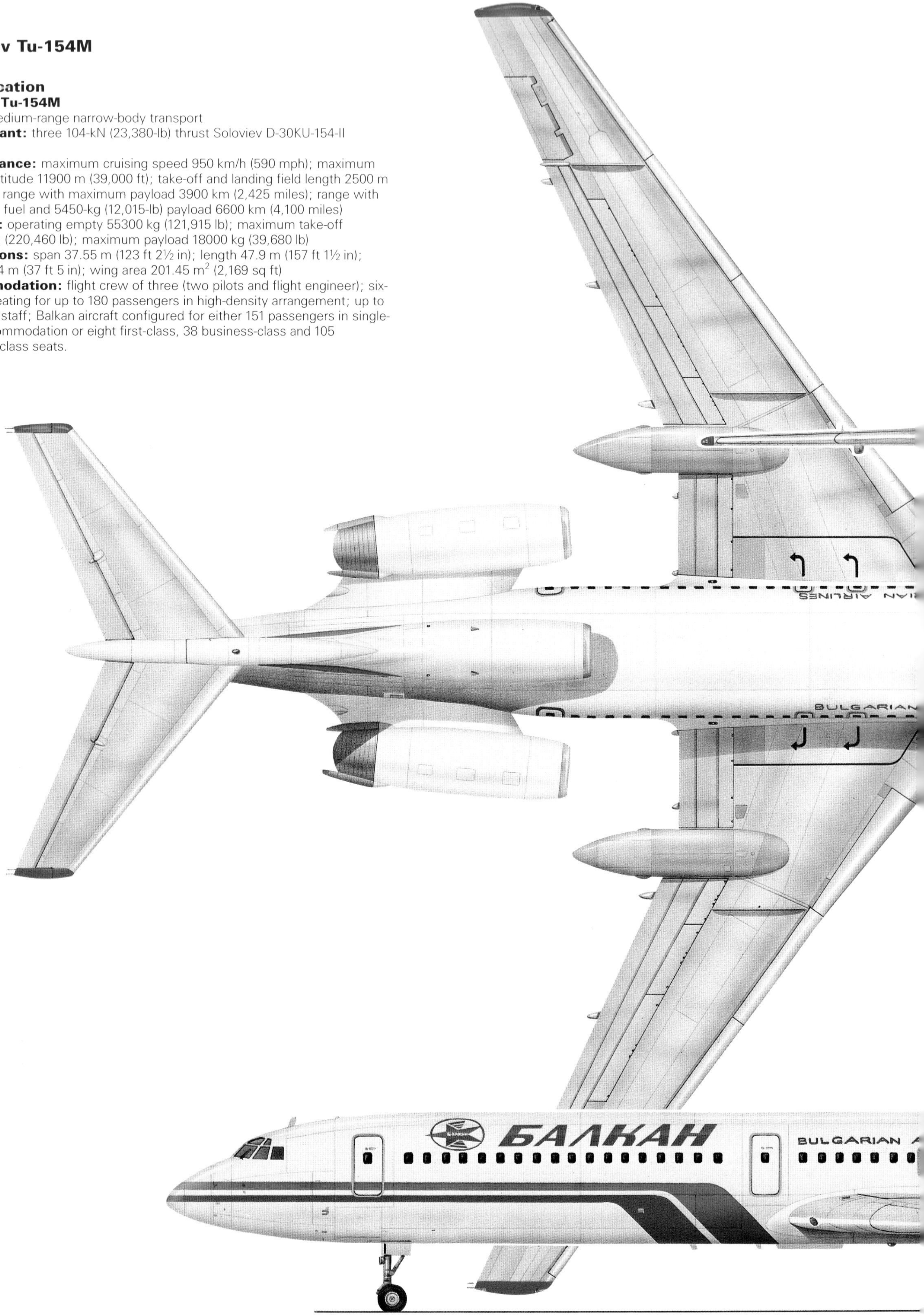

Still in production at Kuybyshev, although ultimately to be replaced by the new-technology Tu-204, the Tu-154 is one of the world's major airliner types. In widespread service with Aeroflot on both domestic and international services, the 'Careless' is also the standard airliner of most Soviet-aligned nations. Although not competing with comparable Western types in terms of performance and fuel efficiency, the Tu-154 exhibits typical Soviet characteristics of being extremely strong and being able to operate from semi-prepared surfaces. A notable feature of this and many other Tupolev jets are the undercarriage nacelles projecting beyond the wing trailing edge. The sturdy main units retract backwards into the nacelles, the bogies somersaulting to lie flat within the fairings. Balkan has a large fleet encompassing the major recent variants, some of its Tu-154Bs being converted from early Tu-154s and Tu-154As. This is the latest Tu-154M.

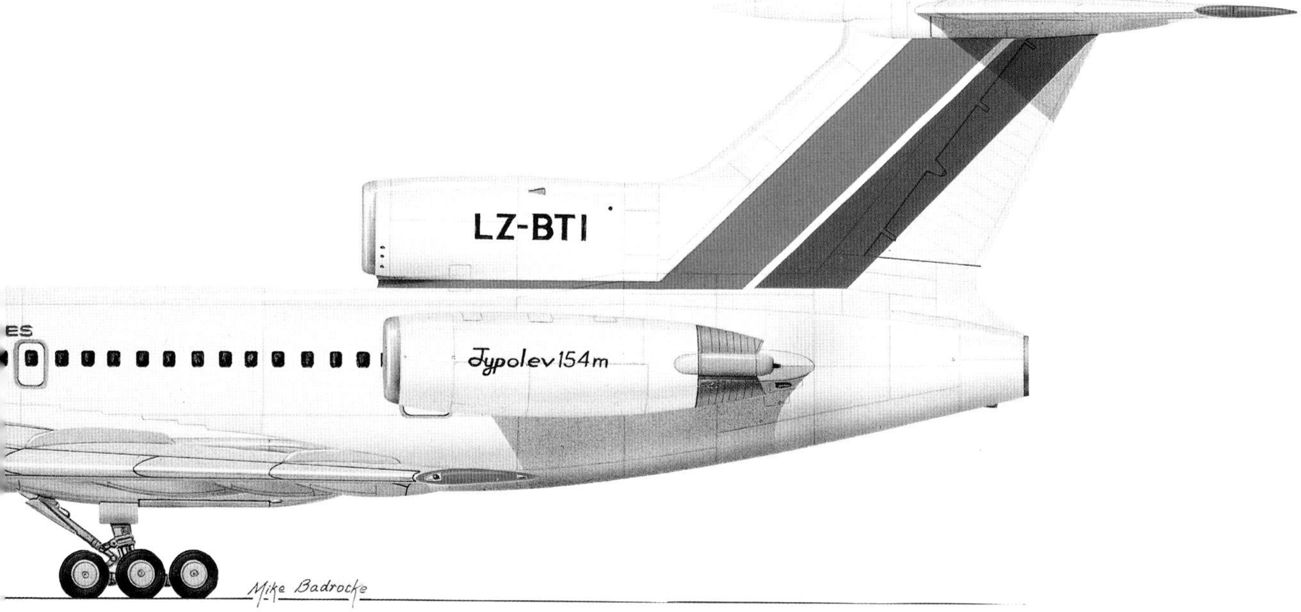

BAe 125-800

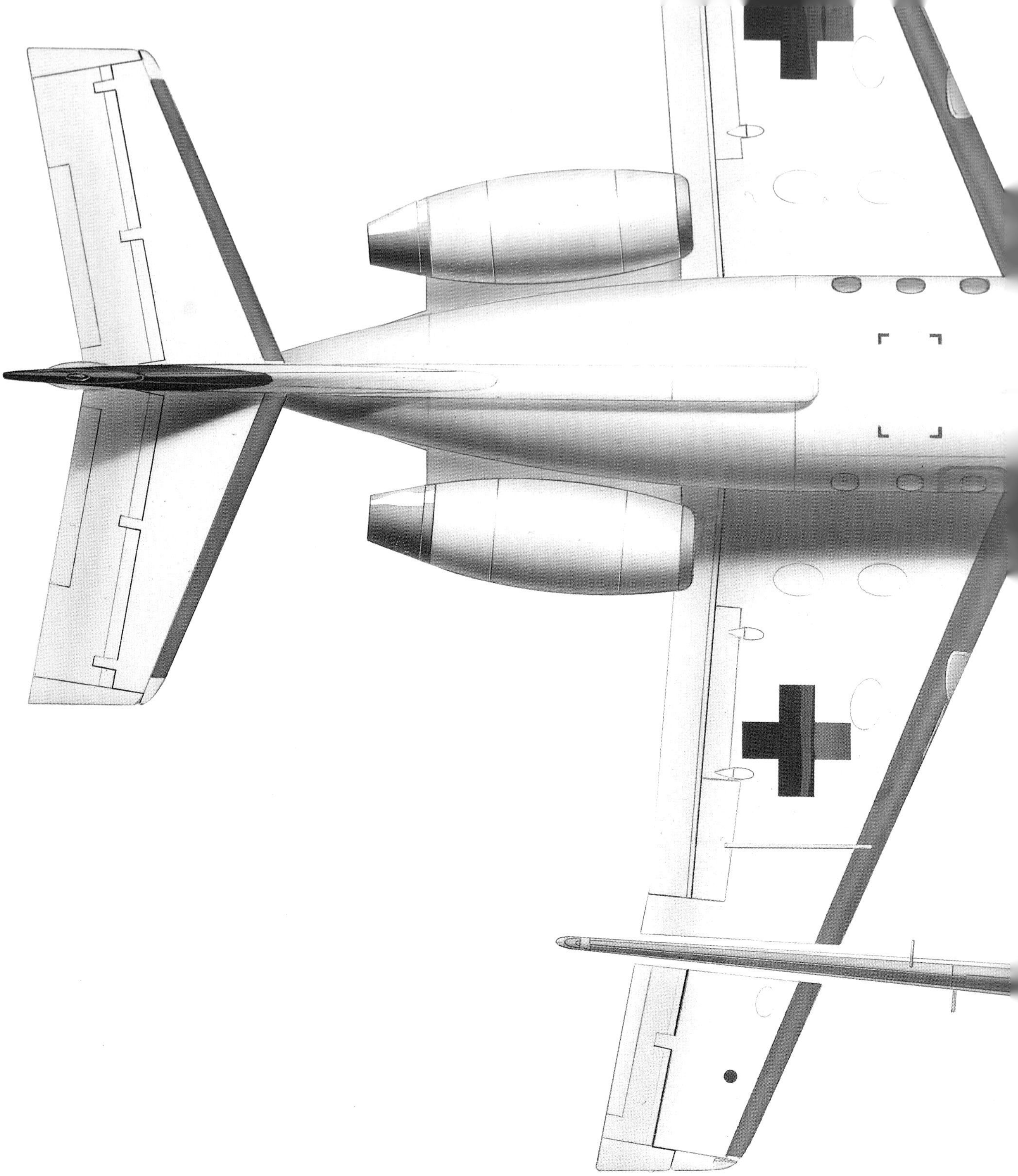

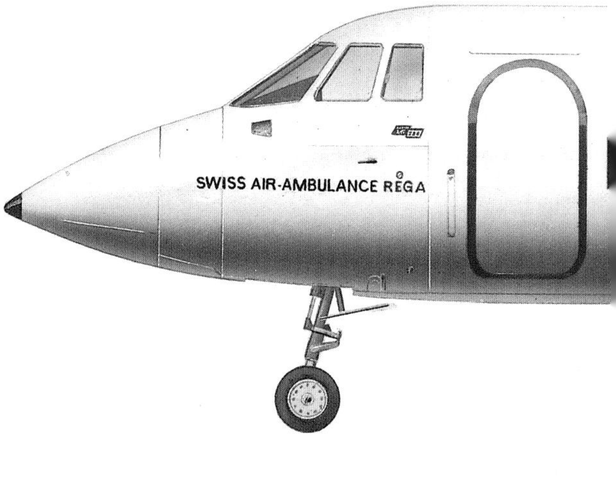

Specification

BAe 125-800
Wing span: 15.66 m (51 ft 4½ in)
Length: 15.59 m (51 ft 2 in)
Height: 5.36 m (17 ft 7 in)
Wing area: 34.74 m^2 (374 sq ft)
Powerplant: 2 × Garrett TFE731-5R, 19.13 kN (4,300 lb st) each
Passenger capacity: 8-14
Empty weight: 6849 kg (15,100 lb)
Maximum take-off weight: 12428 kg (27,400 lb)
Cruising speed: 741 km/h (400 knots)
Maximum speed: Mach 0.87
Service ceiling: 13106 m (43,000 ft)
Maximum range: 5560 m (3,000 nm)
Production total: (all models, including orders) 784 by end of 1990

A pair of BAe 125-800B aircraft fly with the Swiss Air Ambulance service on medical evacuation duties. Provision is made on board for two stretchers and their medical attendants. Executive jets offer the perfect answer for aeromedical flights, being as fast and as long-legged as any commercial jet by offering fuel economy, a smooth ride and fast reaction times to emergencies.

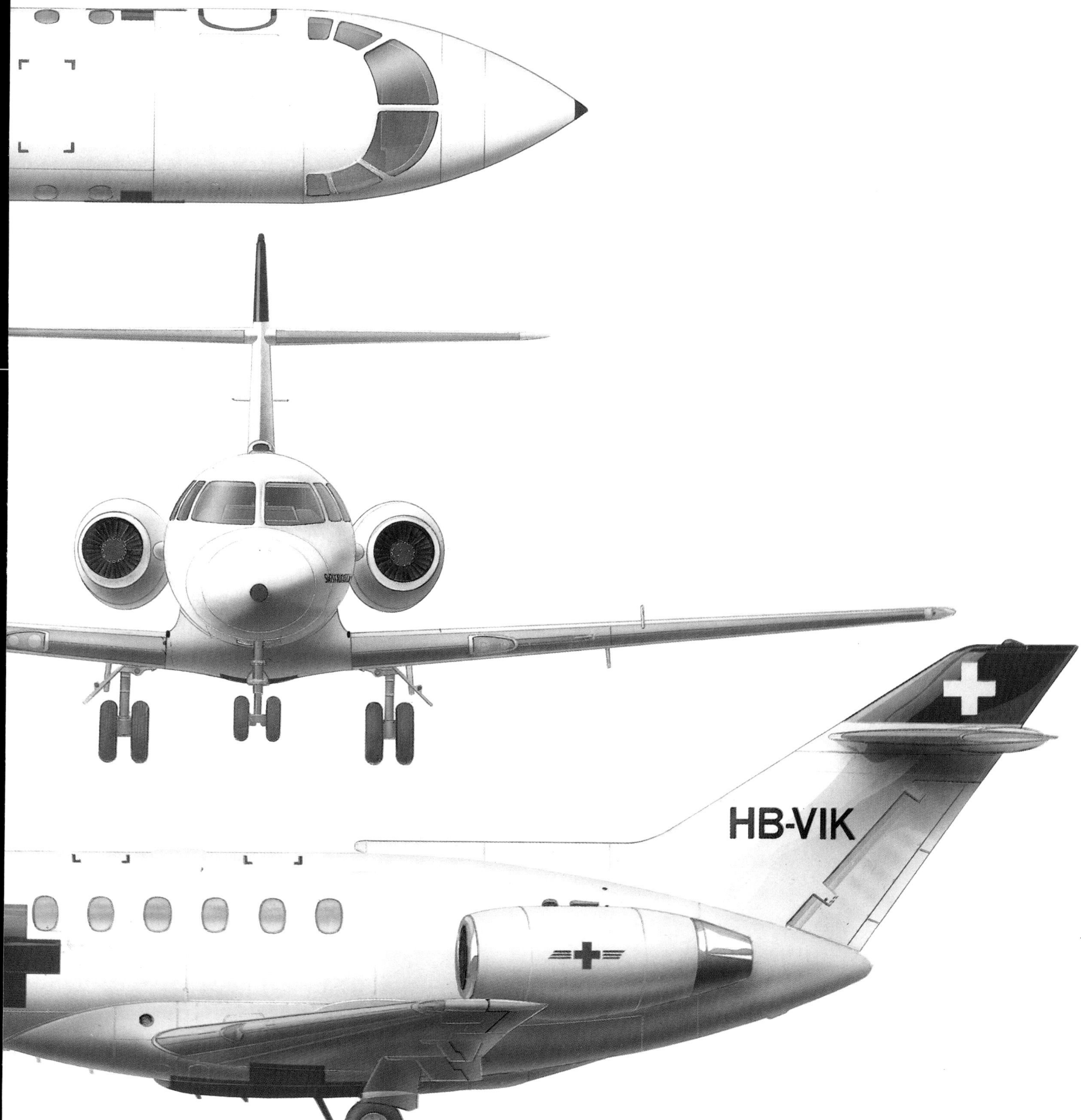

Rhein-Flugzeugbau Fantrainer 600

RFB's house colours adorn this Fantrainer 600, used as part of the test programme and to sell the product. The unusual design results from the desire to provide handling similar to tactical aircraft and incorporate the ducted-fan technology and tandem seating. While RFB figures show the Fantrainer to be a very efficient, economic, sweet-handling and environment-friendly aircraft, and despite spirited displays in front of major customers at such shows as Paris and Farnborough, Thailand is at present the only purchaser. However, the fact that Thai students progress straight from the Fantrainer to the Northrop F-5 is some measure of its potential as a trainer.

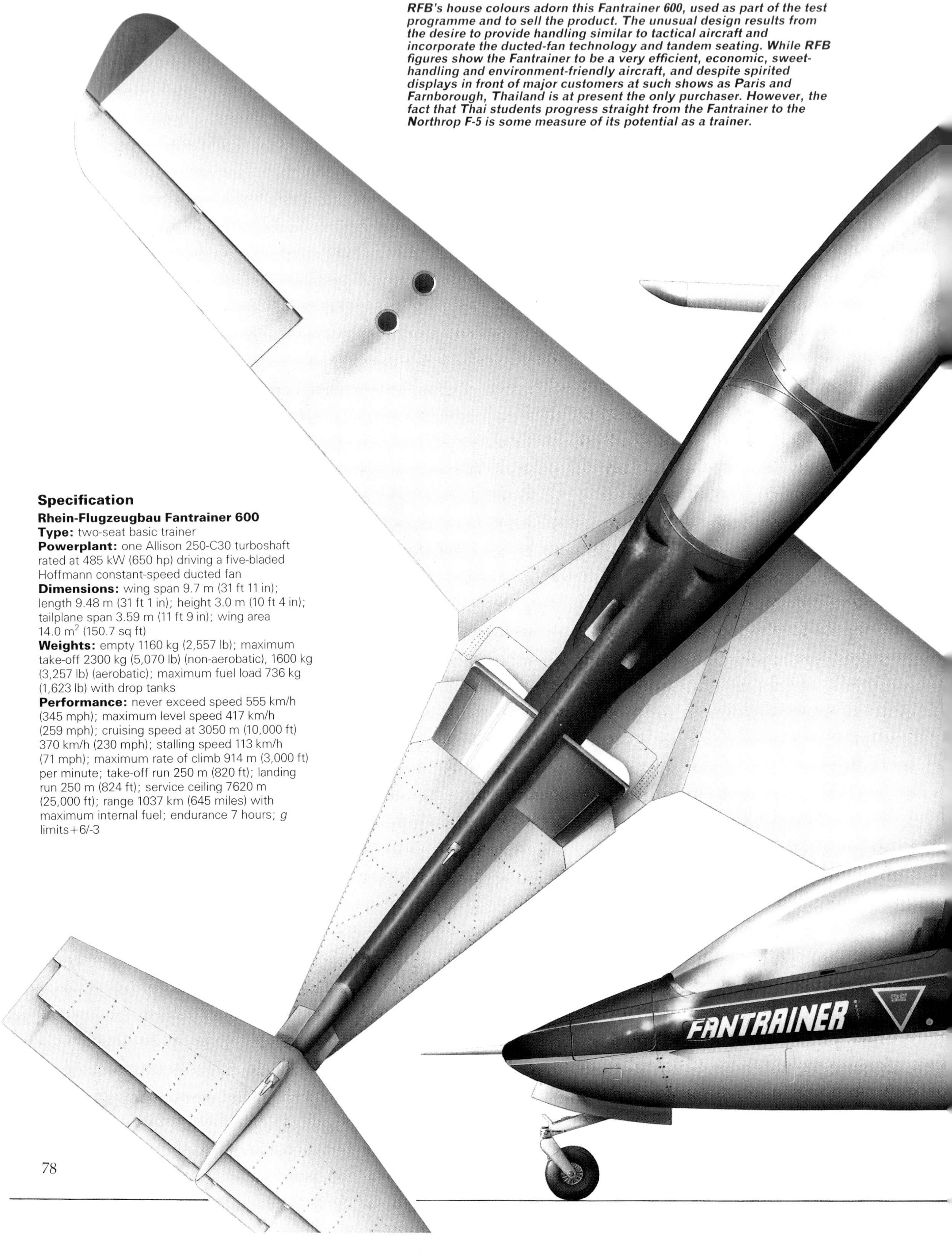

Specification

Rhein-Flugzeugbau Fantrainer 600
Type: two-seat basic trainer
Powerplant: one Allison 250-C30 turboshaft rated at 485 kW (650 hp) driving a five-bladed Hoffmann constant-speed ducted fan
Dimensions: wing span 9.7 m (31 ft 11 in); length 9.48 m (31 ft 1 in); height 3.0 m (10 ft 4 in); tailplane span 3.59 m (11 ft 9 in); wing area 14.0 m^2 (150.7 sq ft)
Weights: empty 1160 kg (2,557 lb); maximum take-off 2300 kg (5,070 lb) (non-aerobatic), 1600 kg (3,257 lb) (aerobatic); maximum fuel load 736 kg (1,623 lb) with drop tanks
Performance: never exceed speed 555 km/h (345 mph); maximum level speed 417 km/h (259 mph); cruising speed at 3050 m (10,000 ft) 370 km/h (230 mph); stalling speed 113 km/h (71 mph); maximum rate of climb 914 m (3,000 ft) per minute; take-off run 250 m (820 ft); landing run 250 m (824 ft); service ceiling 7620 m (25,000 ft); range 1037 km (645 miles) with maximum internal fuel; endurance 7 hours; *g* limits+6/-3

D-EATR
Nick Watton.

Shorts 330-200

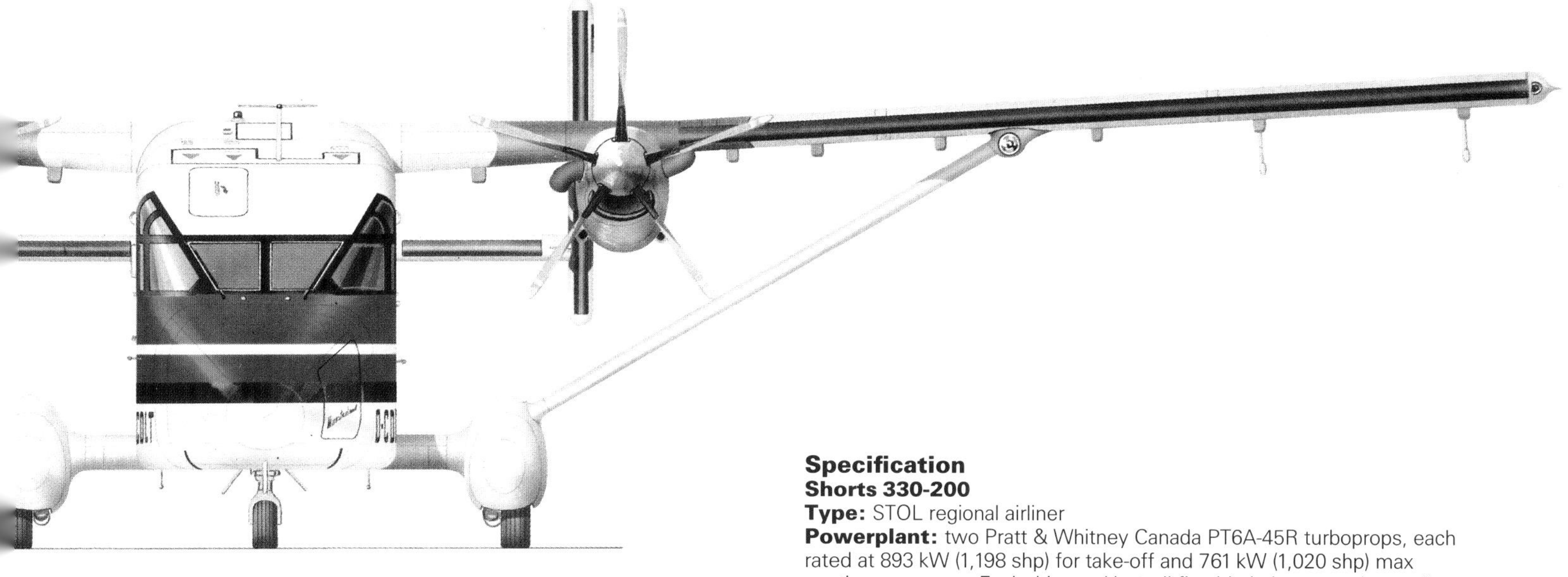

Specification

Shorts 330-200

Type: STOL regional airliner

Powerplant: two Pratt & Whitney Canada PT6A-45R turboprops, each rated at 893 kW (1,198 shp) for take-off and 761 kW (1,020 shp) max continuous power. Each drives a Hartzell five-blade low-speed propeller

Performance: maximum cruising speed at 3050 m (10,000 ft) 352 km/h (218 mph); stalling speed 136 km/h (85 mph); maximum rate of climb at sea level 360 m (1,180 ft) per minute: service ceiling with one engine out 3500 m (11,500 ft); take-off run 1042 m (3,420 ft); landing on run 1030 m (3,380 ft); range with max passenger load 87 km (544 miles); range with max fuel 1695 km (1,053 miles)

Weights: empty equipped 6680 kg (14,727 lb); maximum take-off 10387 kg (22,900 lb)

Dimensions: span 22.76 m (74 ft 8 in); length 17.69 m (58 ft 0½ in); height 4.95 m (16 ft 3 in); tailplane span 5.68 m (18 ft 7¾ in); wing area 42.1 m^2 (453 sq ft)

Accommodation: flight crew of two; one cabin attendant; standard accommodation for 30 passengers in rows of three

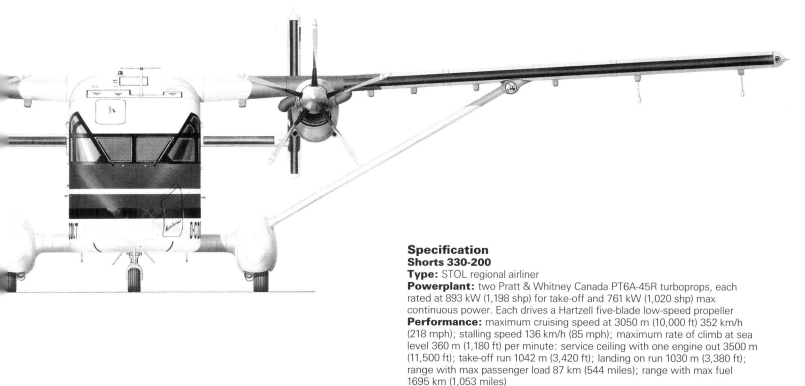

Being derived from the Shorts Skyvan, the 330 has inherited the square-section fuselage and high aspect ratio wings. Allied to the efficient Pratt & Whitney Canada PT6A turboprops, these allow the 330 to take off with a significant load from short runways. Particular success in the commuter field was also due to the low noise profile of the type. DLT at Frankfurt was an early customer, utilising its aircraft on domestic flights around Germany. These have since been withdrawn and sold.

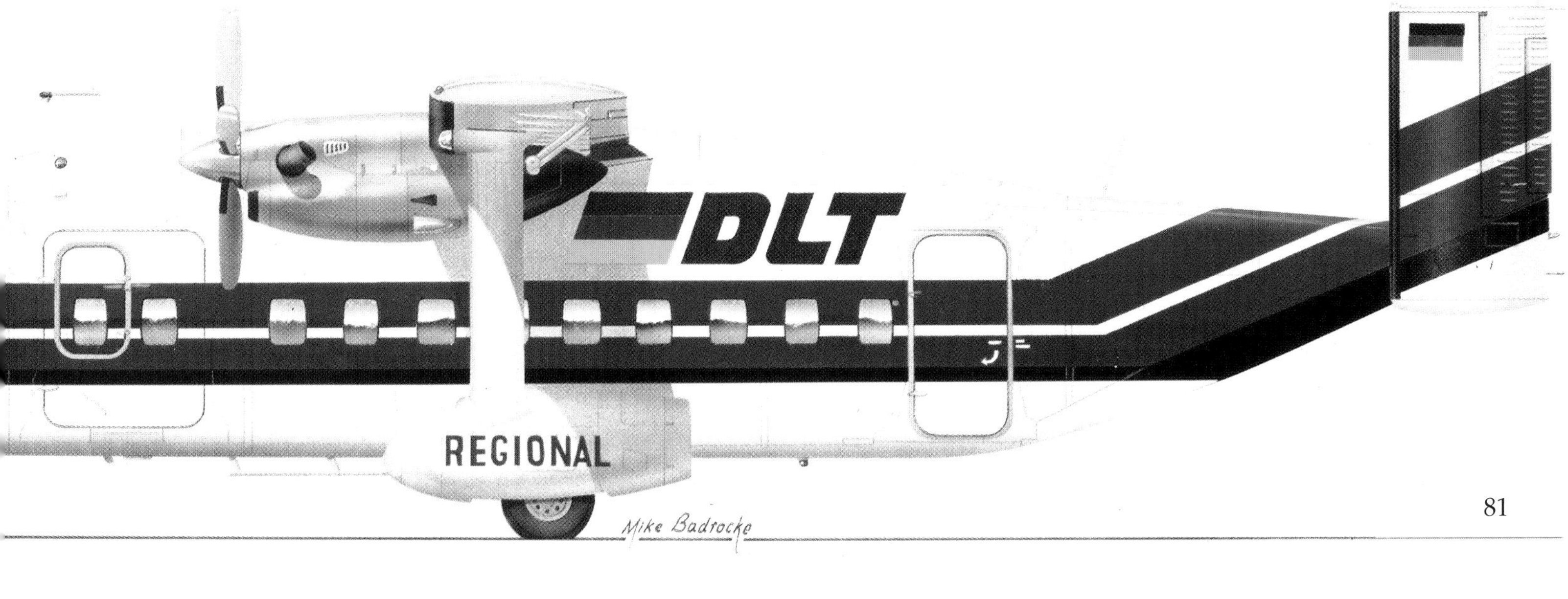

De Havilland (Boeing) Canada DHC-8 Dash 8-101

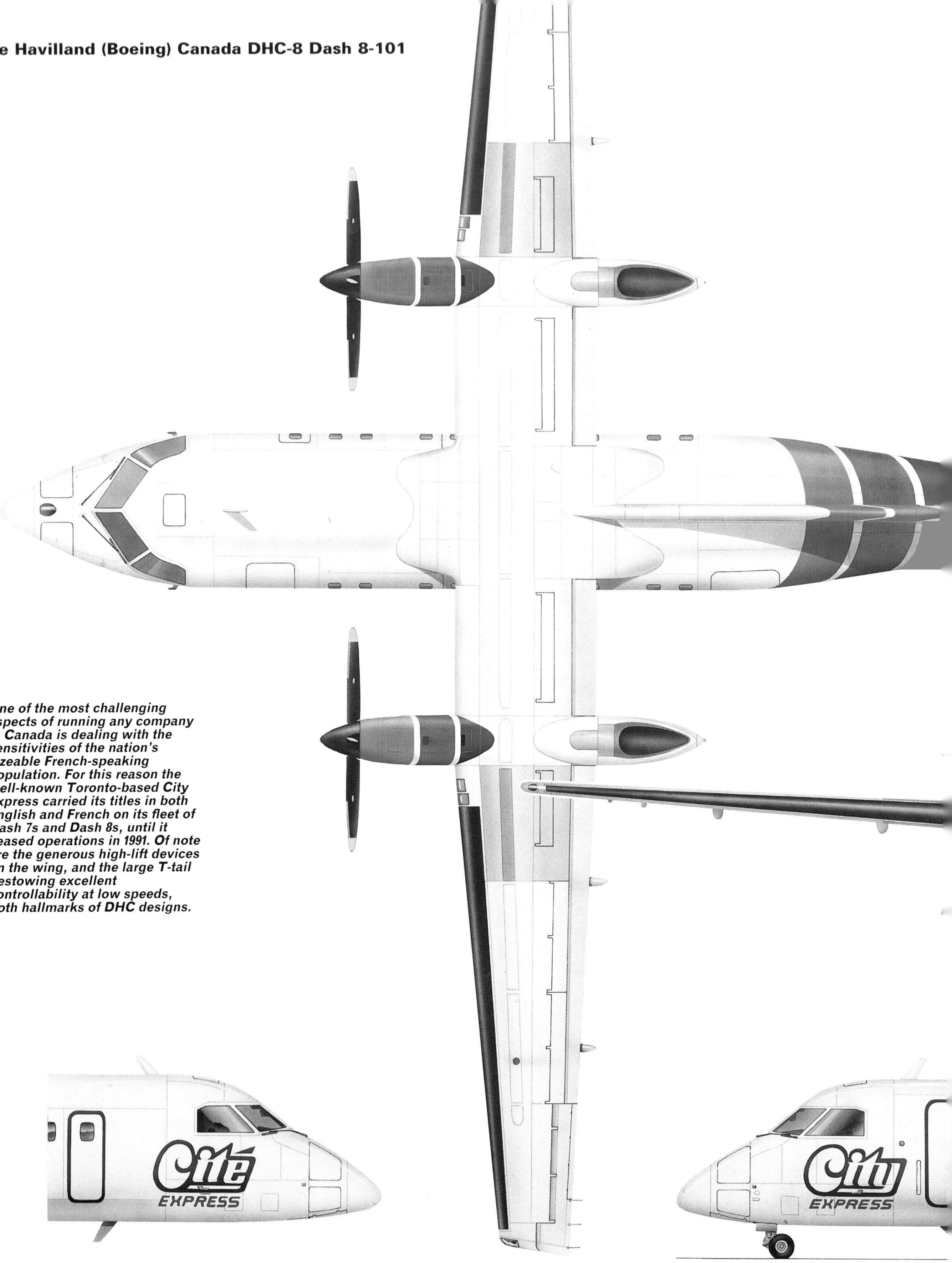

One of the most challenging aspects of running any company in Canada is dealing with the sensitivities of the nation's sizeable French-speaking population. For this reason the well-known Toronto-based City Express carried its titles in both English and French on its fleet of Dash 7s and Dash 8s, until it ceased operations in 1991. Of note are the generous high-lift devices on the wing, and the large T-tail bestowing excellent controllability at low speeds, both hallmarks of DHC designs.

Specification

De Havilland (Boeing) Canada DHC-8 Dash 8-101

Type: short-range twin-turboprop transport

Powerplant: two Pratt & Whitney Canada PW120A turboprop engines, each rated at 1432 kW (1,800-shp) and driving a Hamilton Standard 14-SF7 four-bladed constant-speed propeller; power on one engine can be increased to 1491 kW (2,000 shp) if other engine fails; standard fuel capacity 3160 litres (695 Imp gal)

Performance: maximum cruising speed 497 km/h (309 mph); stalling speed flaps down 134 km/h (83 mph); maximum rate of climb at sea level 631 m/min (2,070 ft/min); rate of climb at sea level with one engine out 162 m/min (531 ft/min); range with full passenger load 1650 km (1,025 miles); range with maximum cargo payload 1019 km (633 miles); take-off run at sea level at maximum take-off weight 960 m (3,150 ft); landing run at maximum landing weight 908 m (2,979 ft)

Weights: empty equipped 10024 kg (22,100 lb); maximum take-off 15650 kg (34,500 lb); maximum landing weight 15375 kg (33,900 lb); standard usable fuel load 2576 kg (5,678 lb); optional maximum fuel load 4646 kg (10,244 lb); maximum passenger payload 4037 kg (8,900 lb); maximum cargo payload 4467 kg (9,849 lb)

Dimensions: wing span 25.91 m (85 ft); elevator span 7.92 m (26 ft); length 22.25 m (73 ft); height 7.49 m (24 ft 7 in); propeller diameter 3.96 m (13 ft); maximum fuselage diameter 2.69 m (8 ft 10 in); wing area 54.35 m^2 (585 sq ft)

Accommodation: two flight crew; standard main cabin commuter layout for 36 passengers in four-abreast seating with a central aisle; alternative 40-passenger layout available, along with other interior configurations to suit individual customers

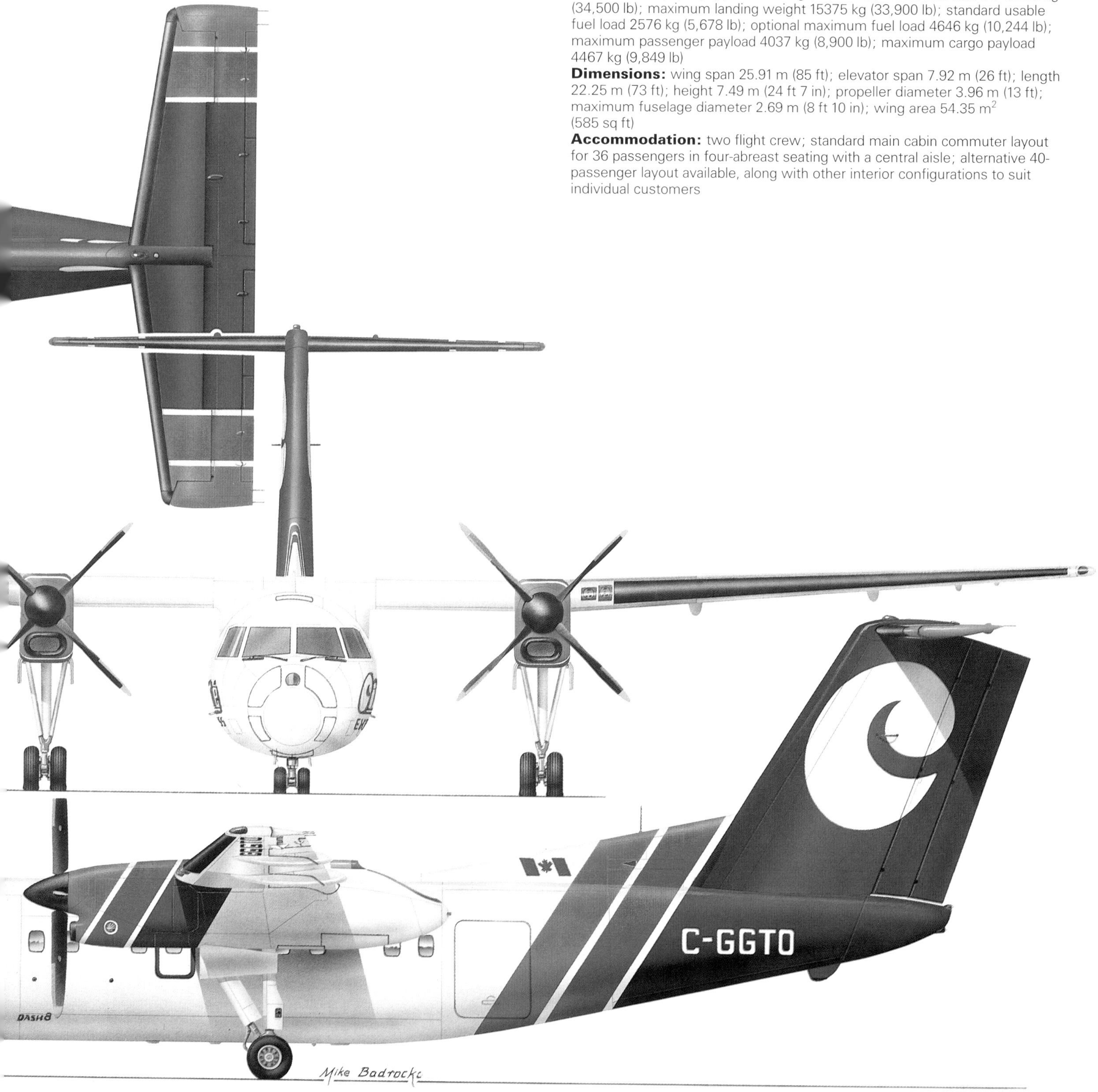

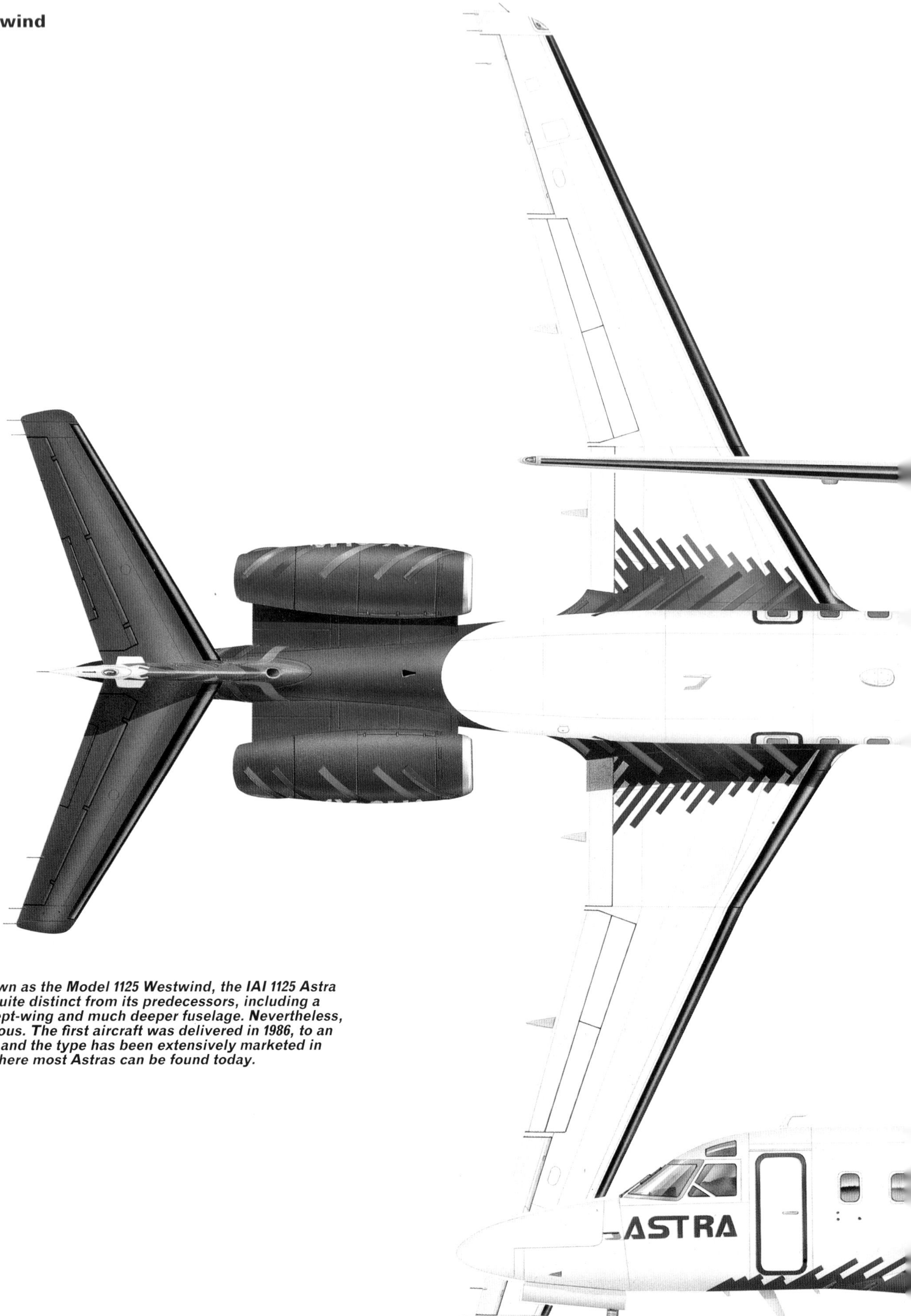

While originally known as the Model 1125 Westwind, the IAI 1125 Astra possesses a shape quite distinct from its predecessors, including a high-technology swept-wing and much deeper fuselage. Nevertheless, its parentage is obvious. The first aircraft was delivered in 1986, to an American customer, and the type has been extensively marketed in the United States, where most Astras can be found today.

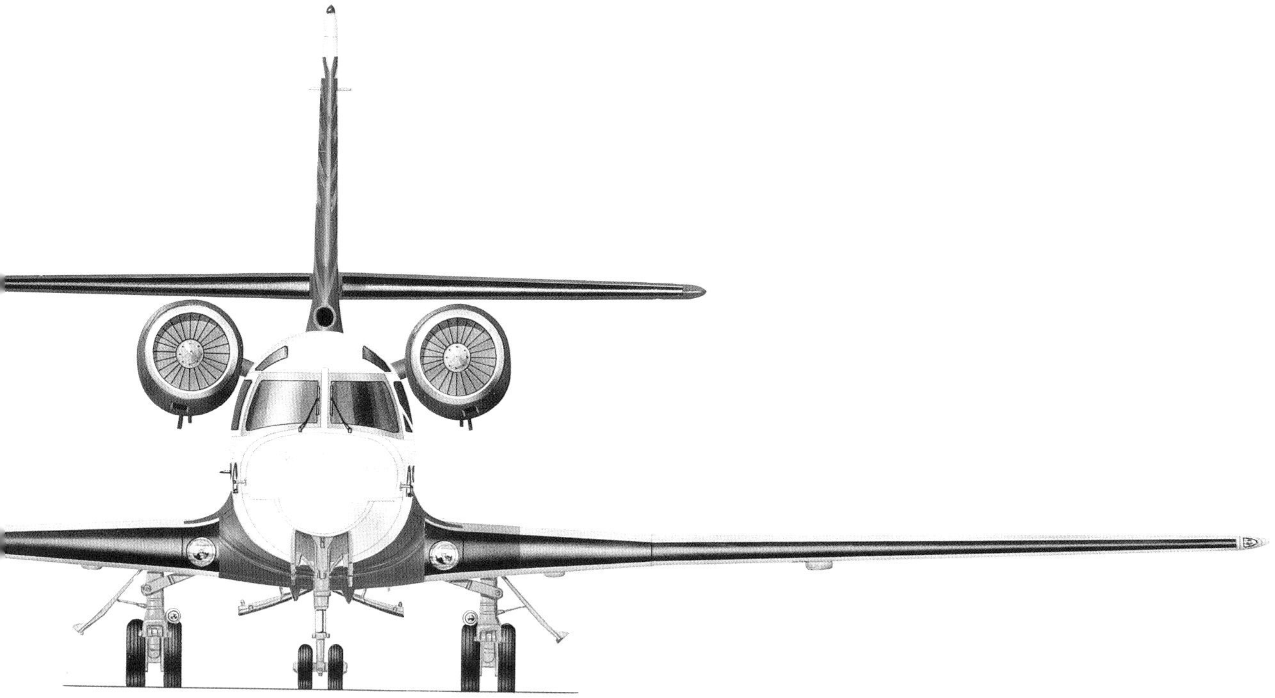

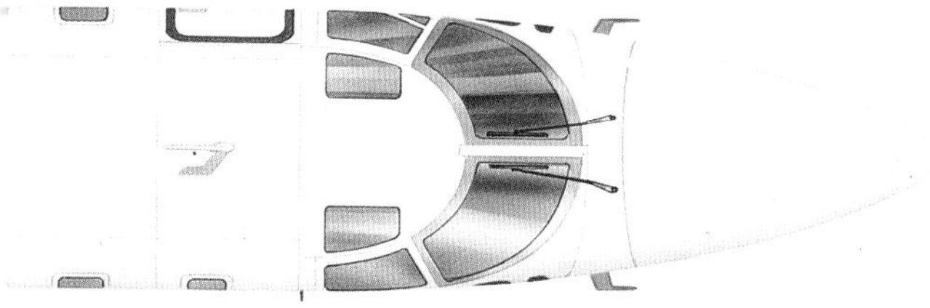

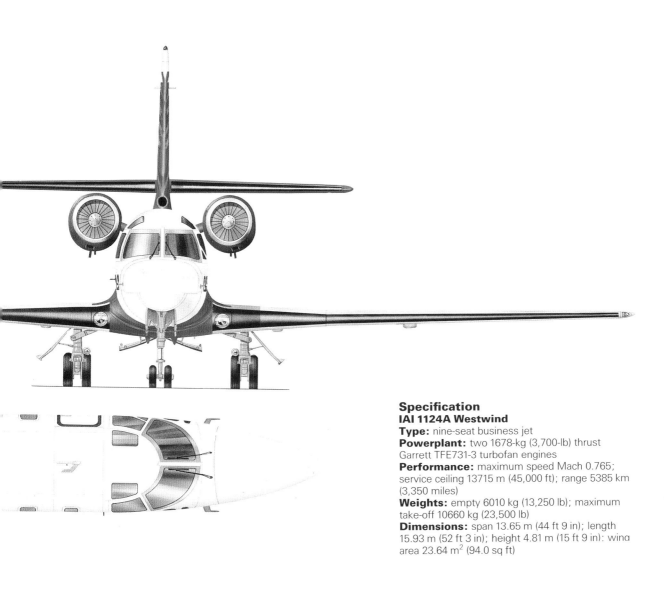

Specification

IAI 1124A Westwind

Type: nine-seat business jet
Powerplant: two 1678-kg (3,700-lb) thrust Garrett TFE731-3 turbofan engines
Performance: maximum speed Mach 0.765; service ceiling 13715 m (45,000 ft); range 5385 km (3,350 miles)
Weights: empty 6010 kg (13,250 lb); maximum take-off 10660 kg (23,500 lb)
Dimensions: span 13.65 m (44 ft 9 in); length 15.93 m (52 ft 3 in); height 4.81 m (15 ft 9 in); wing area 23.64 m^2 (94.0 sq ft)

Dassault Falcon 10/20H/50/900

Specification
Dassault Falcon 10

Wingspan: 12.8 m (42 ft 11 in)
Length: 13.8 m (45 ft 5 in)
Height: 4.6 m (15 ft 1½ in)
Wing area: 7.3 m^2 (259 sq ft)
Powerplants: two 14.38-kN (3,230-lb st) Garrett TFE731-2 turbofans
Passenger capacity: 4-8
Empty weight: 4880 kg (10,760 lb)
Maximum take-off weight: 8500 kg (18,740 lb)
Maximum cruising speed: 494 kt (910 km/h; 566 mph)
Service ceiling: 13716 km (45,000 ft)
Maximum range: 1,918 nm (3552 km/2,207 miles)

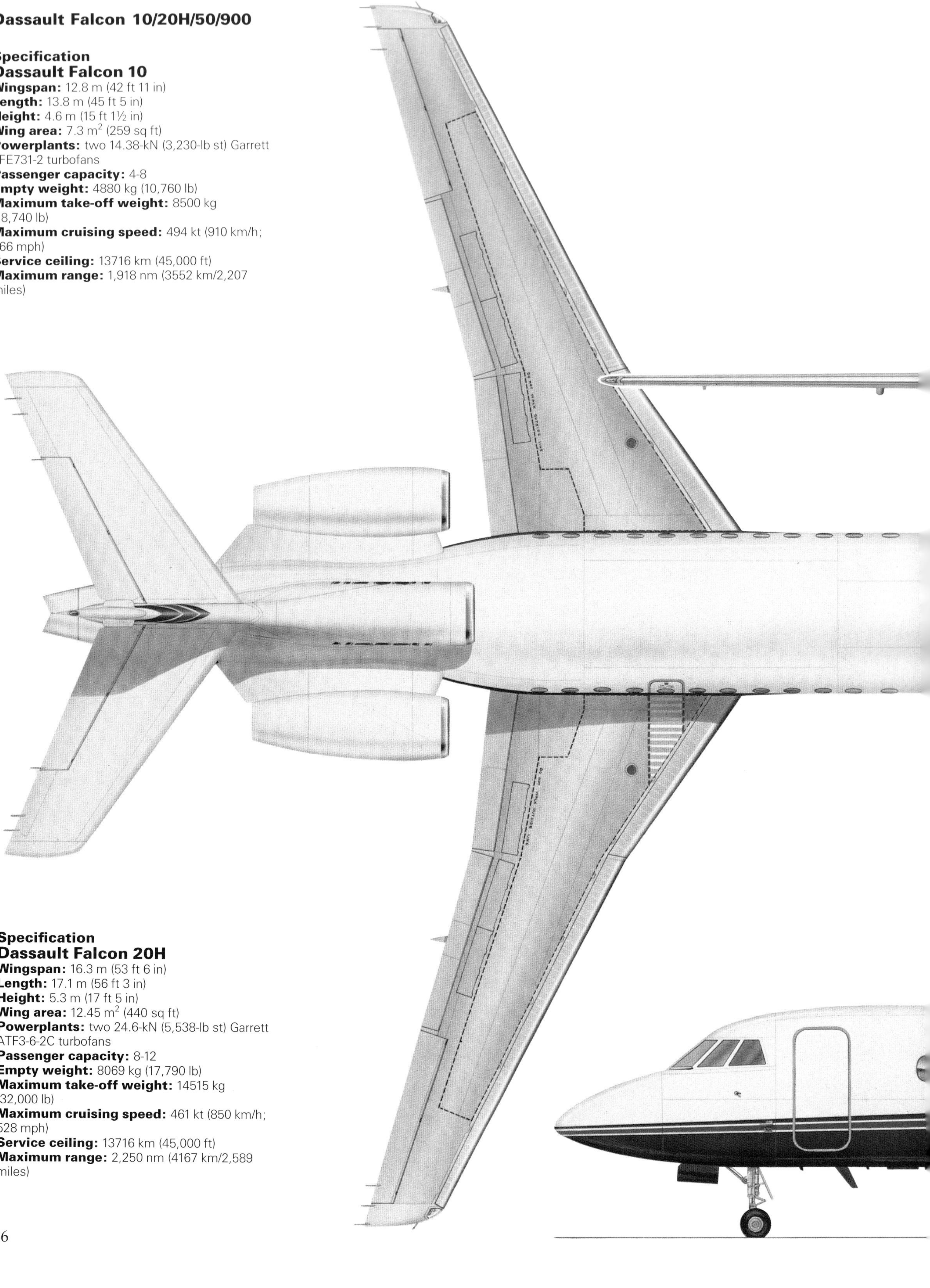

Specification
Dassault Falcon 20H

Wingspan: 16.3 m (53 ft 6 in)
Length: 17.1 m (56 ft 3 in)
Height: 5.3 m (17 ft 5 in)
Wing area: 12.45 m^2 (440 sq ft)
Powerplants: two 24.6-kN (5,538-lb st) Garrett ATF3-6-2C turbofans
Passenger capacity: 8-12
Empty weight: 8069 kg (17,790 lb)
Maximum take-off weight: 14515 kg (32,000 lb)
Maximum cruising speed: 461 kt (850 km/h; 528 mph)
Service ceiling: 13716 km (45,000 ft)
Maximum range: 2,250 nm (4167 km/2,589 miles)

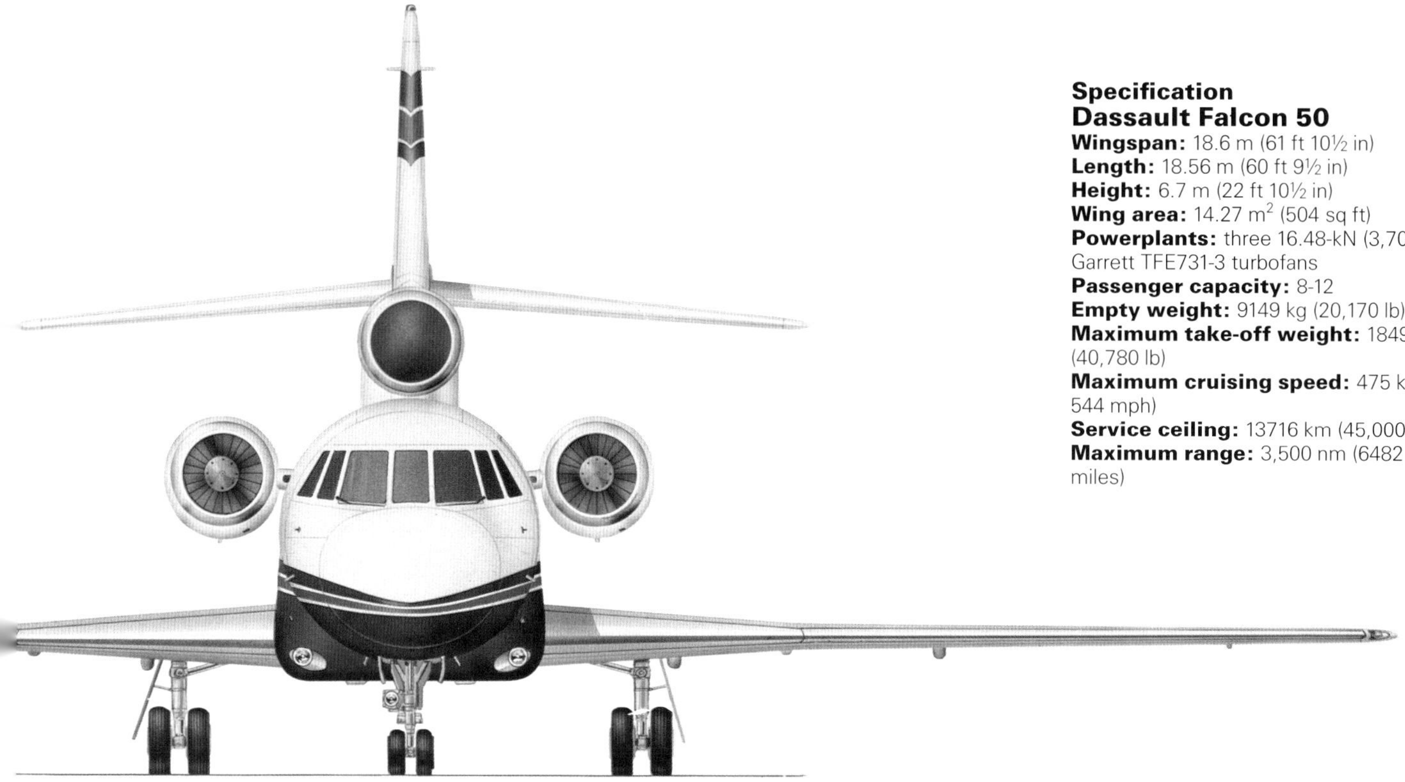

Specification
Dassault Falcon 50
Wingspan: 18.6 m (61 ft 10½ in)
Length: 18.56 m (60 ft 9½ in)
Height: 6.7 m (22 ft 10½ in)
Wing area: 14.27 m^2 (504 sq ft)
Powerplants: three 16.48-kN (3,700-lb st) Garrett TFE731-3 turbofans
Passenger capacity: 8-12
Empty weight: 9149 kg (20,170 lb)
Maximum take-off weight: 18497 kg (40,780 lb)
Maximum cruising speed: 475 kt (875 km/h; 544 mph)
Service ceiling: 13716 km (45,000 ft)
Maximum range: 3,500 nm (6482 km/4,027 miles)

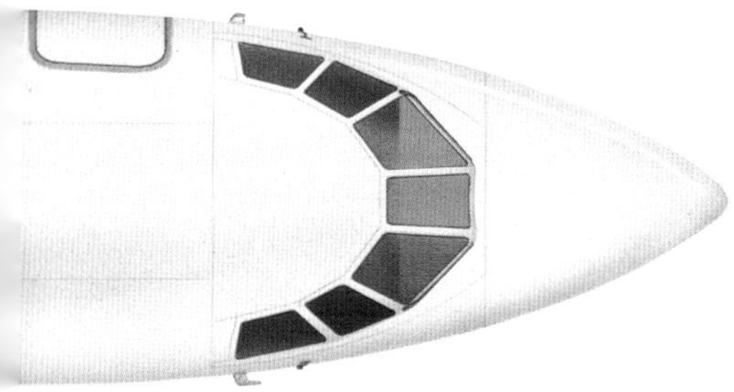

Specification
Dassault Falcon 900
Wingspan: 19.35 m (63 ft 5 in)
Length: 20.2 m (66 ft 6¾ in)
Height: 7.5 m (24 ft 9¼ in)
Wing area: 14.95 m^2 (528 sq ft)
Powerplants: three 18.4-kN (4,500-lb st) Garrett TFE731-5AR-1C turbofans
Passenger capacity: up to 19
Empty weight: 10240 kg (22,575 lb)
Maximum take-off weight: 20639 kg (45,500 lb)
Maximum cruising speed: 500 kt (922 km/h; 572 mph)
Service ceiling: 15544 km (51,000 ft)
Maximum range: 3,900 nm (7222 km/4,488 miles)

The first Falcon 900, named* Spirit of Lafayette, *flew on 21 September 1984. The second aircraft set a new distance record for its class when it flew non-stop from Paris to Dassault's US distribution centre at Little Rock, Arkansas, the same year, covering a distance of 7973 km (4,954 miles) at Mach 0.84. The aircraft shown here is one of a quartet of Falcon 900s operated by the Ford Motor Company and was the third aircraft off the production line.

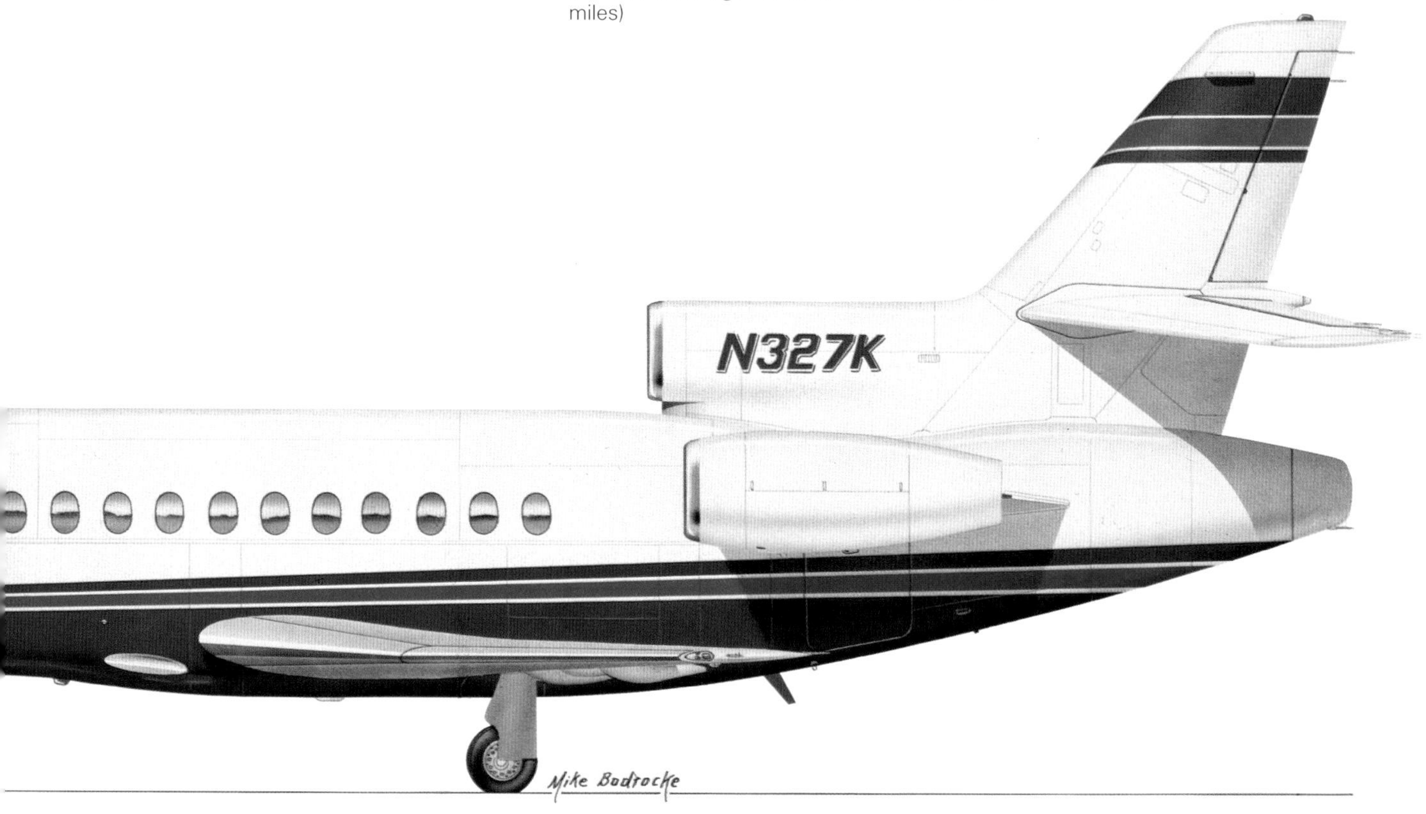

Airbus A310-204

Specification

Airbus A310-204 (CF6 engines – basic fuel configuration)
Powerplant: two General Electric CF6-80C2A2 high bypass turbofans, each developing 222.4kN (50,000lb) for take-off
Dimensions: wing span 43.86m (144ft); tailplane span 16.26m (53ft 4in); length 46.66m (153ft 1in); height 15.80m (51ft 10in); wing area 291m^2 (2,357sq ft)
Weights (243-seat configuration): empty 70016kg (1564,356lb); maximum take-off 138600kg (305,555lb); maximum landing 122000kg (268,959lb); maximum fuel 44089kg (97,197lb)
Performance: Long range cruising speed Mach 0.8; approach speed 250 km/h (155mph); take-off run 1860m (6.100ft); landing run 1480m (4,850ft); range 6690km (4,160 miles)

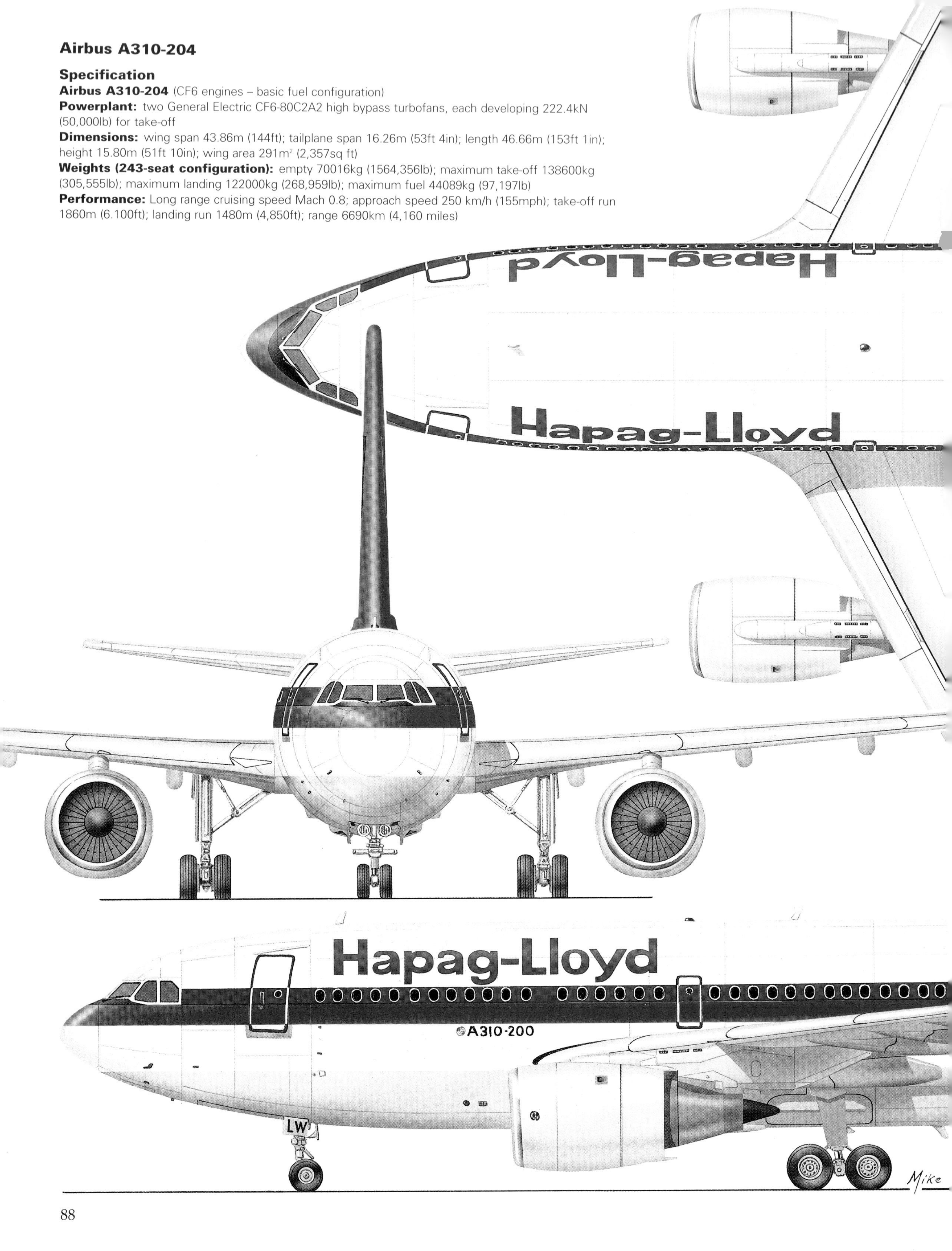

The high technology wing of the A310 allows a high cruise speed and good range thanks to a supercritical wing section. At the other end of the speed scale, numerous high lift devices provide safe operations close to the ground. In addition to extreme reliability and safety, the A310 offers unrivalled economy, available with three of the latest fuel-efficient large turbofans (General Electric CF6, Pratt & Whitney JT9D or PW4152). Hapag Lloyd is a typical operator, having four A310-204s, complete with the wingtip fences introduced as standard on current production aircraft. Other West German operators are Lufthansa (nine A310-203s and three A310-304s) and its charter subsidiary Condor (four A310-203s and two A310-304s).

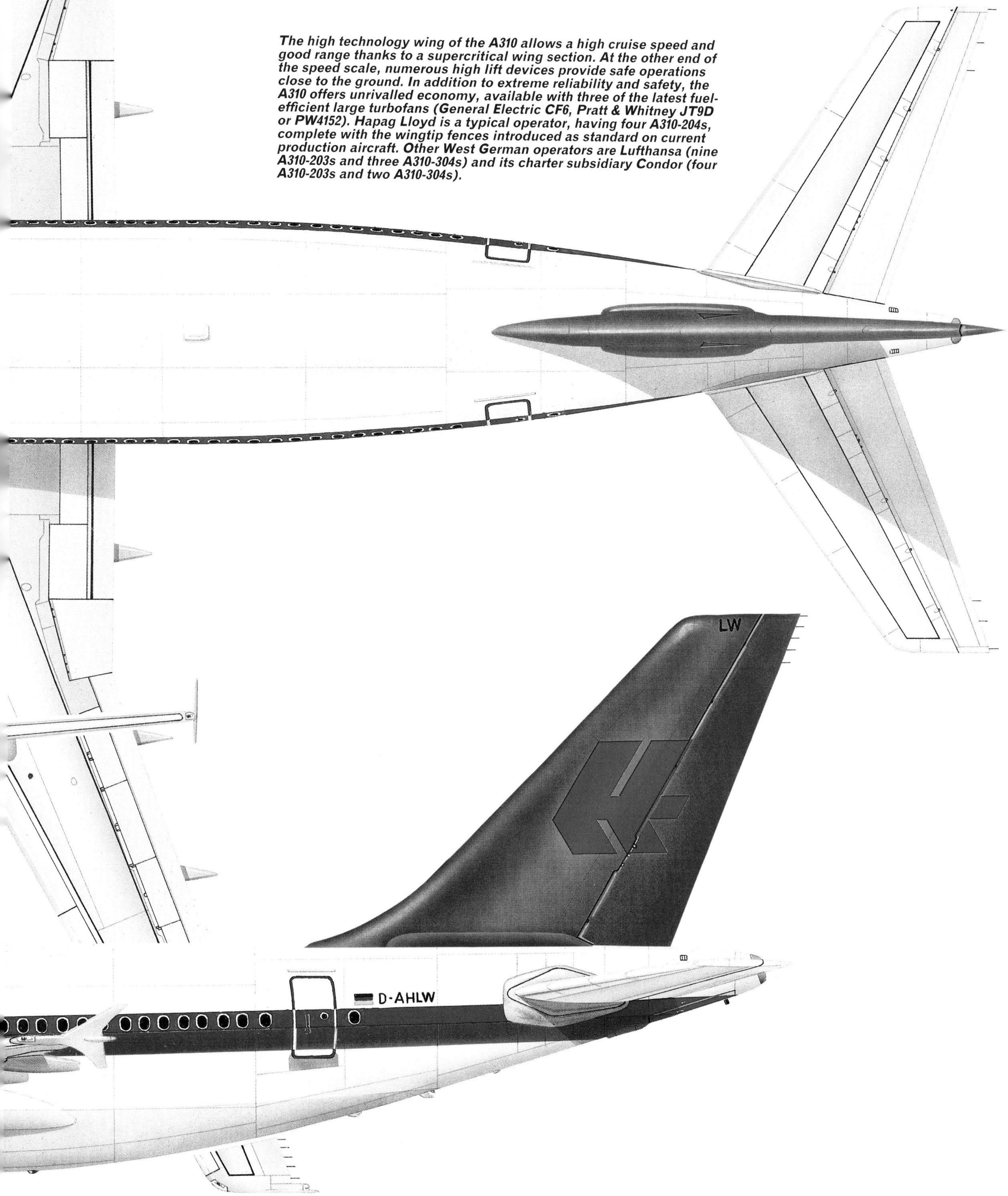

British Aerospace 146 Series 200

Specification

British Aerospace 146 Series 200
Type: short-range passenger transport
Powerplant: four Textron Lycoming ALF 502R-5 turbofans, each rated at 31.0 kN (6,970 lb) thrust
Performance: maximum operating Mach number 0.70; maximum cruising speed 767 km/h (477 mph); stalling speed at 33° flap, max weight 170 km/h (106 mph); take-off run to 10.7 m (35 ft) 1509 m (4,950 ft); landing run from 15 m (50 ft) 1103 m (3,620 ft); range with standard fuel and reserves 2733 km (1,609 miles); range with max load 2179 km (1,355 miles)
Weights: operating empty 23266 kg (51,294 lb); max take-off 42184 kg (93,000 lb); max payload 10753 kg (23,706 lb)
Dimensions: span 26.21 m (86 ft 0 in); length 28.60 m (93 ft 10 in); height 8.59 m (28 ft 2 in); wing area 77.30 m^2 (832 sq ft)
Accommodation: flight crew of two with optional observer's seat; max capacity of 112 passengers in six-abreast seating

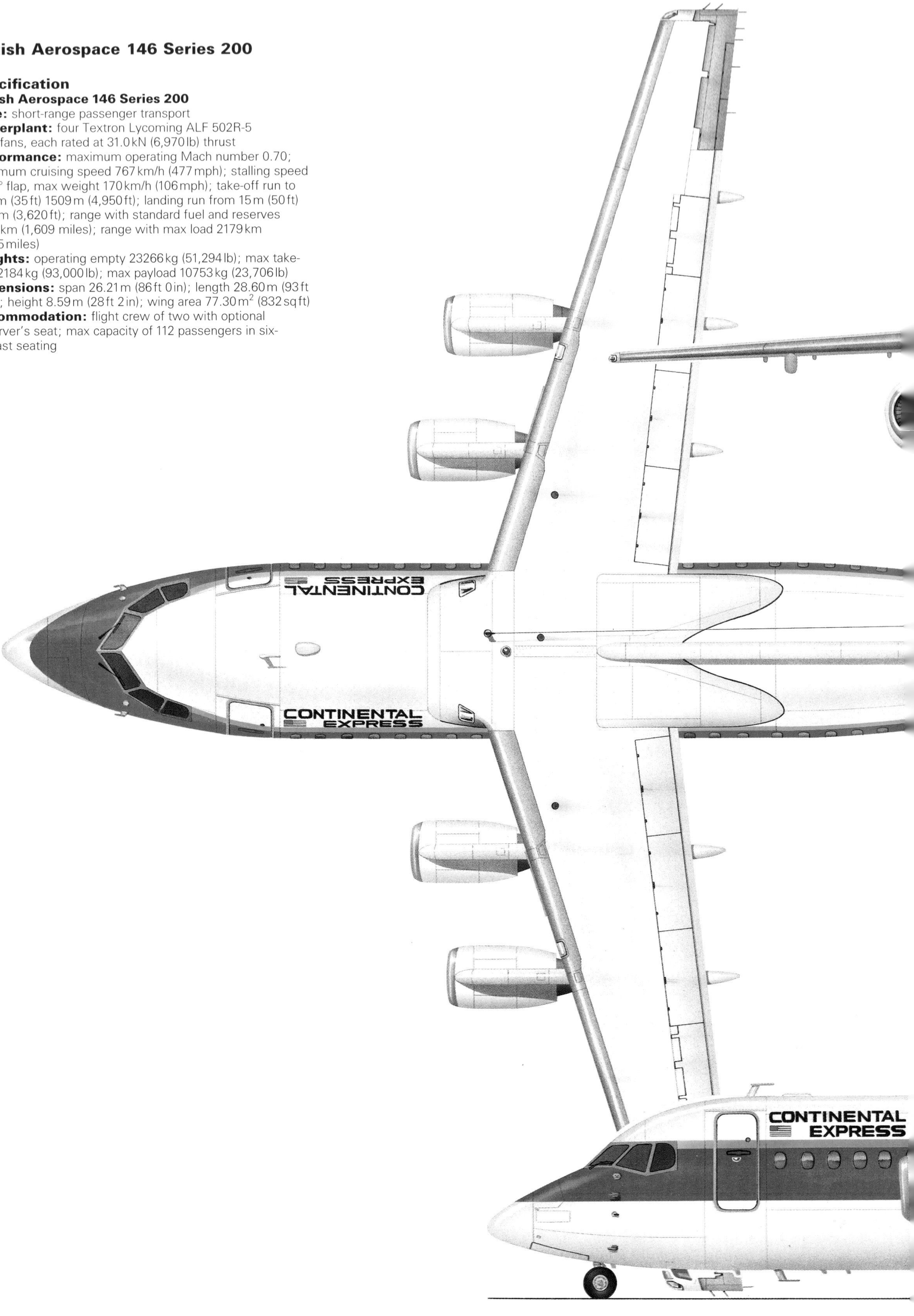

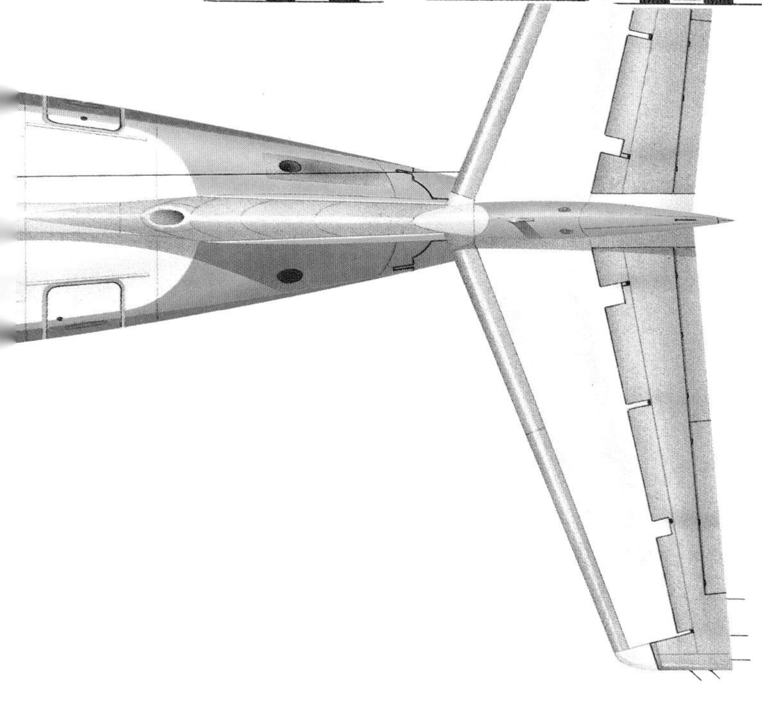

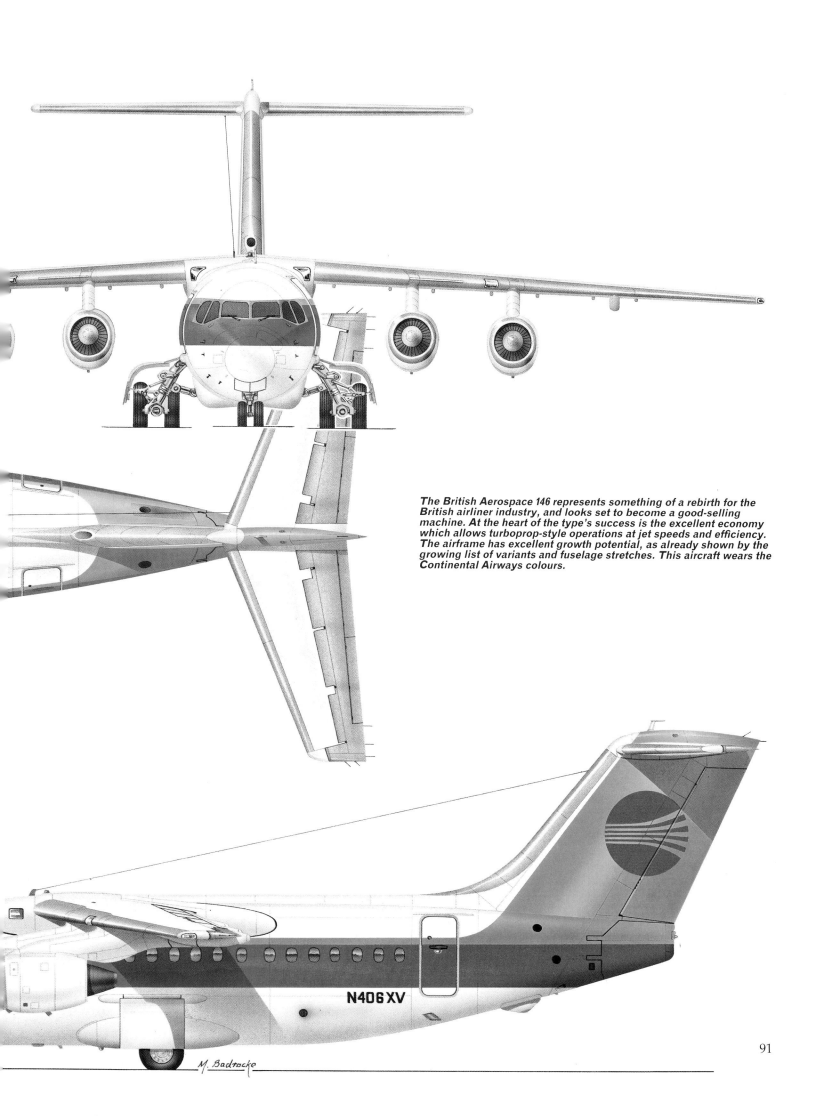

The British Aerospace 146 represents something of a rebirth for the British airliner industry, and looks set to become a good-selling machine. At the heart of the type's success is the excellent economy which allows turboprop-style operations at jet speeds and efficiency. The airframe has excellent growth potential, as already shown by the growing list of variants and fuselage stretches. This aircraft wears the Continental Airways colours.

Saab 340B

Specification

Saab 340B

Wingspan: 21.45 m (70 ft 4 in)
Length: 19.75 m (64 ft 8 in)
Height: 6.89 m (22 ft 6 in)
Wing area: 41.8 m^2 (450 sq ft)
Powerplant: two 1304-kW (1,750-shp) General Electric CT7-9B turboprops
Passenger capacity: up to 37
Empty weight: 8036 kg (17,715 lb)
Maximum take-off weight: 12928 kg (28,500 lb)
Maximum cruising speed: 285 kt (527 km/h; 327 mph)
Long-range cruising speed: 252 kt (466 km/h; 289 mph)
Service ceiling: 9449 m (31,000 ft)
Maximum range: 1,310 nm (2426 km, 1508 miles)

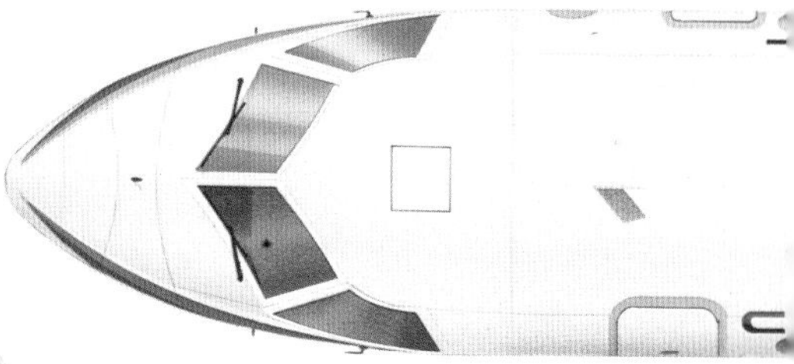

Saab foresaw a considerable market for the 340 in the United States, where the type was aimed at the commuter airlines and feeder networks. They were rewarded with several important sales, including aircraft for the regional networks of American, Eastern, Northwest and Continental, in whose colours this aircraft is seen. Six leased aircraft served with Bar Harbor Airlines at various locations on the eastern seaboard, but when the airline suspended operations in January 1991, the Saabs were returned. The rest of the fleet continued to operate under Continental Express ownership, consisting of Beech 99s and 1900s, Swearingen Metros and EMBRAER Brasilias. The Saabs were 340As powered by the CT8-5A2 engine, configured with 35 seats.

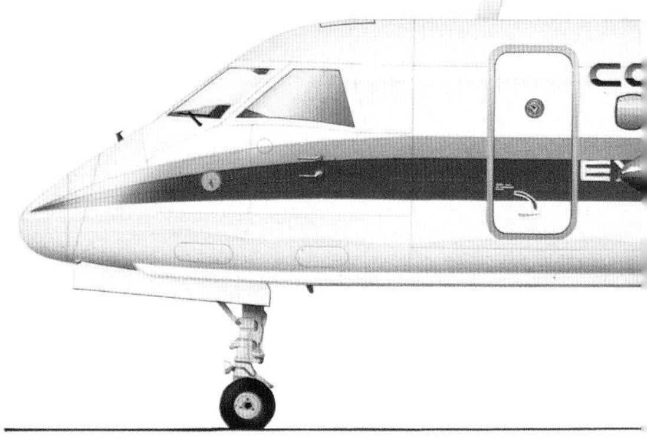

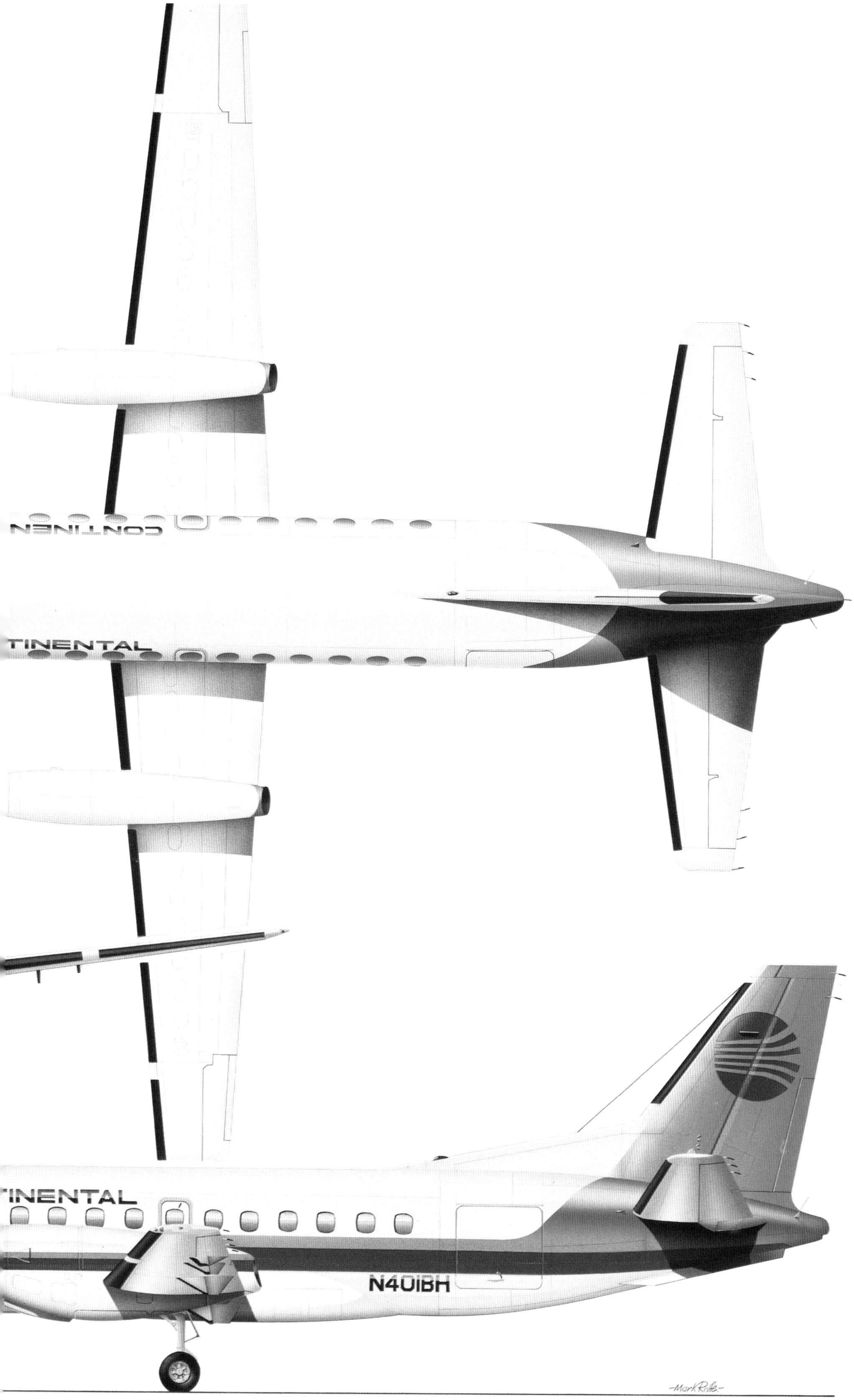
TINENTAL
TINENTAL
N401BH

Specification
Gulfstream I
Type: twin-turboprop executive transport
Powerplant: two 1631-kW (2,190-shp) Rolls-Royce Dart 529 turboprops
Performance: max cruising speed at 7625 m (25,000 ft) 560 km/h (348 mph); service ceiling 11000 m (36,000 ft); range, with max fuel and reserves 4088 km (2,540 miles)
Weights: empty, equipped 9933 kg (21,900 lb); max take-off 15920 kg (35,100 lb)
Dimensions: span 23.87 m (78 ft 4 in); height 6.94 m (22 ft 9 in); length 19.66 m (64 ft 6 in)

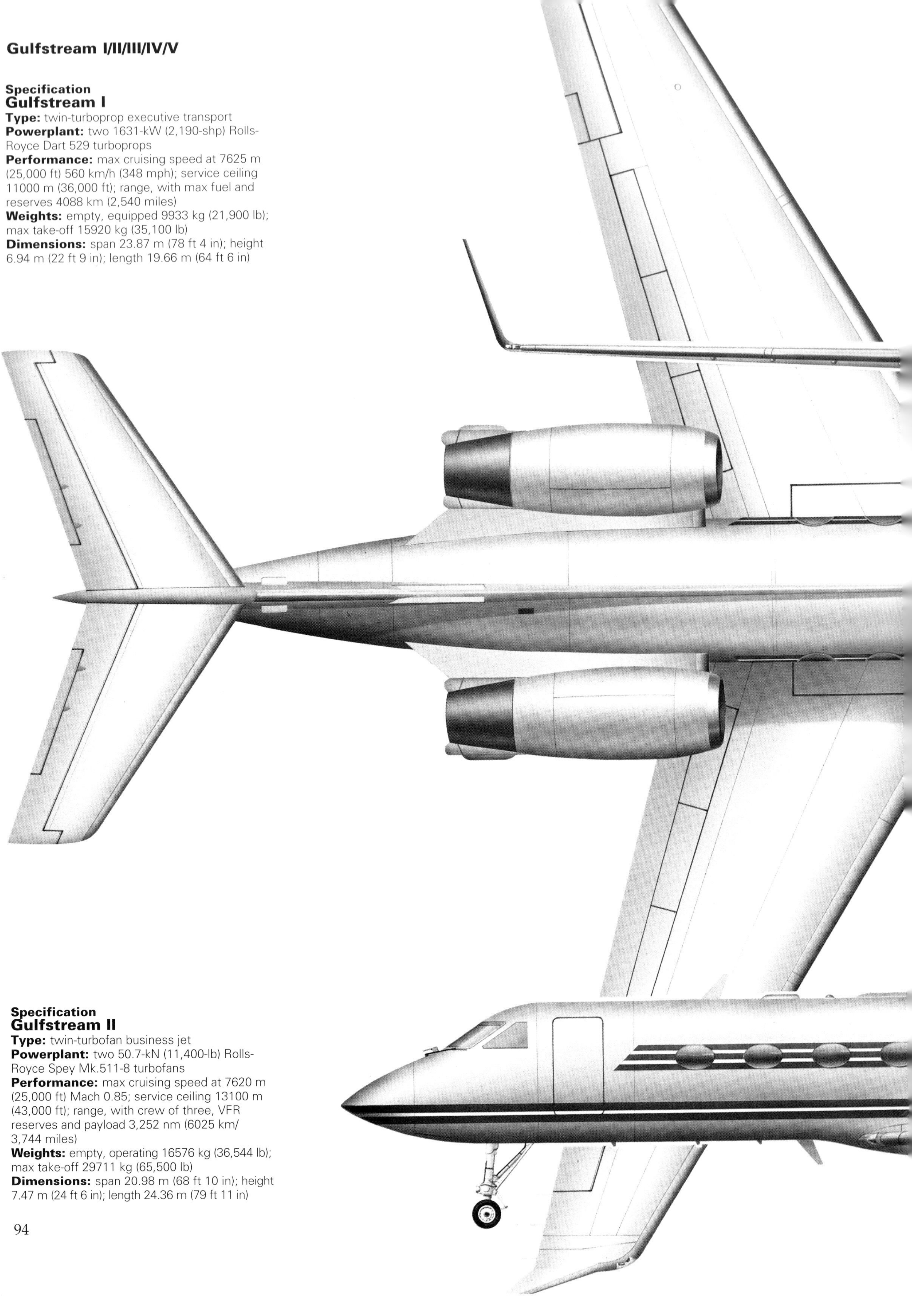

Specification
Gulfstream II
Type: twin-turbofan business jet
Powerplant: two 50.7-kN (11,400-lb) Rolls-Royce Spey Mk.511-8 turbofans
Performance: max cruising speed at 7620 m (25,000 ft) Mach 0.85; service ceiling 13100 m (43,000 ft); range, with crew of three, VFR reserves and payload 3,252 nm (6025 km/ 3,744 miles)
Weights: empty, operating 16576 kg (36,544 lb); max take-off 29711 kg (65,500 lb)
Dimensions: span 20.98 m (68 ft 10 in); height 7.47 m (24 ft 6 in); length 24.36 m (79 ft 11 in)

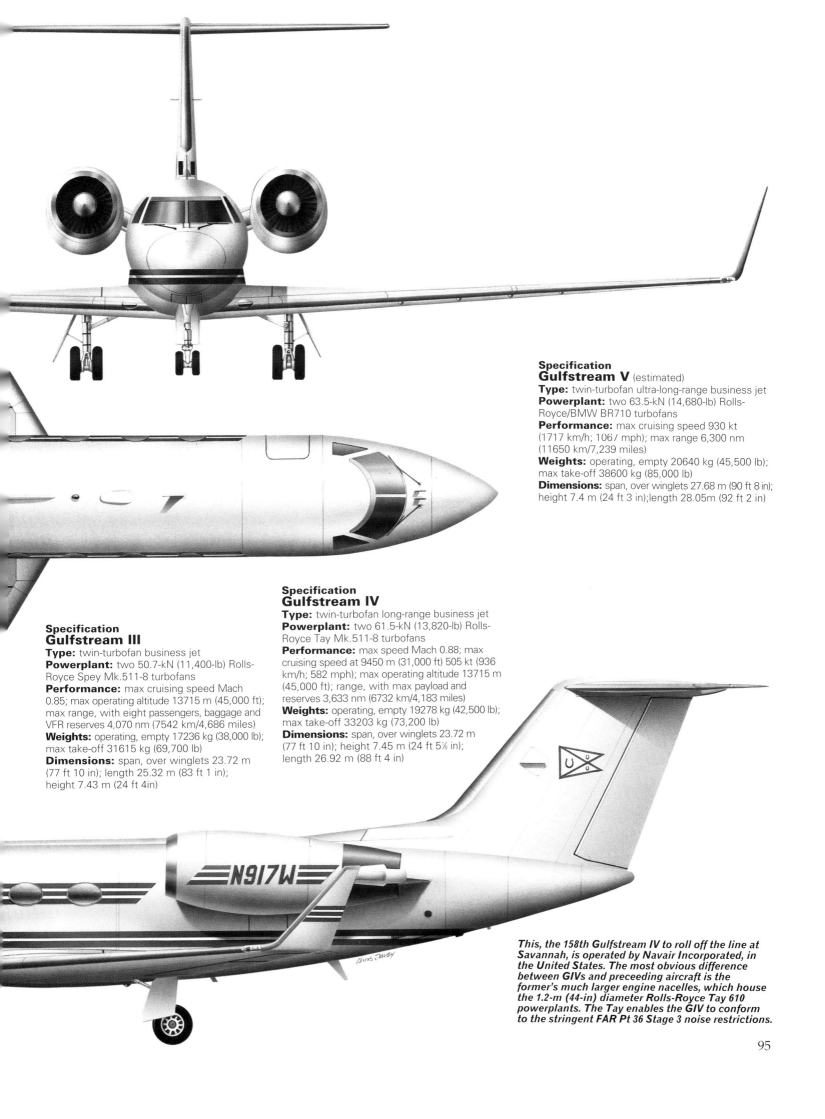

Specification
Gulfstream V (estimated)
Type: twin-turbofan ultra-long-range business jet
Powerplant: two 63.5-kN (14,680-lb) Rolls-Royce/BMW BR710 turbofans
Performance: max cruising speed 930 kt (1717 km/h; 1067 mph); max range 6,300 nm (11650 km/7,239 miles)
Weights: operating, empty 20640 kg (45,500 lb); max take-off 38600 kg (85,000 lb)
Dimensions: span, over winglets 27.68 m (90 ft 8 in); height 7.4 m (24 ft 3 in);length 28.05m (92 ft 2 in)

Specification
Gulfstream III
Type: twin-turbofan business jet
Powerplant: two 50.7-kN (11,400-lb) Rolls-Royce Spey Mk.511-8 turbofans
Performance: max cruising speed Mach 0.85; max operating altitude 13715 m (45,000 ft); max range, with eight passengers, baggage and VFR reserves 4,070 nm (7542 km/4,686 miles)
Weights: operating, empty 17236 kg (38,000 lb); max take-off 31615 kg (69,700 lb)
Dimensions: span, over winglets 23.72 m (77 ft 10 in); length 25.32 m (83 ft 1 in); height 7.43 m (24 ft 4in)

Specification
Gulfstream IV
Type: twin-turbofan long-range business jet
Powerplant: two 61.5-kN (13,820-lb) Rolls-Royce Tay Mk.511-8 turbofans
Performance: max speed Mach 0.88; max cruising speed at 9450 m (31,000 ft) 505 kt (936 km/h; 582 mph); max operating altitude 13715 m (45,000 ft); range, with max payload and reserves 3,633 nm (6732 km/4,183 miles)
Weights: operating, empty 19278 kg (42,500 lb); max take-off 33203 kg (73,200 lb)
Dimensions: span, over winglets 23.72 m (77 ft 10 in); height 7.45 m (24 ft 5⅛ in); length 26.92 m (88 ft 4 in)

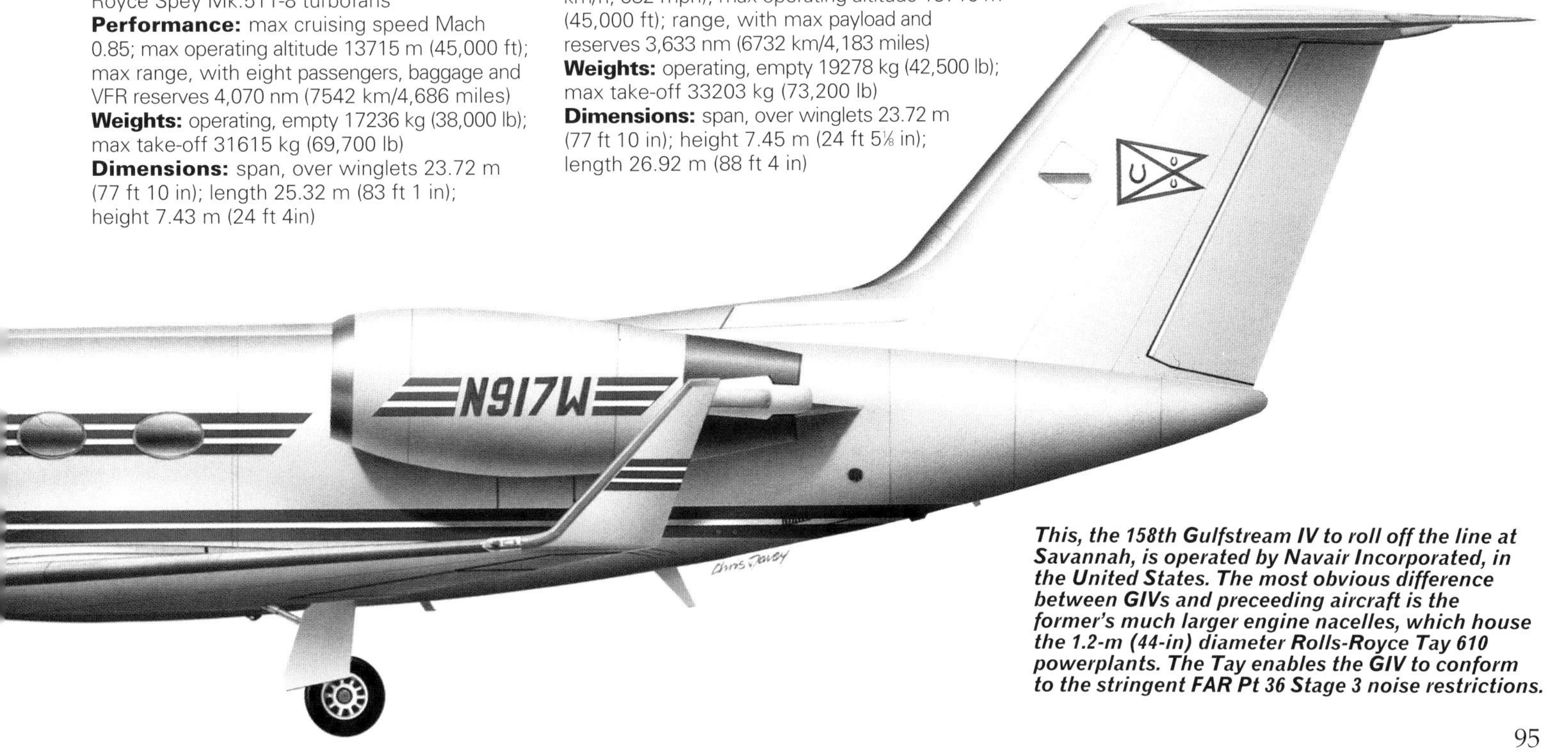

This, the 158th Gulfstream IV to roll off the line at Savannah, is operated by Navair Incorporated, in the United States. The most obvious difference between GIVs and preceeding aircraft is the former's much larger engine nacelles, which house the 1.2-m (44-in) diameter Rolls-Royce Tay 610 powerplants. The Tay enables the GIV to conform to the stringent FAR Pt 36 Stage 3 noise restrictions.

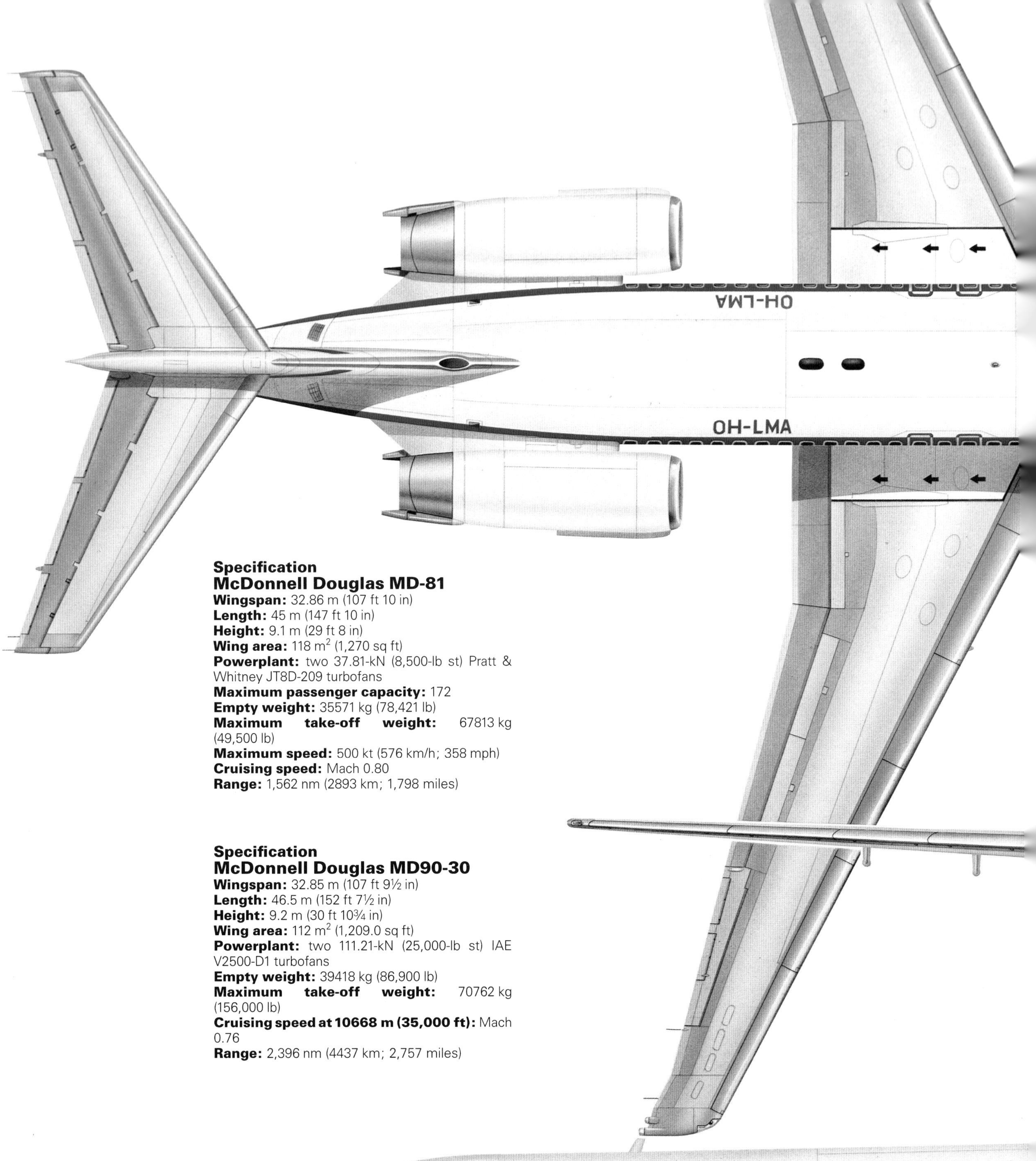

Specification
McDonnell Douglas MD-81
Wingspan: 32.86 m (107 ft 10 in)
Length: 45 m (147 ft 10 in)
Height: 9.1 m (29 ft 8 in)
Wing area: 118 m^2 (1,270 sq ft)
Powerplant: two 37.81-kN (8,500-lb st) Pratt & Whitney JT8D-209 turbofans
Maximum passenger capacity: 172
Empty weight: 35571 kg (78,421 lb)
Maximum take-off weight: 67813 kg (49,500 lb)
Maximum speed: 500 kt (576 km/h; 358 mph)
Cruising speed: Mach 0.80
Range: 1,562 nm (2893 km; 1,798 miles)

Specification
McDonnell Douglas MD90-30
Wingspan: 32.85 m (107 ft 9½ in)
Length: 46.5 m (152 ft 7½ in)
Height: 9.2 m (30 ft 10¾ in)
Wing area: 112 m^2 (1,209.0 sq ft)
Powerplant: two 111.21-kN (25,000-lb st) IAE V2500-D1 turbofans
Empty weight: 39418 kg (86,900 lb)
Maximum take-off weight: 70762 kg (156,000 lb)
Cruising speed at 10668 m (35,000 ft): Mach 0.76
Range: 2,396 nm (4437 km; 2,757 miles)

Finnair has long been a staunch McDonnell Douglas customer and so the MD-87 was a logical choice to supplant the earlier models of DC-9s which continued to serve alongside the airline's more recently delivered MD-82s and MD-83s. The MD-87 is the short-fuselage member of the MD-80 family with seats for up to 130 passengers, compared to 172 in the longer standard versions. It was the first of the family to be fitted with EFIS, AHRS and a head-up display for the pilots, but its most distinctive feature is its resculpted tail and extended low-drag tailcone.

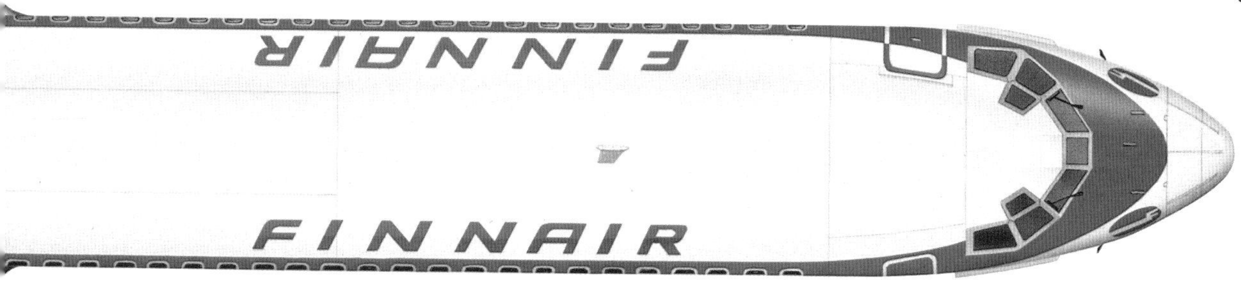

Specification
McDonnell Douglas MD-87

Type: short/medium-range airliner
Powerplant: two Pratt & Whitney JT8D-219 turbofans, each rated at 93.4 kN (21,000 lb) thrust
Performance: maximum speed 925 km/h (575 mph); maximum cruising speed Mach 0.8; cruising speed Mach 0.76; take-off run 1913 m (6,275 ft); landing run 1451 m (4,760 ft); range with maximum fuel (standard tanks) 5522 km (3,431 miles); range with full passenger load (standard tanks) 4457 km (2,769 miles)
Weights: (all with standard tanks) operating empty 33628 kg (74,139 lb); maximum take-off 63503 kg (140,000 lb); maximum fuel 17748 kg (39,128 lb); maximum payload 17112 kg (37,727 lb)
Dimensions: wing span 32.87 m (107 ft 10 in); length 39.75 m (130 ft 5 in); height 9.30 m (30 ft 6 in); tailplane span 12.24 m (40 ft 2 in); wing area 118 m^2 (1,270 sq ft); tailplane area 29.17 m^2 (314 sq ft)
Accommodation: two on flight deck plus observer's seat; Finnair has two-class accommodation for 112 passengers

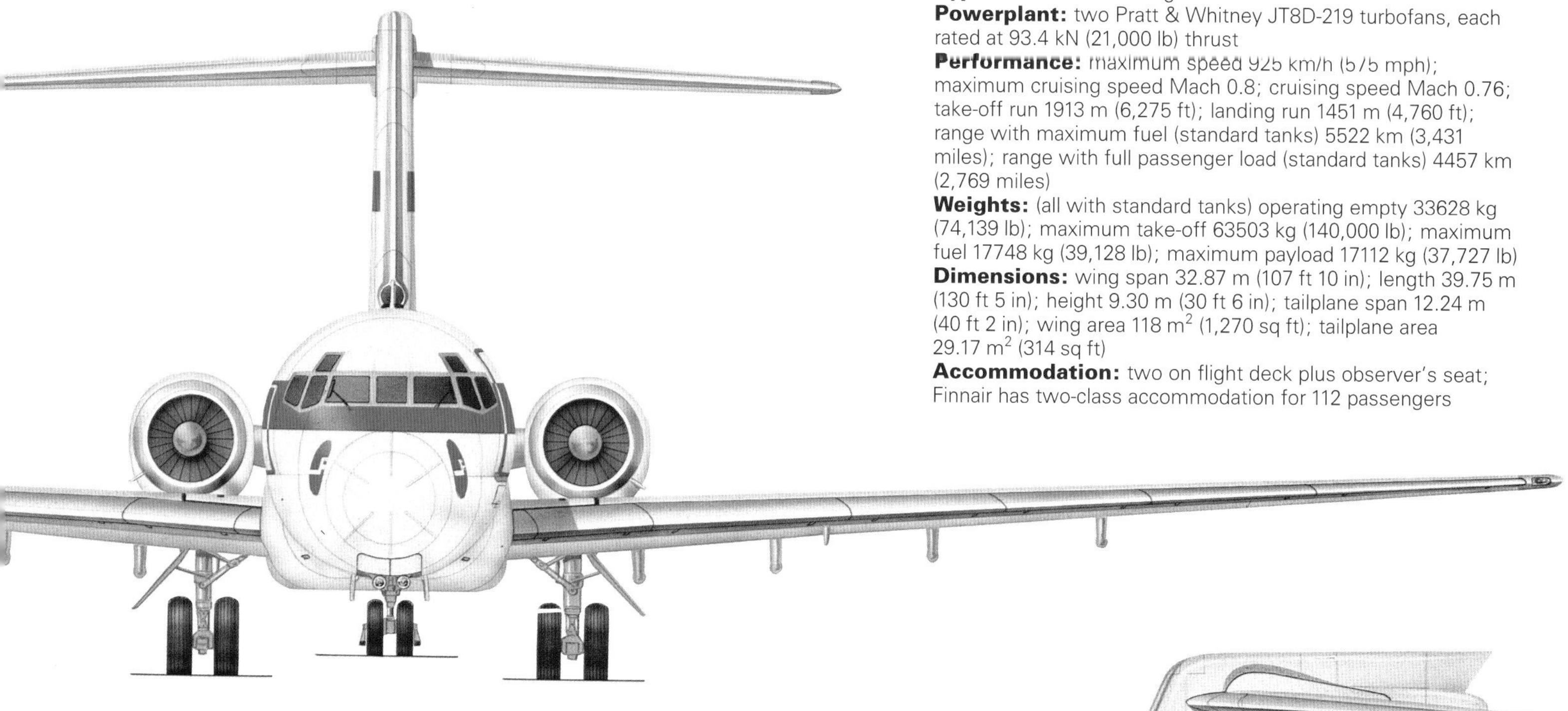

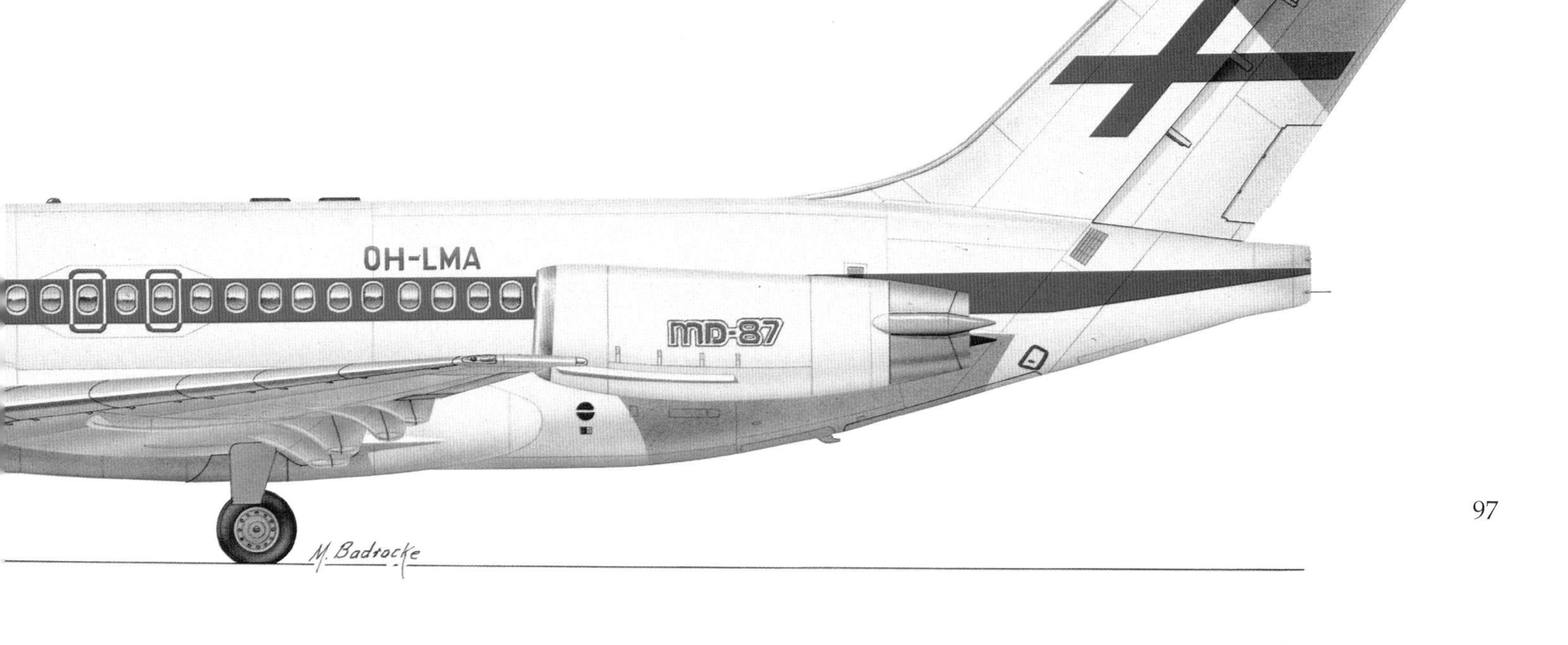

Ilyushin Il-96-300

The first prototype of the Il-96, SSSR-96000, flew from Khodinka on 28 September 1988, and the type made its international debut at the Paris air show the following year. Aeroflot has ordered about 100 aircraft for its long range, high density routes both at home and overseas. Further developments of the type are the Il-96M with 350 seats for medium range sectors, and the Il-90 twin-engined version to fill a similar high density, short range role as the Airbus A330. Western engines such as the Trent and PW400 are under consideration for the latter.

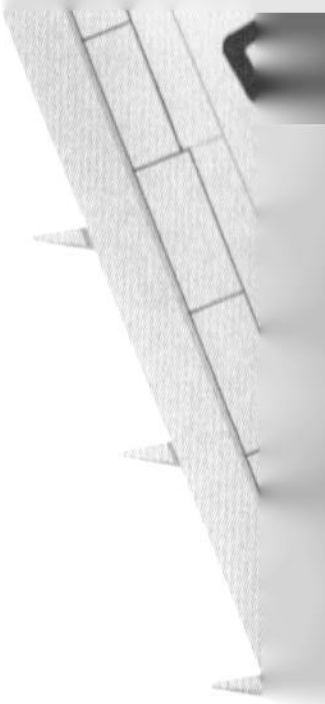

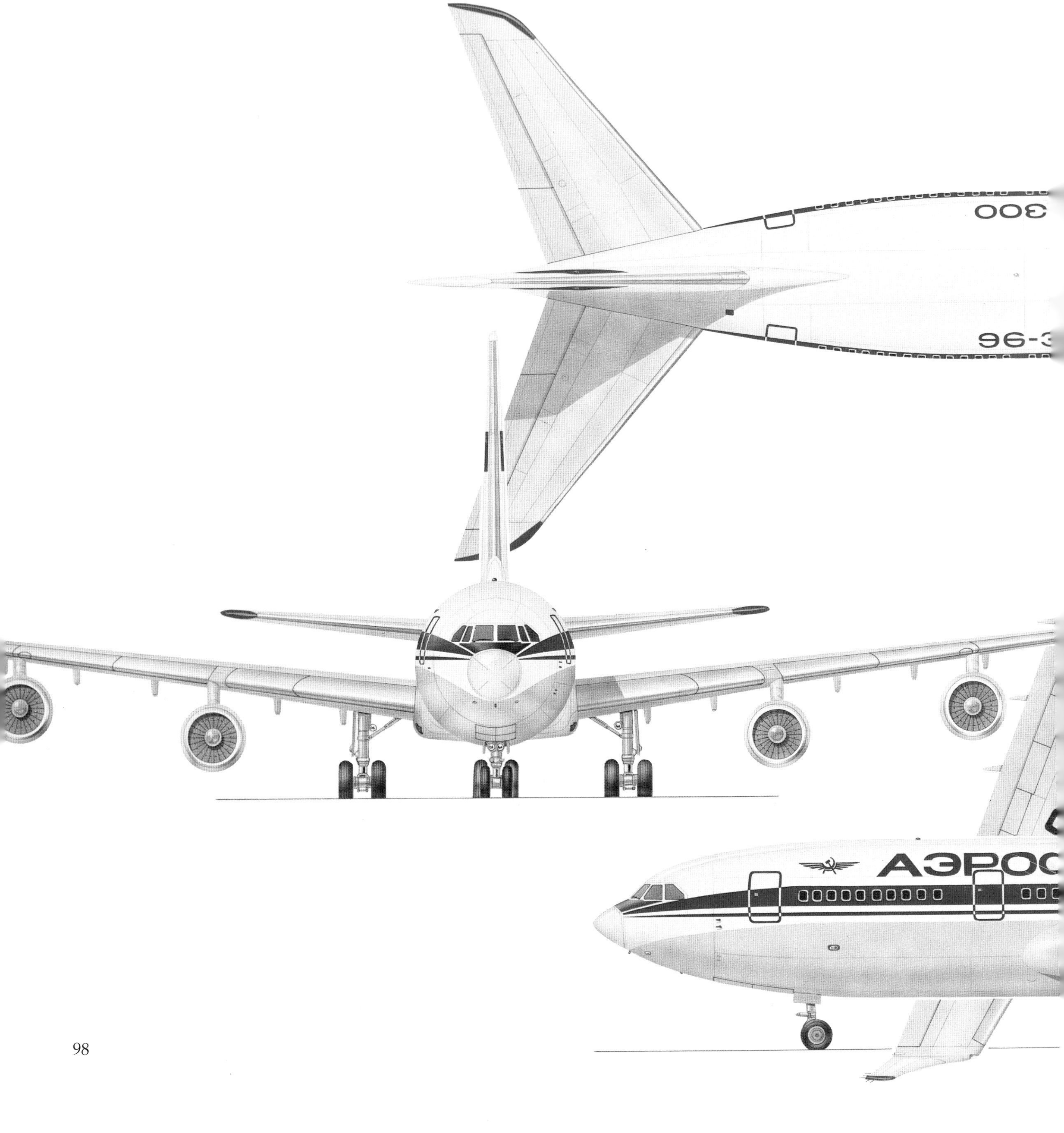

Specification

Ilyushin Il-96-300

Type: wide-body long range passenger transport

Powerplant: four Soloviev PS-90A turbofans, each rated at 156.9 kN (35275 lb) thrust

Performance: normal cruising speed 900 km/h (559 mph); take-off runway length 2600 m (8530 ft); approach speed 260 km/h (162 mph); landing runway length 1980 m (6,500 ft); range with maximum payload 7500 km (4,660 miles), with 30000 kg (66,140 lb) payload 9000 km (5,590 miles)

Weight: basic operating 117000 kg (257,940 lb); maximum take-off 216000 kg (476,200 lb); maximum payload 40000 kg (88,185 lb)

Dimensions: wing span 57.66 m (189 ft 2 in); length 55.35 m (181 ft 7¼ in); height 17.57 m (57 ft 7¾ in); tailplane span 20.57 m (67 ft 6 in); wing area 391.6 m^2 (4,215 sq ft)

Accommodation: pilot, co-pilot and flight engineer on flight deck; 10-12 cabin staff; all-tourist accommodation for 300 passengers in nine-abreast seating; mixed-class layout for 22 first-class passengers (six-abreast), 40 in business-class (eight-abreast) and 173 in economy-class (nine-abreast)

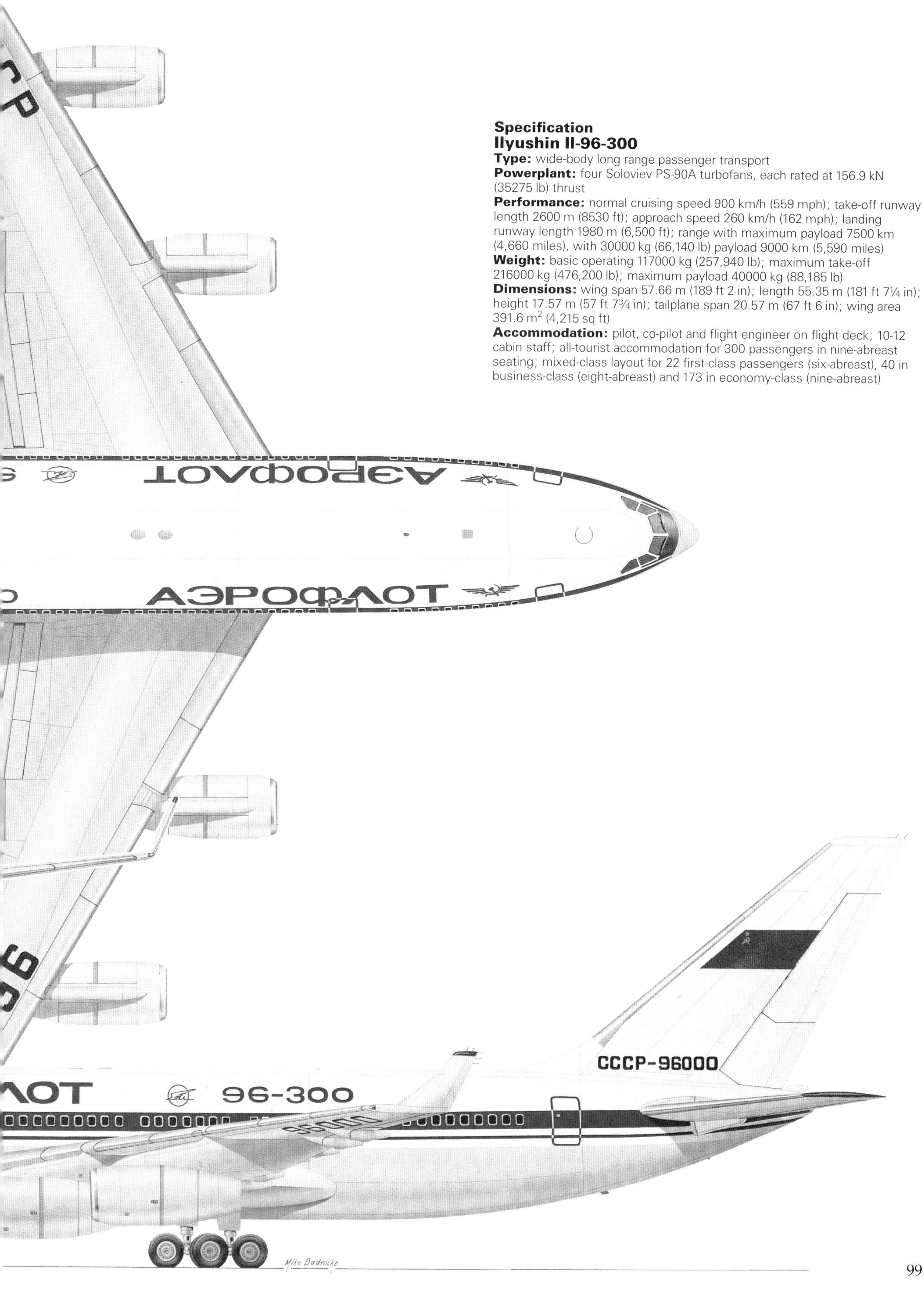

Specification
ATR 42

Wingspan: 24.5 m (80 ft 7 in)
Length: 22.6 m (74 ft 4 in)
Height: 7.3 m (24 ft 10 in)
Wing area: 54.4 m^2 (586 sq ft)
Powerplant: two 1342-kW (1,800-shp) Pratt & Whitney Canada PW120 turboprops
Passenger capacity: 42-50
Empty weight: 10284 kg (22,674 lb)
Maximum take-off weight: 16700 kg (38,817 lb)
Maximum cruising speed: 490 km/h (305 mph)
Economic cruising speed: 450 km/h (279 mph)
Service ceiling: 7620 m (25,000 ft)
Maximum range with full payload: 1946 km (1,050 miles)

Specification
ATR 72

Wingspan: 27.0 m (88ft 9 in)
Length: 27.1 m (89 ft 1 in)
Height: 7.6 m (25 ft 1 in)
Wing area: 61.0 m^2 (656 sq ft)
Powerplant: two 1611-kW (2,160-shp) Pratt & Whitney Canada PW124/2 turboprops
Passenger capacity: 64-74
Empty weight: 12200 kg (26,896 lb)
Maximum take-off weight: 21500 kg (47,400 lb)
Maximum cruising speed: 526 km/h (327 mph)
Economic cruising speed: 460 km/h (286 mph)
Service ceiling: 7620 m (25,000 ft)
Maximum range with 66 passengers: 2666 km (1,440 miles)

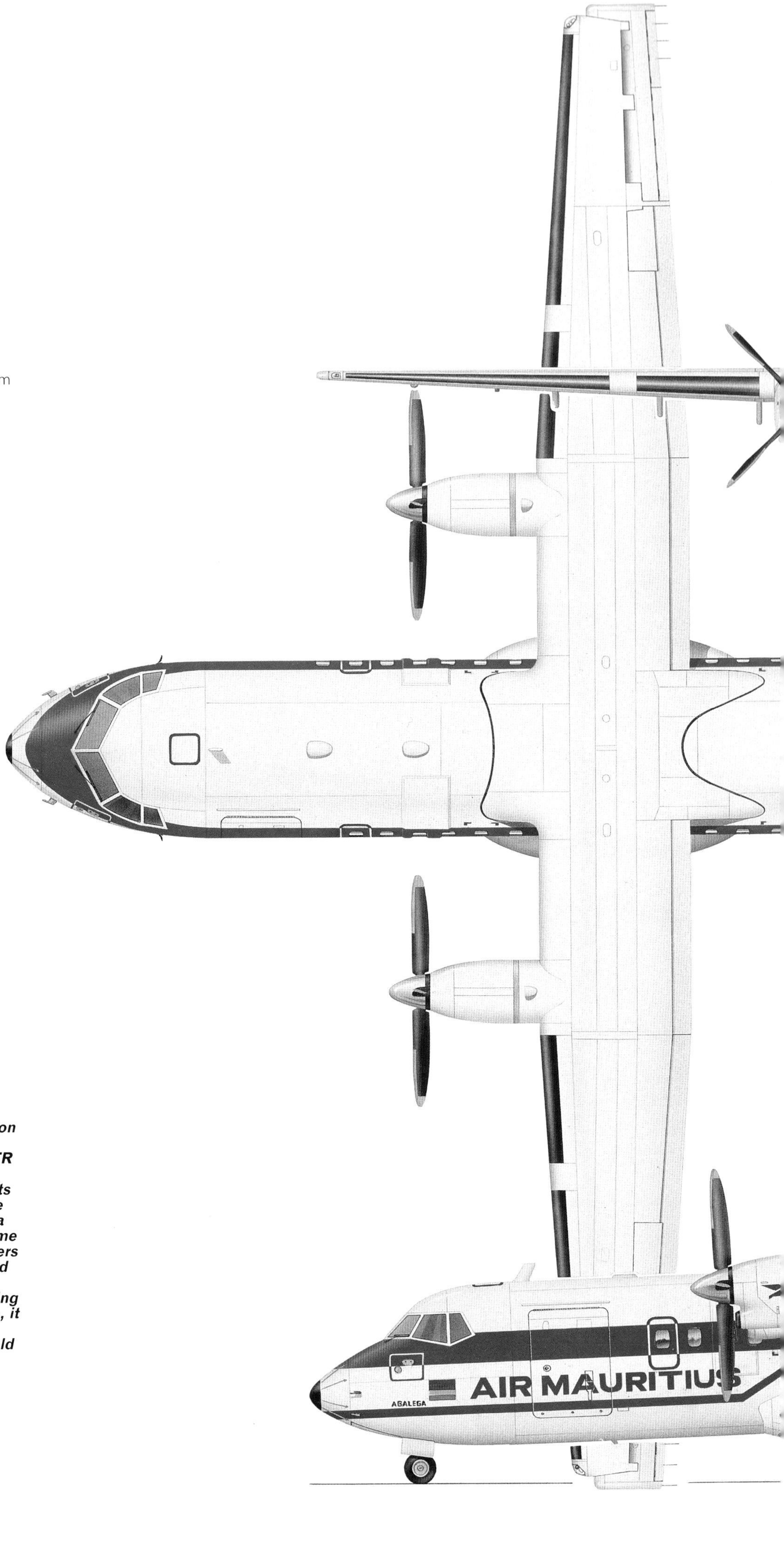

Air Mauritius flies two 48-seat ATR 42-300s on services around the island group, a role to which the type is admirably suited. The ATR family is highly versatile, offering various internal configurations ranging from 42 seats (to 50) in the 42 and 64-74 in the 72. To these basic passenger options have been added a dedicated freighter (ATR 42F) and a maritime patroller (Petrel). In service the aircraft offers excellent economy on the short-range, rapid turn-round sectors that characterise the regional/feeder carriers. Although possessing a respectable take-off/landing performance, it is tailored to operations from airports with standard facilities, trading off true short-field capability against great aerodynamic efficiency.

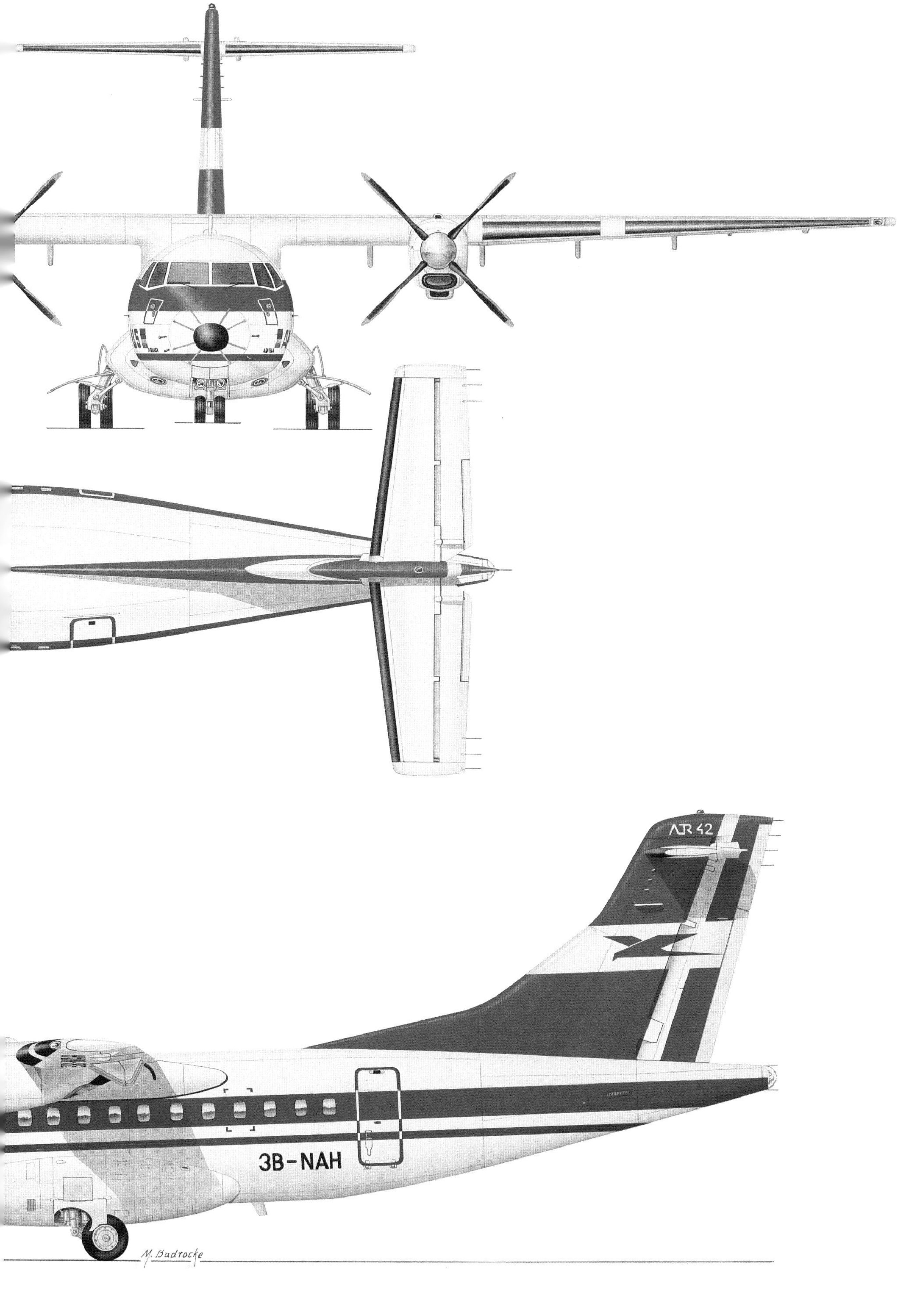
ATR 42
3B-NAH
M. Badrocke

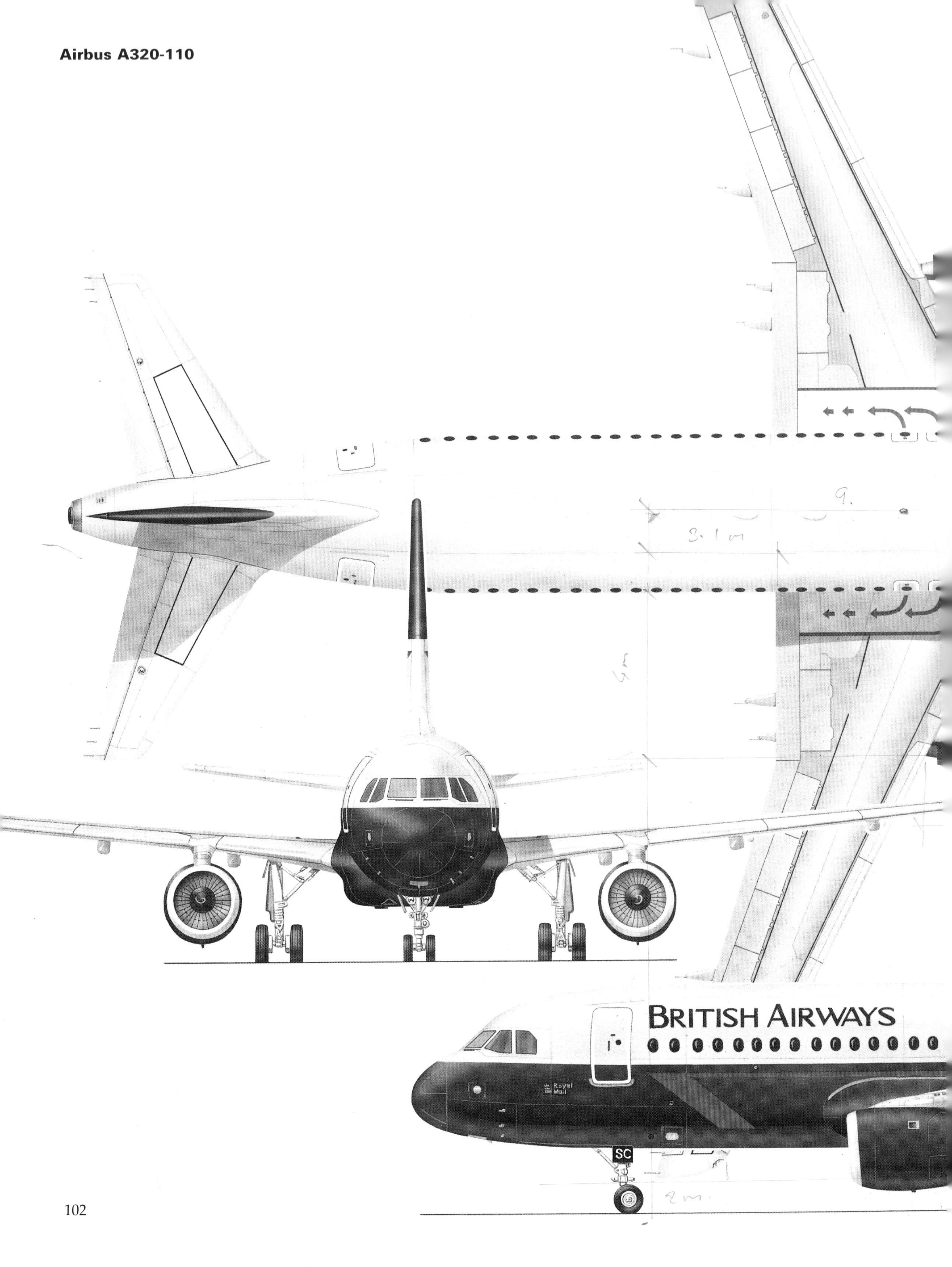
BRITISH AIRWAYS
Royal
Mail
SC

Specification
Airbus A320-110
Accommodation: flight crew of two, up to 179 passengers in high density single-class arrangement;
12 four-abreast in first class and 138 six-abreast in economy class;
84 in business and 68 in economy class (typical)
Powerplant: two CFM International CFM56-5-A1 turbofans of 104.5kN thrust each
Dimensions: wing span 33.9m; length 37.57m; height 11.8m; wing area 122.4m^2; tailplane area 31.0m^2
Performance: (at max T/O weight) cruise speed approx Mach 0.8; take-off distance 1707m; landing distance 1540m; range with reserves approx 5000km

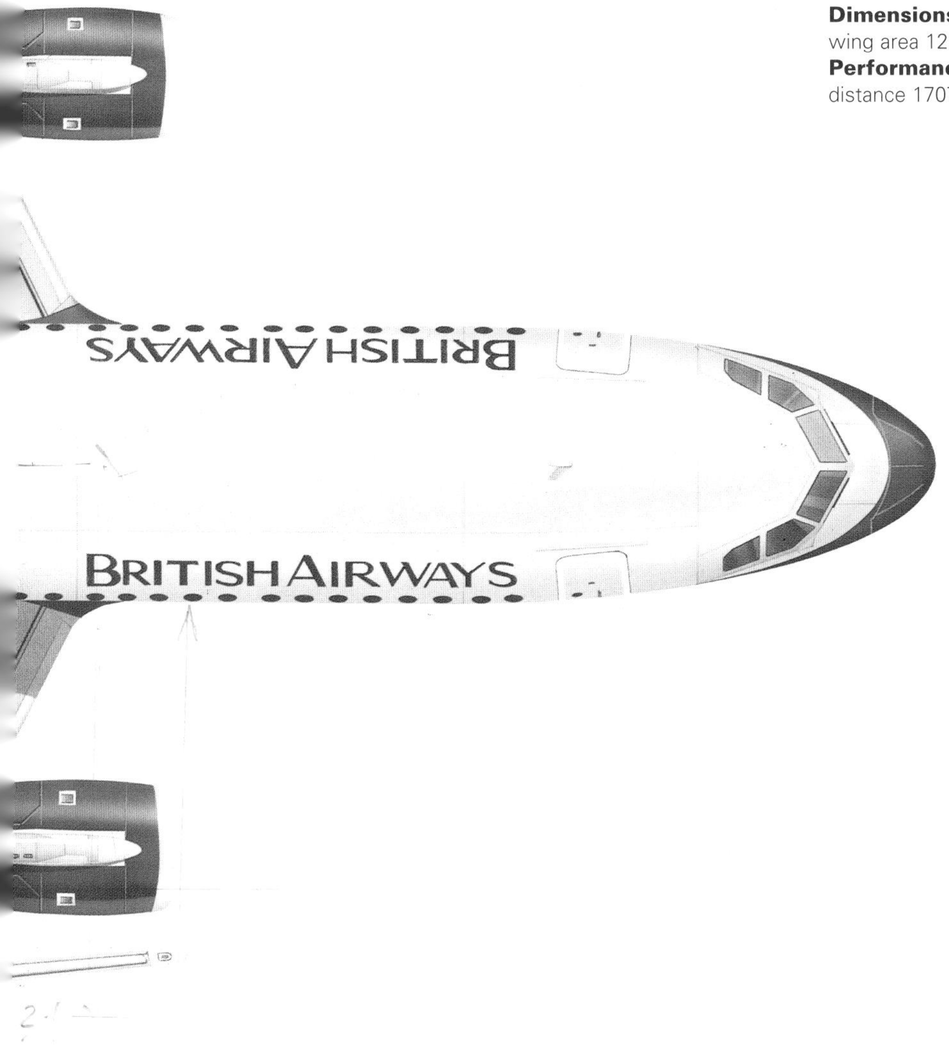

The UK national carrier British Airways has always favoured Boeing products, and despite British Aerospace playing a major role in Airbus design and production, had chosen US products in preference for several years. What was once Britain's second airline, British Caledonian, had ordered the A320 for its short-haul routes to Europe, but the two airlines merged before delivery, meaning that the Airbus aircraft started their careers in British Airways colours. Having somewhat embarrassingly become an Airbus operator, BA is now well-pleased with its A320 fleet, these posting superb reliability rates.

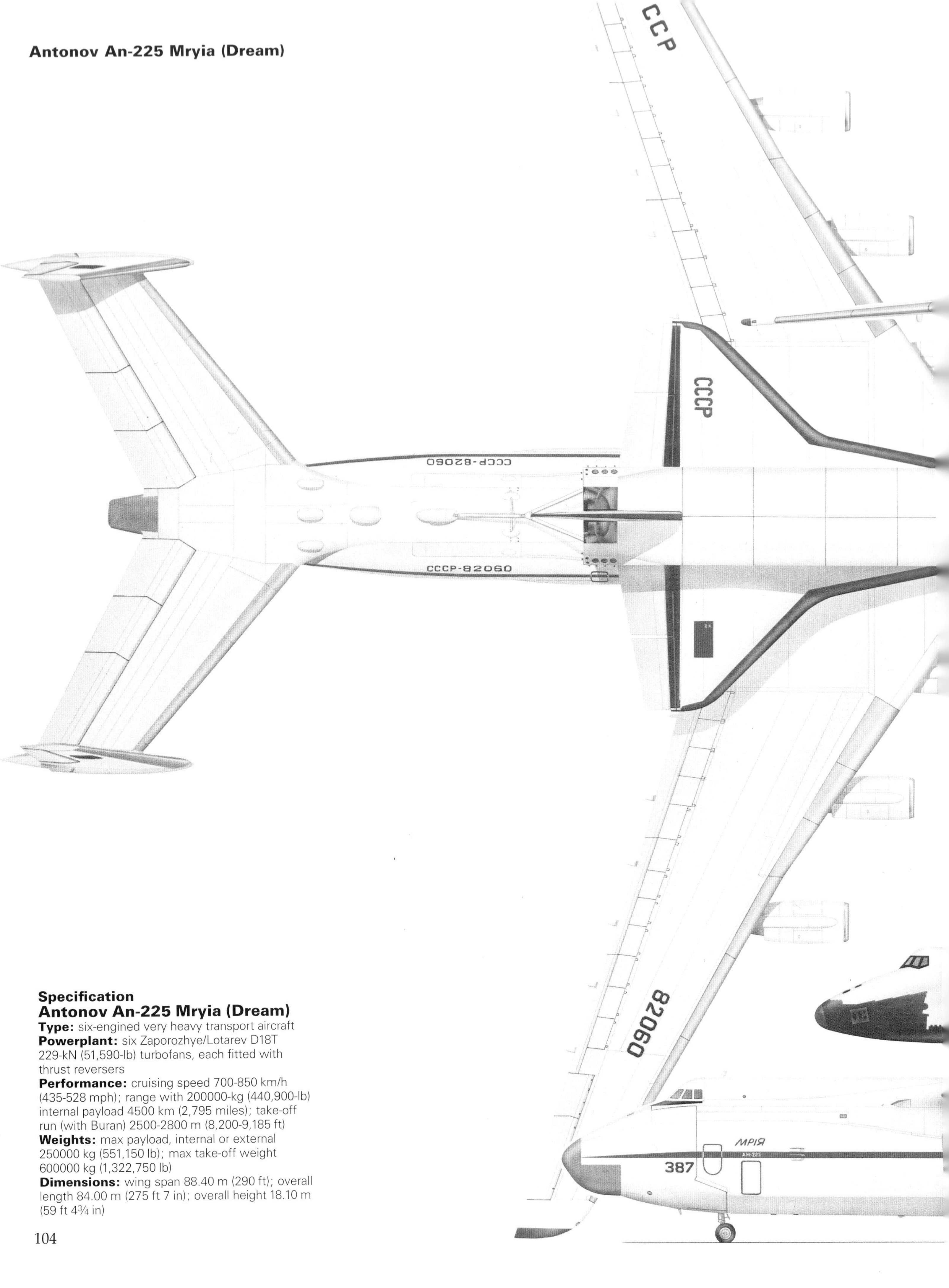

Specification

Antonov An-225 Mryia (Dream)

Type: six-engined very heavy transport aircraft
Powerplant: six Zaporozhye/Lotarev D18T 229-kN (51,590-lb) turbofans, each fitted with thrust reversers
Performance: cruising speed 700-850 km/h (435-528 mph); range with 200000-kg (440,900-lb) internal payload 4500 km (2,795 miles); take-off run (with Buran) 2500-2800 m (8,200-9,185 ft)
Weights: max payload, internal or external 250000 kg (551,150 lb); max take-off weight 600000 kg (1,322,750 lb)
Dimensions: wing span 88.40 m (290 ft); overall length 84.00 m (275 ft 7 in); overall height 18.10 m (59 ft 4¾ in)

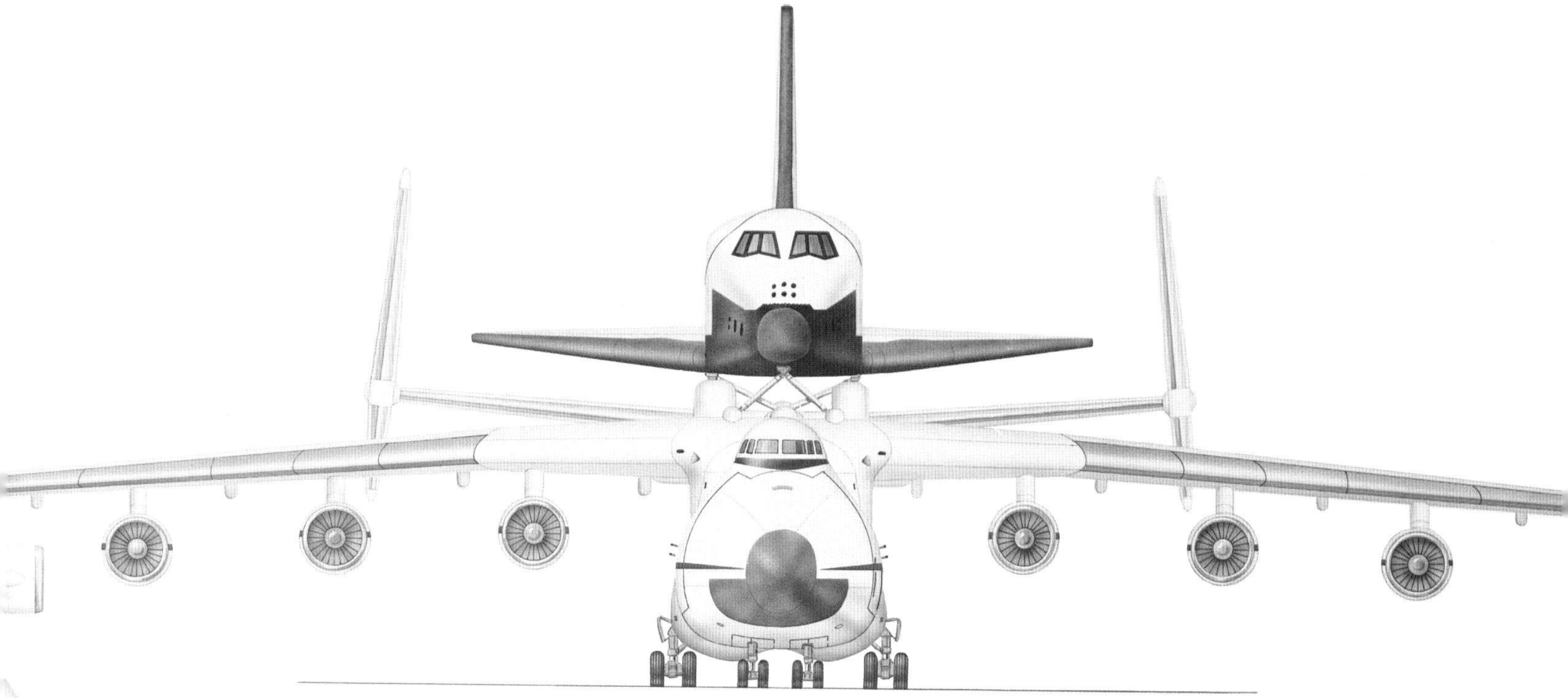

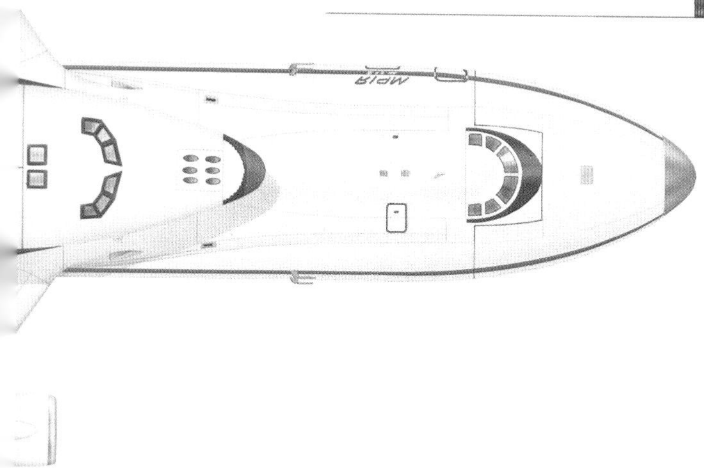

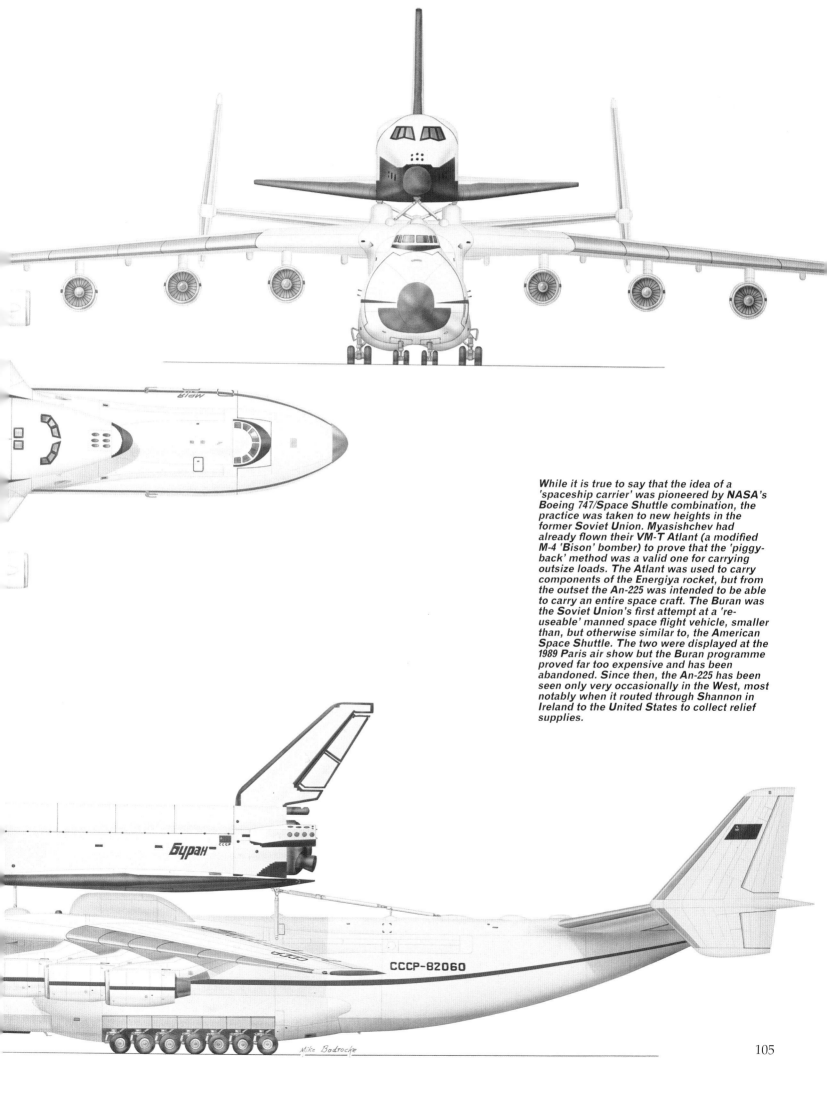

While it is true to say that the idea of a 'spaceship carrier' was pioneered by **NASA**'s **Boeing 747/Space Shuttle** combination, the practice was taken to new heights in the former **Soviet Union**. **Myasishchev** had already flown their **VM-T Atlant** (a modified M-4 '**Bison**' bomber) to prove that the 'piggy-back' method was a valid one for carrying outsize loads. The **Atlant** was used to carry components of the **Energiya** rocket, but from the outset the **An-225** was intended to be able to carry an entire space craft. The **Buran** was the **Soviet Union**'s first attempt at a 're-useable' manned space flight vehicle, smaller than, but otherwise similar to, the **American Space Shuttle**. The two were displayed at the 1989 **Paris** air show but the **Buran** programme proved far too expensive and has been abandoned. **Since** then, the **An-225** has been seen only very occasionally in the **West**, most notably when it routed through **Shannon** in **Ireland** to the **United States** to collect relief supplies.

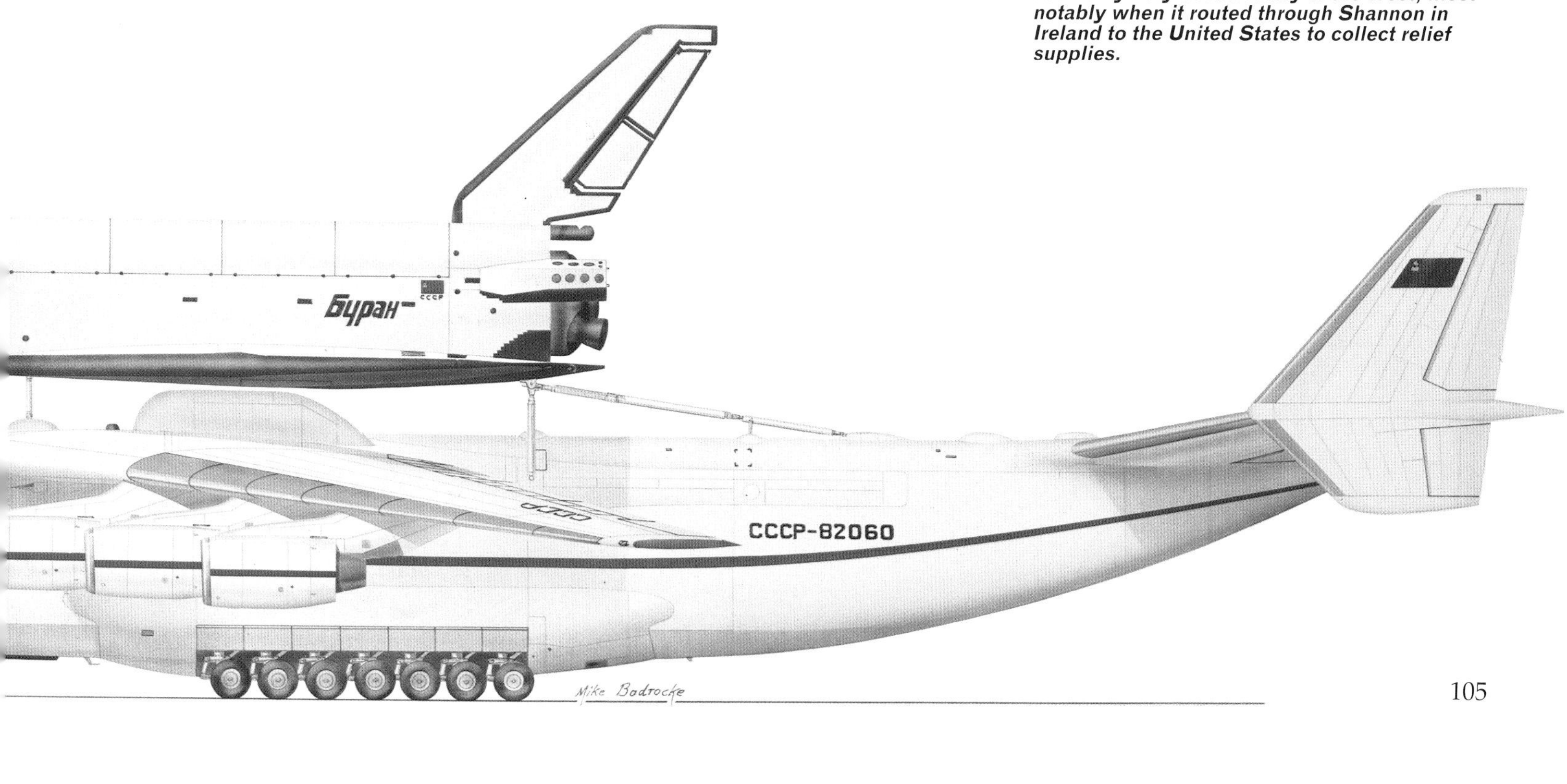

McDonnell Douglas MD-11

Specification
McDonnell Douglas MD-11

Type: long-range wide-body transport
Powerplant: three Pratt & Whitney PW4460 turbofans rated at 256.9 kN (60,000 lb) thrust or alternatively General Electric CF6-80C2D1F rated at 273.57 kN (61,500 lb) thrust
Performance: maximum Mach number 0.945; maximum cruising speed at 9150 m (30,000 ft) 932 km/h (579 mph); stalling speed at maximum take-off weight and 25° flap 263 km/h (164 mph); maximum rate of climb at sea level 944 m (2,770 ft) per minute; service ceiling 9935 m (32,600 ft); take-off run 2207 m (7,240 ft); landing run from 15 m (50 ft) 1966 m (6,450 ft); range with maximum payload 9270 km (5,760 miles)
Weights: operating empty 125870 kg (277,500 lb); maximum take-off 273300 kg (602,500 lb); maximum fuel 117525 kg (259,100 lb); maximum payload 55655 kg (122,700 lb)
Dimensions: wing span 51.66 m (169 ft 6 in); length 61.21 m (200 ft 10 in); height 17.60 m (57 ft 9 in); tailplane span 18.03 m (59 ft 2 in); wheel track 10.57 m (34 ft 8 in); wheelbase 24.61 m (80 ft 9 in); wing area 338.9 m^2 (3,648 sq ft)
Accommodation: flight crew of two; maximum single-class layout for 410 passengers; Swissair aircraft configured for three-class layout with 236 seats; two freight holds forward and aft of wing, and one bulk cargo compartment in rear fuselage

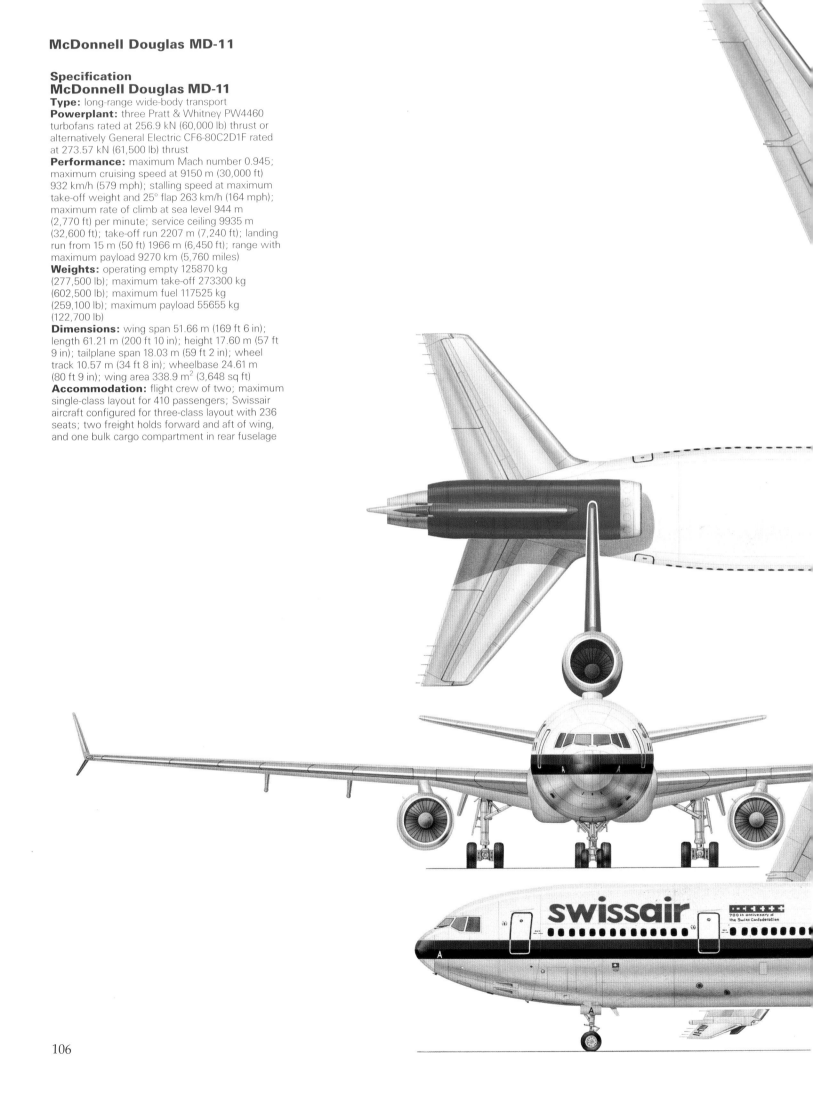

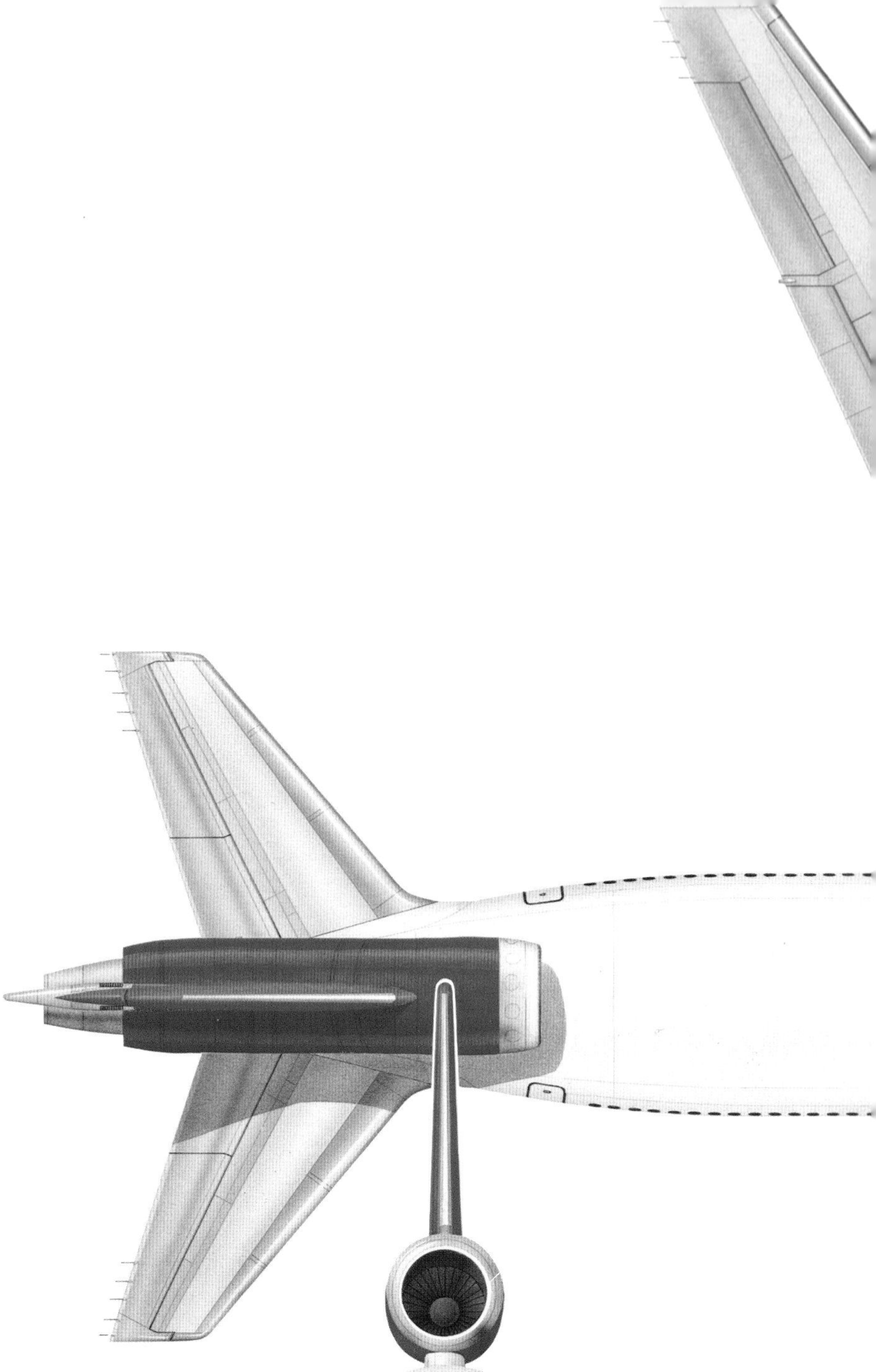

***The MD-11** obviously owes a great deal in design to the **DC-10**, but there are sufficient changes to warrant its classification as a totally new aircraft. The fuselage is considerably stretched to provide great accommodation for both passengers and baggage, while the wings are lengthened and feature winglets. The aerodynamic design is considerably more advanced than that of the **DC-10**, resulting in greater efficiency, and the tailplane holds a fuel 'trim tank'. For the aircrew, the most obvious difference is in the cockpit, where the three-man analog cockpit has been replaced by a thoroughly state-of-the-art, two-man, 'glass' cockpit, with multi-function cathode-ray tube displays.*

*Another early European customer for the **MD-11** was Swissair, which began operations with short-range sectors to European capitals while crews fully familiarised themselves with the aircraft. Later the aircraft were assigned to longer-range routes, displacing **DC-10-30s**.*

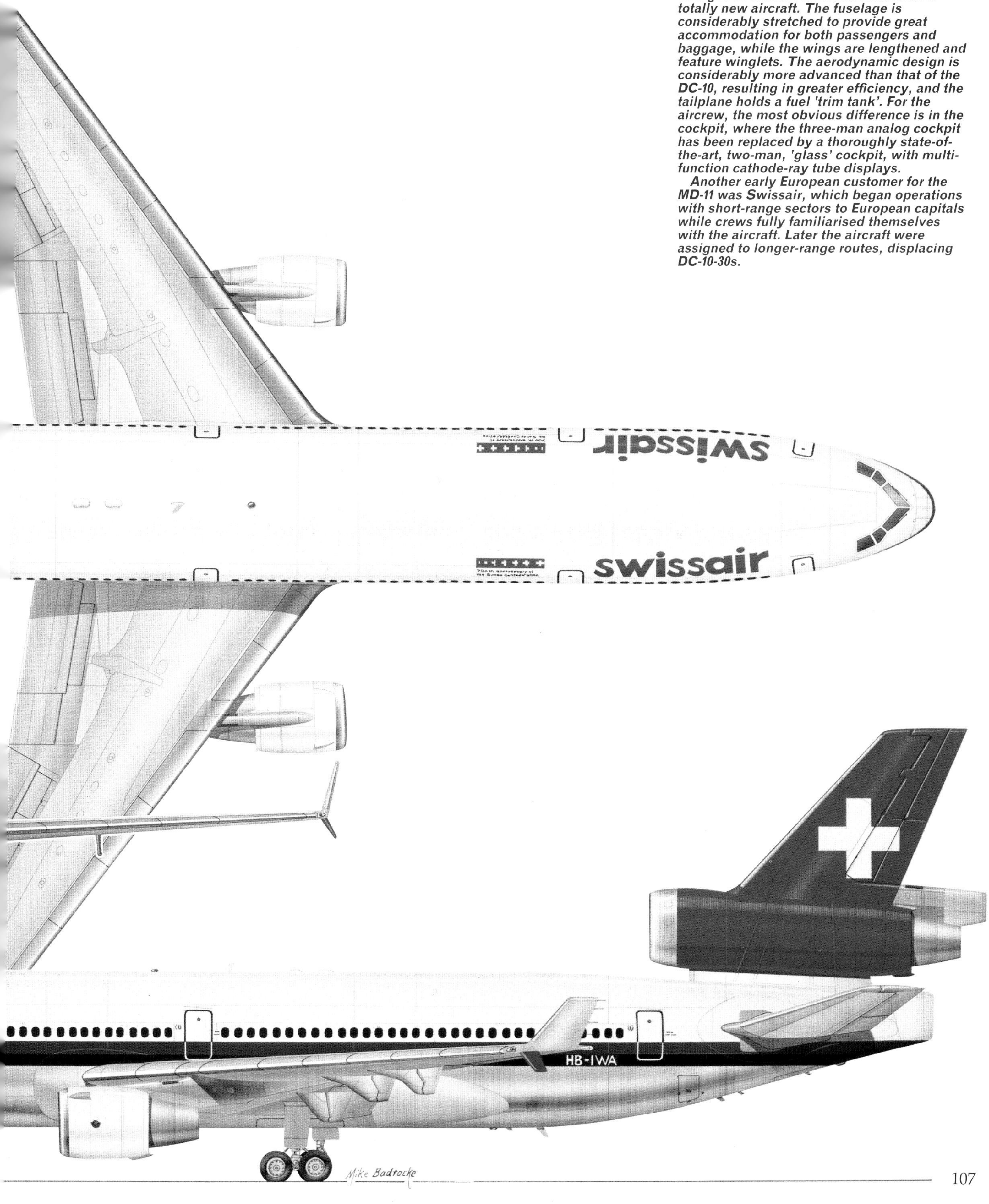

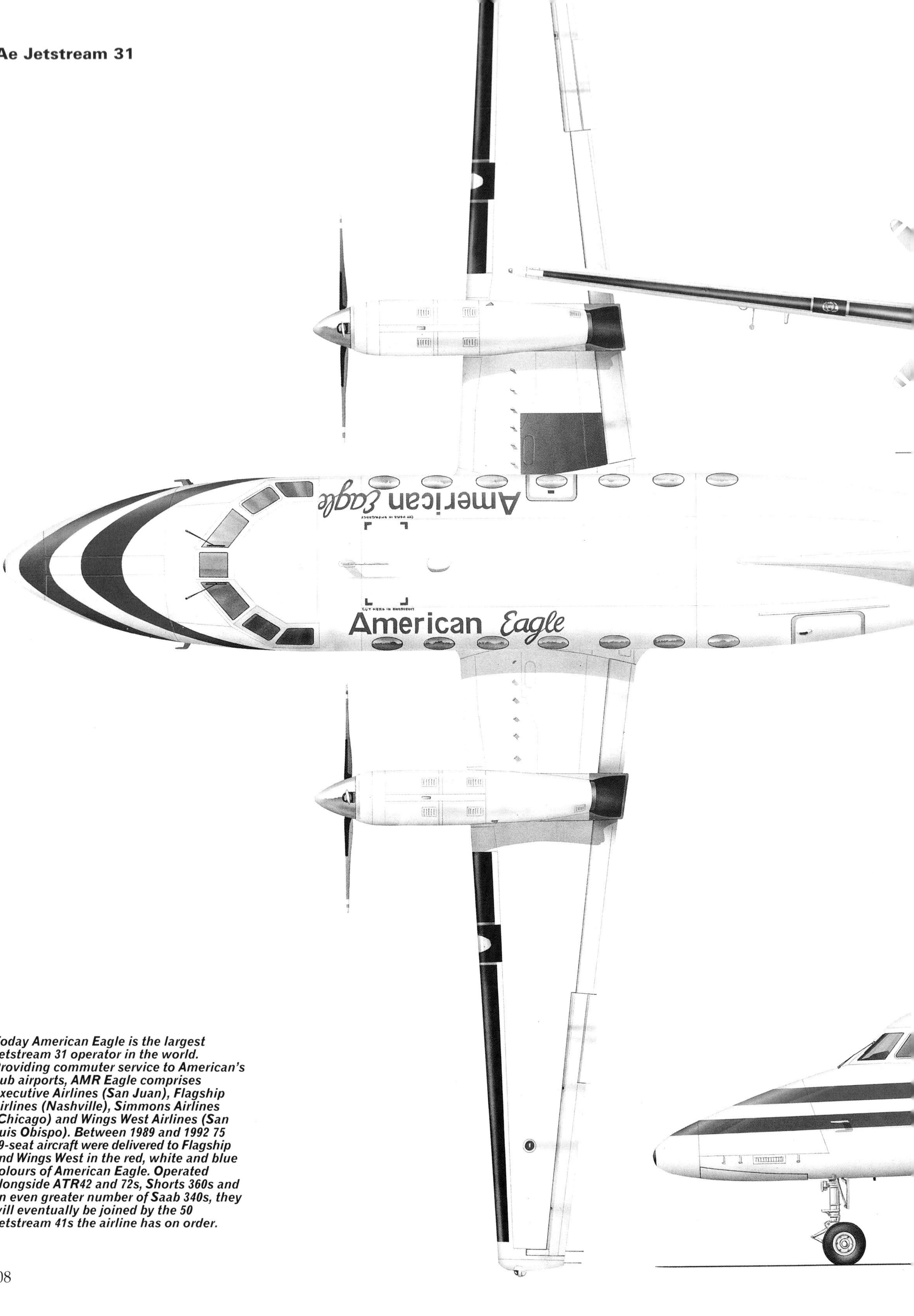

Today American Eagle is the largest Jetstream 31 operator in the world. Providing commuter service to American's hub airports, AMR Eagle comprises Executive Airlines (San Juan), Flagship Airlines (Nashville), Simmons Airlines (Chicago) and Wings West Airlines (San Luis Obispo). Between 1989 and 1992 75 19-seat aircraft were delivered to Flagship and Wings West in the red, white and blue colours of American Eagle. Operated alongside ATR42 and 72s, Shorts 360s and an even greater number of Saab 340s, they will eventually be joined by the 50 Jetstream 41s the airline has on order.

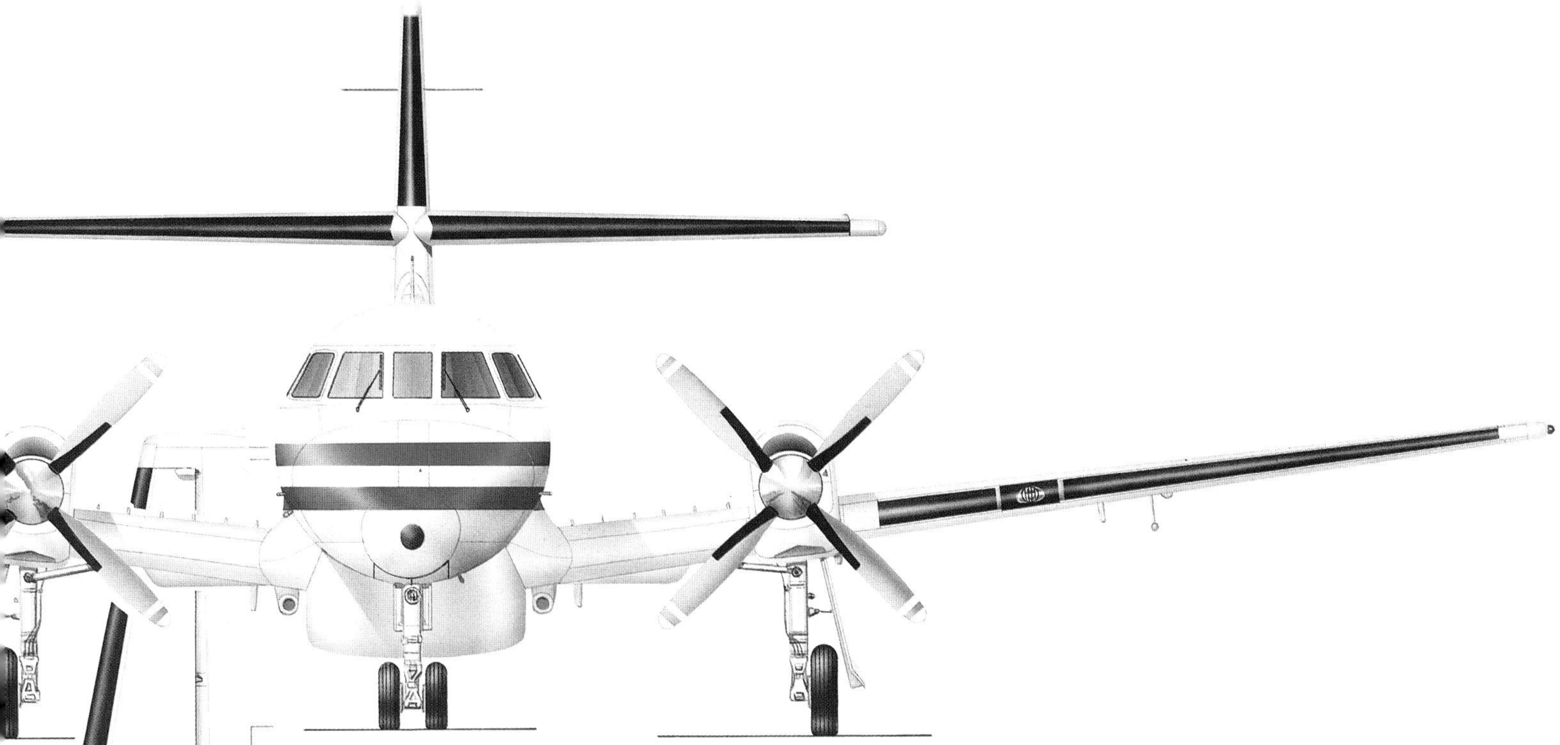

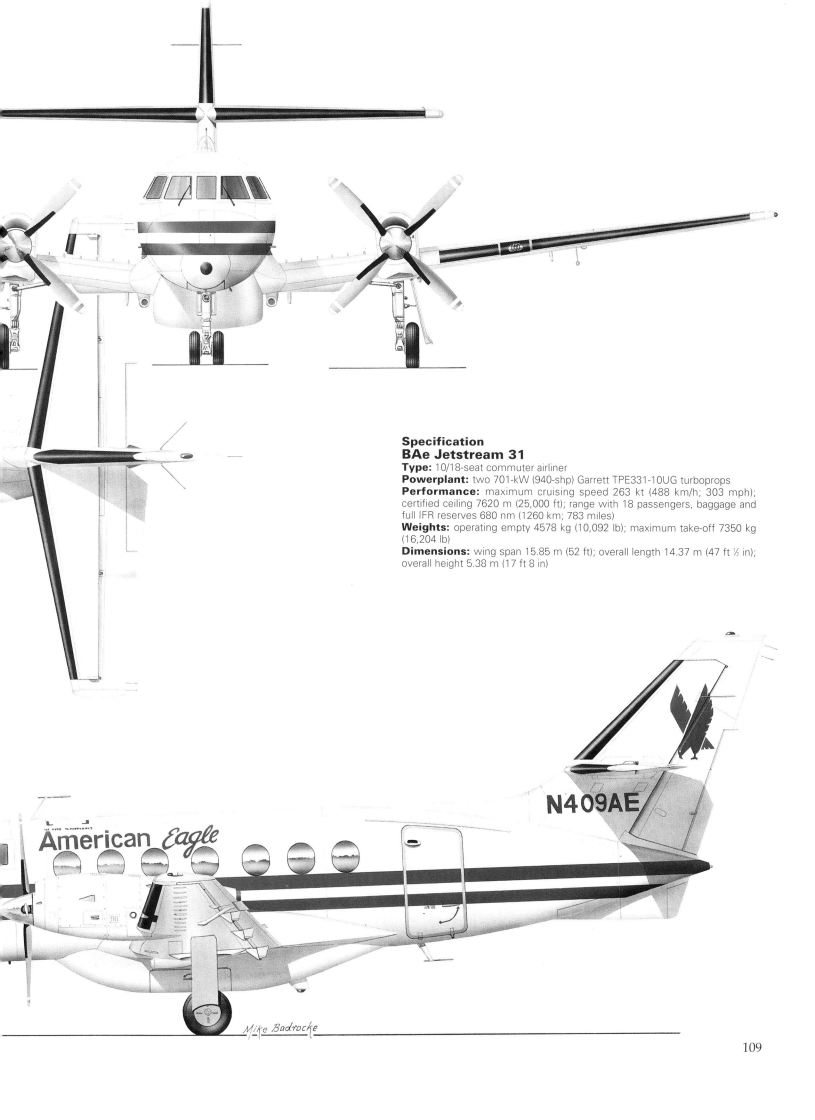

Specification

BAe Jetstream 31

Type: 10/18-seat commuter airliner
Powerplant: two 701-kW (940-shp) Garrett TPE331-10UG turboprops
Performance: maximum cruising speed 263 kt (488 km/h; 303 mph); certified ceiling 7620 m (25,000 ft); range with 18 passengers, baggage and full IFR reserves 680 nm (1260 km; 783 miles)
Weights: operating empty 4578 kg (10,092 lb); maximum take-off 7350 kg (16,204 lb)
Dimensions: wing span 15.85 m (52 ft); overall length 14.37 m (47 ft ½ in); overall height 5.38 m (17 ft 8 in)

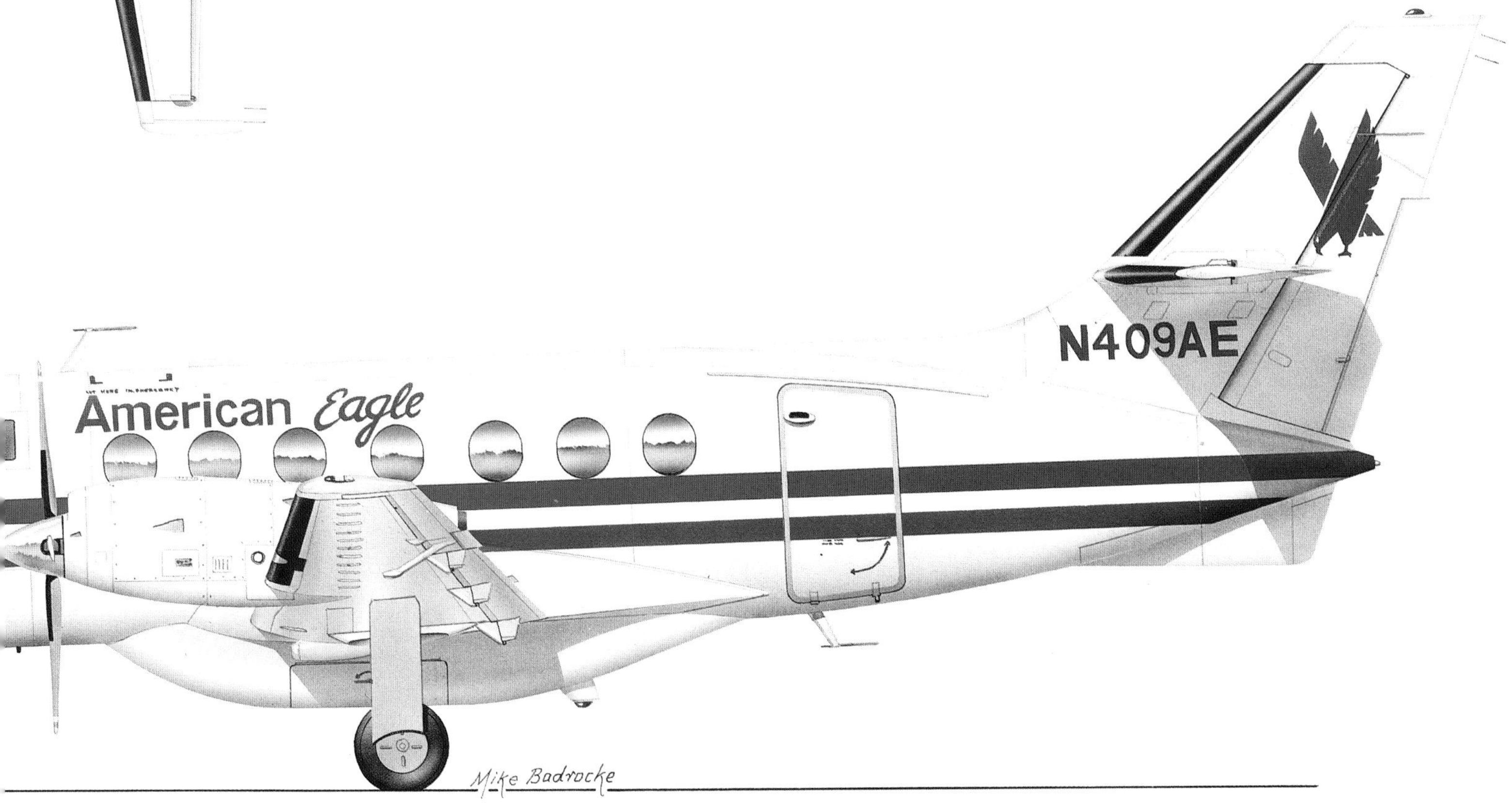

Airbus Industrie A340-311

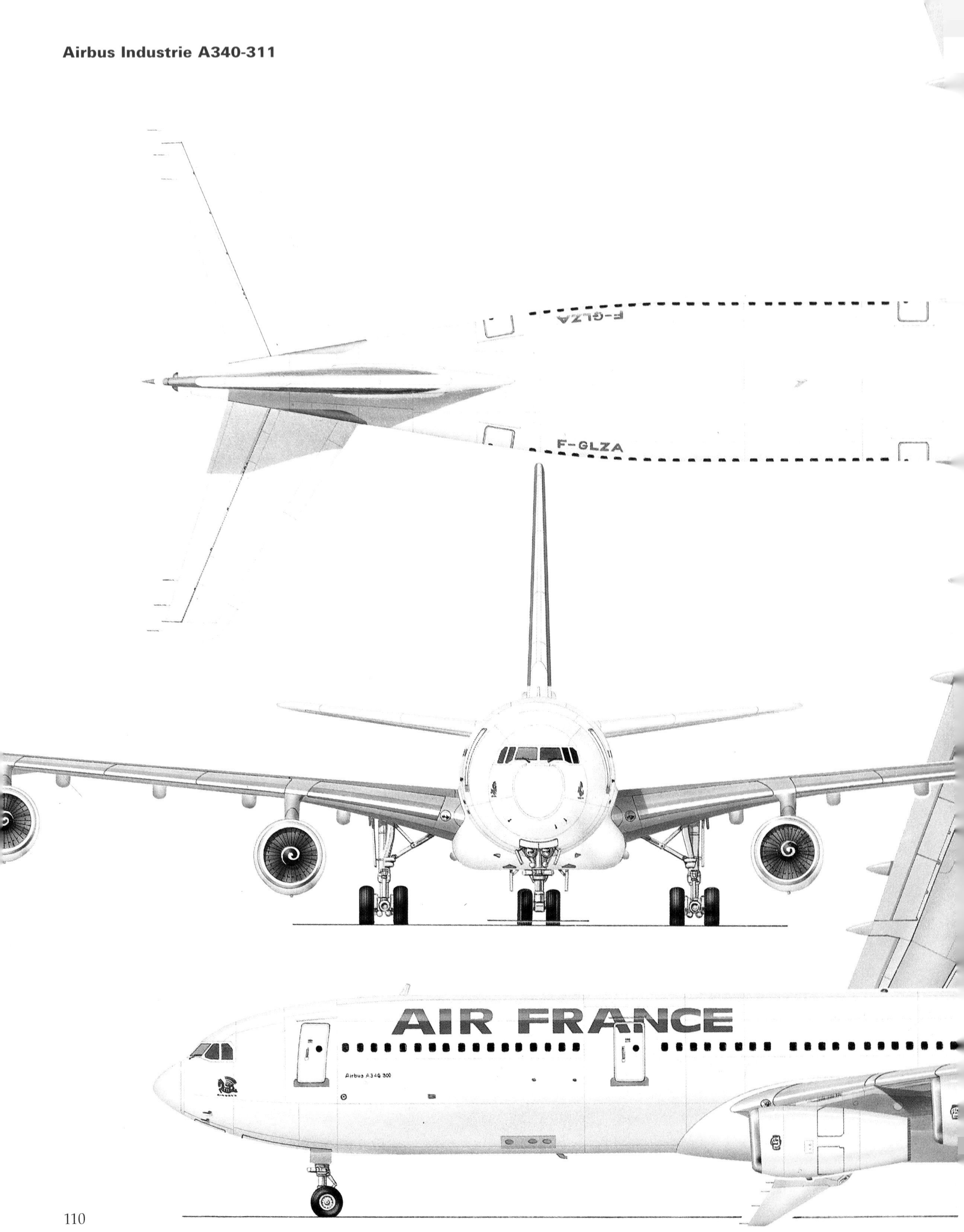

The Airbus story is largely a Franco-German one and, as a result, Air France and Lufthansa have been the launch customers for the majority of aircraft which have rolled off the Toulouse assembly line. Lufthansa has ordered 15 A340s, seven of which will be the ultra-long range A340-211s. The first of these, D-AIBA, will be the first A340 to enter airline service, in January 1993. Air France will have to wait another month for its first A340-311, F-GLZA. Both of these airlines already have the Boeing 747-400 in service and will be one of the few A340 customers to be operating it alongside its main rival.

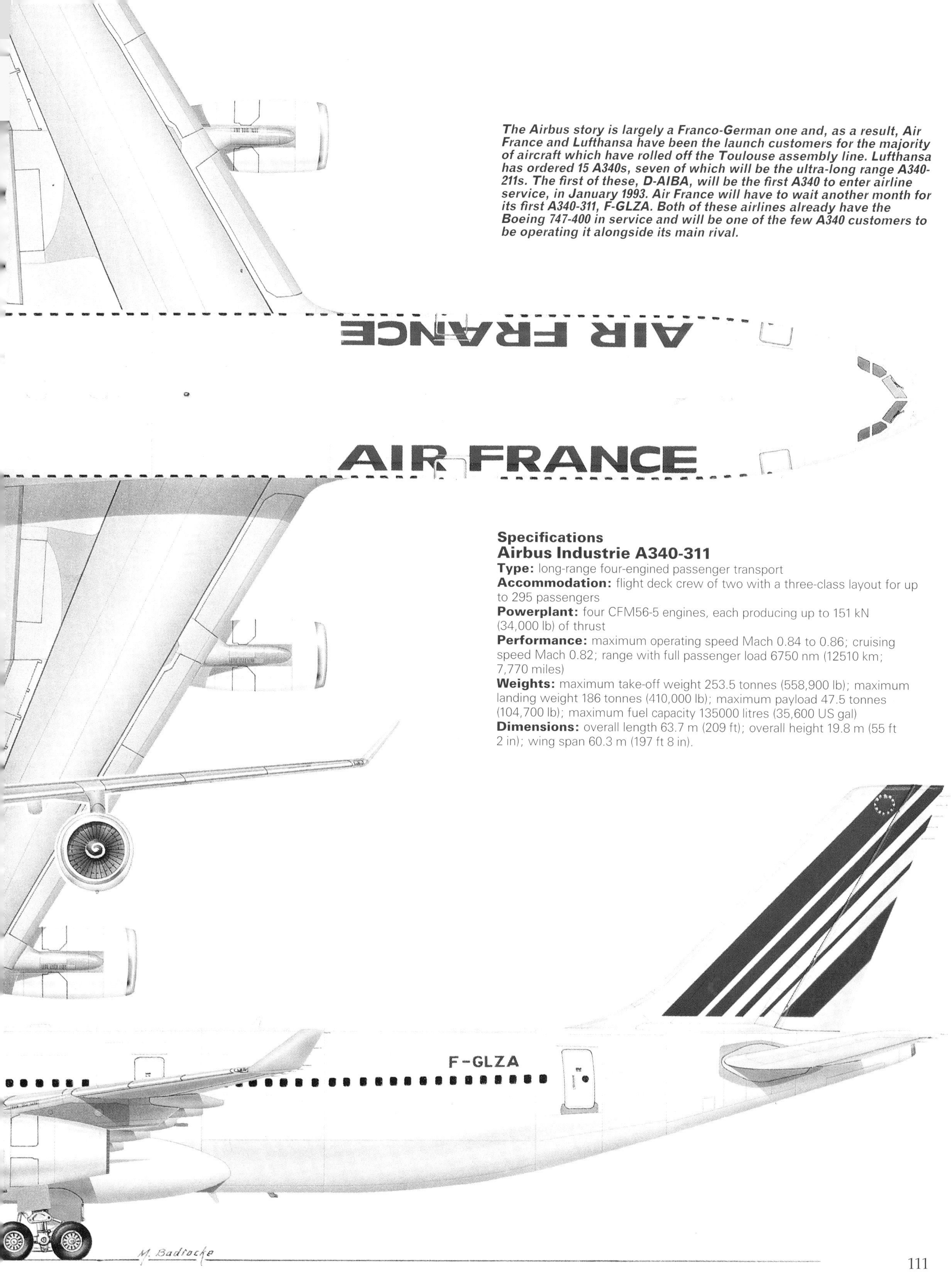

Specifications

Airbus Industrie A340-311

Type: long-range four-engined passenger transport
Accommodation: flight deck crew of two with a three-class layout for up to 295 passengers
Powerplant: four CFM56-5 engines, each producing up to 151 kN (34,000 lb) of thrust
Performance: maximum operating speed Mach 0.84 to 0.86; cruising speed Mach 0.82; range with full passenger load 6750 nm (12510 km; 7,770 miles)
Weights: maximum take-off weight 253.5 tonnes (558,900 lb); maximum landing weight 186 tonnes (410,000 lb); maximum payload 47.5 tonnes (104,700 lb); maximum fuel capacity 135000 litres (35,600 US gal)
Dimensions: overall length 63.7 m (209 ft); overall height 19.8 m (55 ft 2 in); wing span 60.3 m (197 ft 8 in).